D0780221

| MAR 1 8 1985 DATE DUE | | |
|---|---|---|
| FEB 1 7 1986 | | |
| NUV 2 8 1992 APR - 2 1994 | | |
| | | |
| | | |
| | | |
| | | |
| | | |
| | | |

OCT - 4 1984

# THE JEWISH QUEST

## Essays on Basic Concepts of
## Jewish Theology

# Books by Jacob B. Agus

1. *Modern Philosophies of Judaism*. (Behrman House, 1940)
   A study of the philosophies of Herrmann Cohen, Martin Buber, Franz Rosenzweig and Mordecai M. Kaplan.
2. *Banner of Jerusalem*. (Bloch Publishing Co., 1946)
   A study of the thought of Abraham Isaac Kook. Reissued under the title, *Highpriest of Rebirth*.
3. *Guideposts in Modern Judaism*. (Bloch, 1959)
   A book of essays dealing with the central themes of Jewish philosophy.
4. *The Evolution of Jewish Thought*. (Abelard-Schuman, N.Y., 1959)
   A study of the history of Jewish philosophy from the biblical era to the Age of Emancipation. (Published in French and Spanish translations. Reissued by Arno Press, N.Y., 1973)
5. *The Meaning of Jewish History*. Two volumes. (Abelard-Schuman, N.Y., 1963)
   The uniqueness of Jewish experience and the various ways in which it was interpreted.
6. *The Vision and the Way*. (F. Ungar, N.Y., 1969)
   An interpretive anthology of Jewish philosophical ethics. Available in paperback.
7. *Dialogue and Tradition*. (Abelard-Schuman, N.Y., 1971)
   A collection of essays dealing with "the challenges of contemporary Judeo-Christian Thought."
8. *Jewish Identity in an Age of Ideologies*. (F. Ungar, N.Y., 1978)
   An inquiry into the Jewish self-image as it emerged and developed in response to the ideologies of the nineteenth and twentieth centuries.

# THE JEWISH QUEST

## Essays on Basic Concepts of Jewish Theology

JACOB B. AGUS

KTAV PUBLISHING HOUSE, INC.
NEW YORK, NEW YORK

**Library of Congress Cataloging in Publication Data**

Agus, Jacob Bernard, 1911-
The Jewish quest.

Includes bibliographical references and index.
1. Judaism—Doctrines—Addresses, essays, lectures.
2. Judaism—Essence, genius, nature—Addresses, essays,
lectures. 3. Judaism—Relations—Christianity—
Addresses, essays, lectures. 4. Christianity and other
religions—Judaism—Addresses, essays, lectures.
I. Title.
BM601.A38   1983        296.3        83-258
ISBN 0-88125-012-0

MANUFACTURED IN THE UNITED STATES OF AMERICA

# TABLE OF CONTENTS

Dedicated to the loving memories of
my brother
Dr. Haim Agus
and my sister
Esther Stein

# PREFACE

IN THIS, my third, book of essays, the philosophical principles of Judaism are further explored. The ideas expounded in my studies of Jewish thought and of the Jewish self-image in history are here examined from different vantage points.

In this volume, my basic approach is made more evident by the juxtaposition of different essays, written at various times, mostly during the last decade.

Several essays deal with the nature of revelation in an ecumenical setting. The core of revelation is taken to be not the conveyance of concrete information, but an awareness of the numinous and the sublime that develops into a hunger for wisdom, a dedication to goodness, an intensified sense of the holy.

The essays of the second and fourth sections were either presented at interreligious gatherings or written for an ecumenical publication.

The exposition of Maimonides' philosophy of "continuous creativity" and the concepts of what I call, "Neo-Maimonism" are demonstrations of the roots of Conservative Judaism in the rationalistic current of Jewish philosophy.

*The Jewish Quest* is to make oneself and the world fit for the indwelling of the Divine Presence; theologically speaking, it is a yearning for the "kingdom of heaven". Solomon Schechter called attention to the three aspects of this goal—an "invisible" reality in the hearts of people, the redemption of Israel and the universal dimension of messianism. In our day, the many-sidedness of this quest is more apparent than heretofore, but its future course remains uncertain.

We are beginning to emerge from the shadows of recent events. The Holocaust is now being studied objectively and taught in schools. The Arab world is moving, however reluctantly, toward peace with Israel. It is becoming possible to look ahead toward new horizons, reexamining critically our heritage and the import of our history. These tasks have occupied my attention in all my previous books. The essays in this volume deal with parts of this general theme. They are here reprinted virtually unchanged.

vii

# INTRODUCTION—WHO WE ARE

EVERY HISTORIC community establishes its specific character by reflecting on three aspects of its life—its self-image, its attitude to the universal values of culture and religion, its posture toward other groups and humanity generally. Naturally, these phases of culture interact and affect one another. But, as a rule it is easy enough to study them separately.

In the case of the Jewish people, each of the three orientations of collective consciousness is problematic.

The relationship of the Jewish people to God was affirmed to be unique by the Jews themselves and in the Christian world. Their metaphysical status was believed to be inherent in their ethnicity and destiny, and it was irrevocable. Naturally, the self-image of Jewish people and their attitude to their neighbors were determined in large part by this dogma of the Chosen People.

It is commonly asserted that in Jewish life, there is no distinction between nationality and religion. But Jewish thinkers could not be unaware of the dividing line between these two categories. The majority of the Jewish people lived in the Christian world, where this line of demarcation was carved out through centuries in bloody revolutions and civil wars. The movement of Jewish people from the periphery of western European life to its center depended upon and coincided with the progressive separation of church and state. In countries of the *ancien regime*, Jews could only be heretics and pariahs. Religious hostility overflowed often enough into the categories of nationality and race. In Spain, the theory of *limpieza* was evolved. It asserted that Jewish "blood" was corrupted by centuries of unbelief. This decay of religious bias into racist contempt was foreshadowed by the belief, which preachers read into the New Testament since the second century, that the Jewish people had been "rejected" by the Supreme Being, for having failed to recognize their Savior. Weaker and less dogmatic versions of this dogma persisted into the twentieth century in all the lands of Europe. It was widely believed that the Jew was separated from Christian society by a metaphysical barrier. In addition to the categories of race, nationality and

1

religion, which distinguished other groups from one another, the Jew bore the stigmata of a special mystery, compounded of both a blessing and a curse, the grace of chosenness and the doom of rejection. The metaphysical gulf which set the Jews apart was encrusted in the course of time with many and diverse canards, which formed the mythology of Antisemitism.

A mirror-image of this complex of myths and fantasies has often be-deviled the self-consciousness of the Jewish people. The Jewish self-image was at times lifted out of the complexities of history and viewed as if Jews were a "people that dwells alone and is not counted among the nations". (Numbers 23.9) It does not merely cherish a specific body of beliefs and practices. It occupies a unique status, in relation to Providence, and in respect of all the nations of the world.

Collectivities are victims of vanity even more than individuals, and it is easier for the former to mask their pride in the adornment of idealism than it is for the latter. Once a tradition has taken root which appeals to the idealism of people as well as to their self-love, it becomes exceedingly difficult to disentangle the threads and to restore the original state of normalcy.

## Jewish Image in Past and Present

In my book, *Jewish Identity in an Age of Ideologies*, I traced the diverse changes in the Jewish image and self-image that resulted from the movements of thought in the modern world.

So central was the Jewish heritage to the history of the western world that every change in the intellectual climate of Europe implied a subtle alteration in the image of the Jew, for better or for worse. Theology in the most general sense was long the "queen of the sciences," and a unique position in theology led to special consequences when in the last two centuries theologies evolved into ideologies. Every new vision of society influenced the character of the Jewish image and the nature of Jewish identity, whether it was a new understanding of nationality, or of social justice, or of the course of world history, or of the nature of evolution, or of the interpretation of Holy Scriptures; every upheaval in thought and society affected the concept of the Jewish people. Still, the more the Jewish image changed, the more it remained the same, in that it retained references to ancient stereotypes and the resonance of folk mythologies.

Is this situation likely to continue into the distant future? No one can answer this question with dogmatic certainty. The contemporary scene has been radically altered by the following sea-changes:

First, the vast majority of Jewish people now live in North America and in Israel. The American state is based on the principle of individual citizenship, with no special privileges being granted to any ethnic group. The ideology of American nationalism embraces all its citizens, regardless of race, color or creed. Naturally, the actual life of the American people does not always correspond perfectly with its ideal vision. There have always been some islands of exception, if not exclusion, in the American ideology— notably in the case of the American Indian, the Negro, the Mexican and others. But, the official ideology is the dominant force in American life, determining the main currents of its culture. Here is a nation that appreciates and celebrates the diverse ethnic components which generated it. So strong is its unity in law and culture that its pluralistic heritage can only reinforce its solidarity and its message to mankind.

The security of Israel is now included within the range of vital interests of America. While political alignments may be changed, the Israeli alliance with the United States appears to be firm and enduring. Even if America and Israel should go their separate ways in the unforeseen future, Israel is quite able to defend itself against its enemies. Furthermore, Israel's dependence upon American economic and military help serves to cement the relationship between American Jewry and Israel. American Jews feel that it is their duty to interpret Israel to America and America to Israel.

Second, the Christian world is engaged in a basic transformation of its view of the Jewish people. Since the Second World War there have appeared some fifty declarations on Jews and Judaisn, which have reversed the traditional "teaching of contempt" of Judaism, and set a new policy of appreciation of the Jewish heritage. The effects of the new educational approach will be felt in the future, though history teaches us that occasional reverses may still be expected.

In a society so vast and diverse, we cannot expect to see sudden transformations. Traditions of evil as of goodness possess a momentum that is roughly proportionate to their age and ubiquity. But, on the highest levels there is now a fresh sensitivity to the horrors of Antisemitism which are latent in the history of western society. Hopefully, the memory of the Holocaust will not easily be put out of mind.

Third, in the lands of Central Europe, where Antisemitism was an endemic mass-religion, there are few or no Jews. In Poland, Rumania, Hungary and in the smaller contiguous states, the Holocaust left only stray remnants, abandoned cemeteries and mute monuments. That area, extending from the Baltic states to the shores of the Black Sea, was at one time the heartland of the Jews of the world, and the fertile source of mass-emigration. Out of it Jewish people, bearers of Yiddish culture and traditional loyalties, flowed for centuries westward and to the lands of the New World. It was also the home and center of economic Antisemitism, with the ancient heritage of hatred being buttressed by the desperate pressure of an impoverished peasantry bent on acquiring positions in the urban centers, where Jews had long been entrenched.

Fourth, the mythological component of Antisemitism was given some plausibility by the pre-Israel image of the Jew as an individual and the Jewish people as a collectivity. As individuals, Jews appeared to be uprooted, detached from the soil, shallow, skeptical and critical. In the eyes of the recently urbanized masses, barely a generation away from plows and pigs, Jews seemed to be foreign invaders, barring their way to progress. Jews were seen by the uprooted peasants as unnatural people, "city slickers", eking out a living by tricks and deceptions.

As a collectivity, Jews were seen as a ghostly phenomenon, a people landless and helpless, a "pariah"-people, cowardly and self-centered.

The emergence of the state of Israel served to cast these images into the dust-bin of the past. In Israel, the Jews proved themselves to be superb farmers and excellent soldiers. They have taken their place in the concert of nations, with the plow and with the sword. They are no longer a "wandering" people, homeless and helpless, but a people of flesh and blood, of passion and pride, altogether human.

## The Emergence of Anti-Zionism

Strange are the ways of history. When old movements disintegrate, some of their momentum is taken over by new ideologies. Antisemitism, nurtured under the auspices of Christianity for centuries, erupted with volcanic force in the nineteenth century under the aegis of secular ideologies—chiefly romantic nationalism, utopian socialism, Germanic historicism and Nietzschean glorification of power.

In the last decades, the ideology of Anti-Zionism has begun to assume the momentum of Antisemitism, especially in the Muslim and Third World countries. This phenomenon may well preoccupy Jewish leaders in the future, for the Muslim world is rising like a giant who is slowly waking up and shaking off the cobwebs of sleep.

Anti-Zionism is far more than a rational expression of antagonism to this or that policy of the state of Israel, or even to its very existence. In certain countries, Anti-Zionism may be used as a "code word" for the old social disease of Antisemitism, but it is essentially a new phenomenon. The U.N. resolution equating Zionism and racism is a serious danger-signal, an attempt to launch a world-crusade. In the long run, the significant aspect of Anti-Zionism is the mythology in which it is enveloped.

Israel is viewed through a distorting lens and seen as a titanic force of global dimensions, sinister and even satanic. It is not examined in its true proportions as a small state struggling to survive in a cruel world, but it is viewed "through a glass darkly" as the tip of a mighty mystery, a monstrous "conspiracy" of the industrial democracies to capture and conquer the underdeveloped world. The myth of the "Protocols of the Elders of Zion" is taking new shape in the minds of millions.

When Jacobo Timmerman, editor of a daily in Buenos Aires, was kidnapped by right-wing terrorists and interrogated by army leaders he was asked three questions—"Are you a Jew?" "Are you a Zionist?" "Are you part of the Zionist Conspiracy?" He replied in the affirmative to each of the questions. In his view, his affirmative answer to the third question saved his life, for the Argentinian generals thought they could use him for a show-trial.

To us, the amazing phenomenon is the concern of Argentinian nationalists with a "Zionist conspiracy". How many lives does a myth have? — How deep and dark is the fantastic credulity of those who are suspicious of all intellectuals!

Anti-Zionism does have a "religious" basis, not only in Muslim but also in Christian countries. There, the impetus of popular prejudice and medieval myths is likely to persist even when the higher echelons of leadership have arrived at a more humane and progressive position. To be sure, even in Protestant countries, pro-Zionist sentiment was often inhibited, especially in liberal circles, but as a general rule, Zionism in England and America enjoyed widespread support.

In his careful study of "Vatican Diplomacy and the Jews during the Holocaust, 1939-1943", Father John F. Morley writes:

> "According to Maglione, Catholics all over the world looked to Palestine as a sacred land because it was the birthplace of Christianity. If, however, Palestine were to become predominantly Jewish, then Catholic piety would be offended and Catholics would be understandably anxious as to whether they could continue to peacefully enjoy their historic rights over the holy places". (p. 93)

This attitude was doubtless reinforced by the vague feeling that the reconstitution of the Jewish state would undo the belief that Jerusalem was destroyed in punishment for the crucifixion of Jesus.

However, with the passage of time, the state of Israel has been gaining in acceptance by nearly all Christian national organizations. The theological tradition of the Christian world contains the prophecies of the Hebrew Scriptures as well as the opinions of the Church Fathers. It is therefore natural for Christians to associate the Holy Land with the Jewish people. Also, in the face of an Islamic resurgence, Christians are likely to become more aware of their kinship with the Judaic heritage. Theological doctrines are not immune to changes induced by the great events of history.

Furthermore, Israel was born in response to basic human needs and by the freely expressed vote of an international body, the Assembly of the United Nations. It was therefore an all-human achievement, an attempt by the family of nations to provide some reparation for the horrendous crimes of the Holocaust. Christian nations shared in the burden of guilt for the crimes of Germany, because they participated in the millenial teaching of contempt for Jews. Hence, a special glow of idealism illuminated the image of the Jewish state. The sacrificial devotion of Jewish people all over the world was reinforced by the high regard of the western world. Nor was this attitude confined to an elite of moralists. The common people of the West were won over by the spectacle of a largely European people beating back the invasion of hordes of enemies, who were non-European and non-Christian. In the successive wars of 1948, 1956, 1967, and 1973, the decisive victories of Israel contrasted starkly with the global retreat of European nations from their colonial strongholds in Asia and Africa. While the British, French, Dutch and Portuguese withdrew from their colonies, the Jews drove home the lesson of Europe's supremacy in industry and science. By the same token, Israel became the mighty symbol and cutting edge of western imperialism, in the eyes of Arabs and Third World nations.

The negative image of Arabs in the western world was exacerbated by their military defeats, their seemingly hopeless impoverishment and their political ineptitude. Israelis had come to feel that if they must have enemies, they were fortunate that their enemies were Arabs—fanatical, incompetent, mostly illiterate and torn by parochial loyalties.

However, the war of '73 demonstrated that a radical change had taken place. The war coincided with the emergence of OPEC as an all-powerful factor in the economy of the West. Suddenly, the Arab case acquired immense international weight. The wheels of industry, it turned out, could grind to a halt at the pleasure of Arabs. It became equally clear that the Palestinian Arabs were no longer ignorant peasants, but that the children of the *fellahin*, herded in wretched camps which were set up after the wars of '48 and '67, had become college-trained executives and engineers. Aided by scholarships from the oil-rich countries, the young men and women from the refugee camps filled the campuses of American universities, as graduate students, specializing in oil technology and petrochemical studies. Many of the young Palestinians penetrated into crucial positions within some of the oil-states. They acquired powerful leverage on the international scene. Yet, their newly won affluence did not cool their nationalistic ardor, and their sense of having been wronged. On the contrary, they nurtured the anger and anguish of their people in the refugee camps and wherever they were dispersed. The growth of Arab nationalism could no longer be disregarded by the statesmen of the industrial democracies.

To be sure, a widely dispersed people, like the Arabs, may take several generations to attain the unifying mentality of a nation. Political intrigues and conflicting ambitions, along with rival sectarian suspicions, are likely to frustrate this goal, time and again. But, as in the case of nineteenth-century Italy and Germany, the national ideal becomes steadily more and more irresistible.

We must also take note of the fact that the moral image of Israel declined at the very time when the Arab case gained in credibility and power. The increasing nervousness of the Israeli government, the anxious haste to establish new settlements in the midst of Arab lands, the rough tactics used to suppress Arab demonstrations—all these factors helped to remove the aura of moral greatness from the cause of Israel. "The house of Israel" had become "like all the nations".

## Dilemma of American Jewish Leadership

With the Jewish state besieged by enemies and perpetually in need of financial help and moral-political support, the leaders of American Jewry were impelled to center their collective efforts on aid to Israel. Even while the old rhetoric of Jewry as a religious community continued to be used, the substance of Jewish loyalty insensibly shifted from the pole of religion to that of nationality.

The needs of Israel fighting for its life was necessarily ranked ahead of any other concern.

Only on rare occasions do American Jewish leaders take an independent attitude, in keeping with their humane tradition of philanthropy. The Soviet Jews, who refuse to settle in Israel and elect to go to America and the West, continue at this writing to receive aid from American Jews. No one can tell how long the present situation will last—whether only a small trickle of emigration will be allowed, whether the Soviets will use their power to affect the situation one way or the other, whether American Jews will continue to put the individual rights of men and women above the manpower needs of Israel.

Jewish leadership in America today is in need of more subtlety and sophistication than ever before. It must not allow a temporary and partial coincidence of interests to distort its awareness of its enduring allies and antagonists. Traditionally, American Jews enjoyed the support of the liberals in politics and in religion. But in the case of Israel, the support of the liberals was always qualified. They could sympathize with Jewish needs and, when Israel was established, they could welcome the Jewish state as an ally of the democracies. But, this sympathy was counterbalanced and limited by the plight of the Palestinian refugees. As the moral claims of the Palestinians were pushed to the foreground by the commercial pressures of the oil-rich countries, a paradoxical situation developed. Liberals and Fundamentalists changed places vis-à-vis Israel.

The liberals, traditional friends of the Jews, began to temper their enthusiasm for the Jewish state, which they saw as a regressive force, that might become one day the flash-point of another war. The future must be based on states granting equal rights to all citizens, not on the presumed rights of nations and their collective historic rights. On the other hand, the religious Fundamentalists and political Conservatives, previously hostile to Jews as unbelievers, humanists and social progressives, now joined the advocates of an aggressive anti-Soviet posture, hailing Israel as a military outpost on the battlefront against Communism. The possibility of an all-out war does not faze them, since their apocalyptic view of history anticipates an Armageddon. So, the preachers of "Christian politics", "Christian Yellow Pages" and a "Christian America" are at this moment in favor of a "strong" Israel. At the same time, the liberal ministers of the mainline churches, whose staunch opposition to Antisemitism is unquestioned, became skeptical and even resentful of the "expansionist" claims of Israel.

This paradoxical reversal of roles may be only temporary. In any case, it must not be countered by stultifying slogans, such as "Zionism is Judaism", or "Anti-Zionism is Antisemitism".

Once an ideal has become a political reality, it cannot be protected by the immaculate banner of supernatural grace. The Ayatollah Khomeini has reminded us all of the sad truth that when religion bursts into the political arena, it becomes subject to the distortions of chauvinism, the limitations of earthly politics and the corruption of earthly instincts. No people has suffered more than the Jews from the unnatural union of politics and religion. Indeed, it has been the glory of historic Judaism to put in question the claims of sheer power, and to rank the law of God above all the laws of states and their rulers. The Jewish people emerged upon the stage of history, dedicated to the task of becoming a blessing "to all the families of the earth" (Genesis 12:2).

Of course, it is possible to criticize this or that policy of an Israeli government, without indicting either Judaism or the Jews of the world, and vica versa. This point need hardly be argued. But, we must acknowledge that in practice, a resolute policy of anti-Zionism may, if sustained over a period of time, turn into the dripping venom of Antisemitism. Anti-Zionists may seek allies by reviving the old myths of a Jewish conspiracy; also, they may seek to put Jews in the industrial democracies on the defensive by awakening the slumbering demons of Antisemitism. Jewish leaders may also assist unwittingly in this tragic train of events by their uncritical support of an aggressive Israeli policy. For example, the claim that the West Bank belongs to Israel because "God gave it to us" invites the injection into world politics of ancient mythologies, by Muslims as well as by Christians. And the occasional efforts of Jewish leaders in the free countries to put the cause of Israel above all other considerations of the national interest cannot but awaken the resentment of the free nations. The reasoning of the widely respected U.S. Senator Charles Mc.Mathias in his article on the distortion of American policy by the pressure of ethnic groups is a case in point (*Foreign Affairs*, Spring 1982).

More than a century ago, Leo Pinsker attributed the international pathology of Antisemitism to the homelessness of the Jewish people. A landless people acquires a ghostly quality in the eyes of the populace. And people fear ghosts. With the emergence of Israel, this source of the Antisemitic mythology is now blocked. But, we may well see a new kind of Antisemitism based on the myth of a Zion-centered people that keeps apart from the nations while manipulating and distorting their policies. In question is not the old bugaboo of "dual loyalty" but of a singular, meta-historical loyalty to Israel, a mystique that transcends all national loyalties.

The formation of the Jewish state occurred under special circumstances, when hundreds of thousands of refugees crowded the camps of Europe. At that time, the need of a "haven of refuge" for Jews was clear and pressing. The discomfort and displacement of Palestinian Arabs seemed in human terms but a small price to pay for the solution of the Jewish tragedy. The years of "the ingathering of exiles" generated additional momentum and led to the evacuation of Jews from Arab and some European lands. The case of Soviet Jewry was more problematical. A large number of Russian Jews feel that in the Soviet world they are not allowed to become either "good Russians" or "good Jews". On the other hand, the masses of Russian Jewry are largely assimilated. After more than a decade of mass-emigration, the number of Jews in Russia is only slightly diminished. Also, most of the emigrants prefer to settle in the countries of the western world. It is freedom and the western style of living that they prize so highly, rather than the life and culture of Israel.

Once Zionism is perceived as no longer answering a great human need, it is questionable whether many nations would rank the nationalistic ideals of American Jews above the basic human rights of an indigenous population to dwell securely in the land in which they were born.

The task of Diaspora Jewry is to help Israel acquire fresh dimensions of moral and cultural greatness. With the aid of the Diaspora, Israel can attain new heights of achievement that will be meaningful to all men and women of good-will. In the field of interreligious understanding, Israel can become the natural center for basic studies and cultural events, celebrating the plural truths of the three great religions of the West. In the field of intercultural fraternity, the groundwork is already laid, since people from 50 different lands are living in Israel. In the field of scientific research and development, the greatest natural resource is the human brain and the resolve to apply it to the solution of human problems.

Hemmed in on all sides, the open frontier for Israel is the domain of intellectual and cultural greatness. If this horizon is explored, Israel may yet regain the adulation of the free world and demonstrate to the new nations of the world that it is through the high roads of culture that a nation attains its place in the sun.

In France and in Argentina, a new kind of Antisemitism is raising its head. If Israel does not gain peace, and does not regain its moral prestige, it is likely to become the source of a vile mythology in the lands of Islam primarily, but also in the countries of the West.

How shall we deal with this danger, especially as it is now barely "a cloud, the size of a man's hand" on the eastern horizon?

While we cannot plan the details of our strategy in advance, we can sharpen our intellectual perception of the choices confronting us at any point. We can learn to recognize our self-mythification, as it arose in history and provided the tar, which made the feathers of mythology cling to our image. We can note how the biblical claims of singularity and uniqueness were twisted into weapons which were turned against us. We can learn to repudiate the seductive fantasies of self-glorification and confront rationally and humanely the problems that trouble us. We can learn to build bridges of understanding with our Christian brothers, and, possibly also, our Muslim brothers.

These are the themes of the essays in this volume.

# JEWISH SELF-DEFINITION

*Classicism And Romanticism: Our Basic Alternatives*

WE LIVE in a post-ideological age. While great decisions may have to be made in our generation, we continue to feed on the ideologies of two or more generations ago, when the Jewish world was rocked by contending messianic movements: Zionism, Herzlian and Ahad Ha'amist; Socialism, Marxist and nationalist; religious modernism, Reform, Conservative, or Neo-Orthodox. Today, we continue to act as if the old philosophies were still completely relevant, though we recognize that they have lost their youthful exuberance.

Actually, each of the earlier ideologies has been fulfilled as well as frustrated. The modernist forms of Judaism maintain a firm façade of solid strength, but their vitality is questionable. Socialism, in its mild as in its extremist forms, has lost its messianic aura. And Zionism, which has been so largely fulfilled, now presents us with the most difficult problem:

Should Israel, the country and its leadership, be regarded as the sole "heir of Jewish history," the living nucleus of the Jewish future? Or should we think in terms of the welfare of all Jewish people, wherever they live, and the supreme value of the Jewish faith and its ideals, wherever they are upheld? Should our working image be that of a circle with the State of Israel in the center, or of a circle with the Jewish people in the center, or of a circle with the Torah, in all its interpretations, as the center? Or should we think of an ellipse, with two foci, America and Israel, as our preferred image? Or, finally, should we abandon geometry altogether and seek our image in the human sphere?

Are we, then, a family, patriarchal and old-fashioned, with parents living in the ancient home, while their prodigal children roam the highways of the world, hoping to find the pot of gold before they return home? Or are we a modern family, with an ancestral estate—a family of mature children, ready

Originally published in *CCAR Journal*, 1972.

to come to the assistance of the brother or the sister that is in trouble; a family whose members have formed marital alliances with other families, without losing their love for their own primary family traditions and spiritual heritage? Strangely, it is the latter image of a family that is suggested in the Talmud, where the Father is God and the Mother is the congregation of Israel, Kenesset Yisroel, (*Berochot* 35b).

Many are the factors which we need to take into consideration, in order to find the right answer to these questions. Perhaps the most basic ingredient of a healthy response is the fundamental posture that a people assumes. So much depends on the vantage point of our reflections. We can rise above the prejudices and pieties of our time only if we recognize that they frequently pre-judge our conclusions.

In this paper, I propose to discuss the viability of the approach of the classicist to the evaluation of present-day Jewish life and thought.

Amidst all the twists and turns of human thought, we may discern a perennial philosophy that breathes the spirit of serenity and harmony. It may be termed classical because, whenever we encounter it, we feel certain that it corresponds essentially to the wisdom of the ages. It is the philosophy of those who have overcome the turbulence of youth and have penetrated through the smog of pride and prejudice that torments the masses of humanity. Its chief traits are the qualities of wholeness, balance, and reasonableness. It glories in a dispassionate evaluation of all opinions, and it shuns all forms of extremism. It values truth above all other virtues, objective truth that does not vanish like a dream in sober daylight.

In classical philosophy, as in the famous *Midrash*, truth is a fallen angel that springs out of the soil of experience (*Genesis Rabba* VIII, 5). But it is an angel that plays no favorites—open to all men, yet no one can hope to embrace it entire and pure. Even Moses, who passed through the forty-nine gates of wisdom, stood helpless and mute before the fiftieth and final one (*Rosh Hashono* 21b).

Along with the quest for universal truth, the classical temper includes an inner assurance that all human values are essentially coherent. Goodness and beauty, compassion and reverence are diverse facets of the one reality. The quest of reason leads beyond itself toward a vision, which is also reached by the other self-transcending drives of the human spirit—goodness, beauty, and holiness.

Thus far, classical philosophy reaches out on its own power. An Aristotle, a Spinoza, a Goethe, or a Hermann Cohen conveys a sense of the harmonious resonance of human values and cosmic truth. In the words of

Albert Einstein, "subtle is the good Lord, but He is not malicious" (*"Raffiniert ist der Herr Gott, aber boshaft ist er nicht."* Einstein, by Ronald Clark, New York, p. 390).

Religious thought introduces a fresh note into the selfless serenity of the classical philosopher, a note of re-assurance and dedication. Whether one's faith is generated by the cumulative impact of tradition or whether it springs full-blown out of the mysterious depths of one's being, faith is the felt resonance between personal values and cosmic reality. If God be conceived in personal terms, then faith is not simply a generalized trust, as Martin Buber affirms, but it is a trust that our own highest will is congruent with His Will. In a world view that transcends personalism the same assurance prevails, though the term Will is then applied to God metaphorically.

In both cases, we cherish a hierarchy of values and a conviction that it corresponds to the ultimate nature of things. We affirm that communion between God and man is not only possible—it has taken place. Our outstretched hands have been grasped. Our duties have become commands; we are filled with strength.

The great values of our culture were generated by such thrusts of the Divine. There is ground for hope, both personal and historical. If man can reflect the creative Will of God, he shares somehow in the glow of eternity. If history contains authentic records of inspiration and revelation, then its course is not altogether blind and fortuitous. The progressive thrusts of the Divine are not annulled by the many and painful lapses into technocratic barbarism. We see God in the miracles of the human spirit, such as brought victory over Hitler and refused to allow Auschwitz to beguile us into the adulation of Satan. It takes but one flash of lightning to illumine the entire horizon, even if it be for only a moment. The ensuing darkness cannot rob us of the memory of that piercing light

Thus, religious philosophy re-inforces the placid assurance of the classical philosopher, granting him literally the kind of peace that passes understanding. Moreover, it compels him to act out his convictions and to involve himself in the anguished concerns of his contemporaries. The religious philosopher cannot separate himself from the community to seek solace in contemplation. He is committed, or covenanted, for his values have become orders from above. He knows himself to be complete only insofar as he stands before God: *tamim tihye im Adonai Elohecho* (*Deuteronomy* 18:13).

Religious classicism is generally regarded as a synthetic product, hence unstable. In our Western history it emerged in full bloom following the confrontation of Hellenism with Biblical religion. In later centuries, it reappeared whenever the Biblical religions encountered afresh the genius of Hellenic philosophy. In this view, Philo and Maimonides and Mendelssohn and modern classicists are intellectual acrobats; they stand with one foot in the Biblical-rabbinic world, seeking to plant the other foot in the radically different worlds of Plato and Aristotle.

Whenever Judaism was thrown back upon its own resources and compelled to make do with its own original creations, it reverted back to a pragmatic, romantic, or mystical outlook—which, it was argued, is the authentic philosophy of authentic Jews. By the same token, Hellenism, liberated from the stifling embrace of Biblical faith, was enabled to re-assert its nontheistic, secularist genius in the various philosophies of the modern world.

The artificial synthesis which subsisted for sixteen centuries, from Philo to Spinoza, fell apart simply because its components were disparate, perhaps even contradictory. And any attempt to recombine them, it is maintained, is patently a violation of the inner genius of Judaism, which is unique and complete within itself. A modern version of the presumed dichotomy between religion and philosophy is to harp upon the distinction between the "idea of God" and an "existential encounter of the Divine," as if the two were necessarily mutually exclusive.

This is not the way I, as a religious classicist, see the nature of man, nor is it the way I see the course of our spiritual history. Classical religious philosophy is a basic human endeavor to take account of life as a whole. Man knows that he reflects a reality which transcends his understanding. Socrates, the fountainhead of Hellenic thought, is religious in his quest and philosophical in his method. He rejects Protagoras' thesis: "Man is the measure of all things—of things that are, that they are; of things that are not, that they are not." He knows that man's outreach is greater than his grasp, and he remains loyal to the infinite quest. Biblical faith begins with the same intuition: man is not alone; he stands before God, Who wills righteousness and justice.

In the ancient world, the feeling of dependence upon the gods, or any particular god, was widespread and unquestioned. The newness of Biblical faith consisted in its blend of religious feeling, rational wisdom, and ethical ardor. The ultimate Power is God, Whose Will is also the source of the feeble stirrings of conscience in our hearts, of our distinction between the holy and the unclean, of our irrespressible surges of hope and joy. While the Word of God impinges upon us from without, it is in essence one with our own deepest longings, even if the correlation is not immediately apparent. He is neither Power nor Person, but the Unknowable, in Whom Power and

Person, "the Life of life," "the Soul of souls," "the Will of wills," to use the terms of *Kabbalah*, co-exist with the secular goals of the True, the Good, and the Beautiful.

The Divine Word comes at us from many directions at once; there is the tradition of the priests and the elders, the living message of the prophets, the sober wisdom of the sages. But all these partial intimations of His Truth are, we affirm in faith, inwardly coherent. The unity of values within us reflects this unity in Him. The priest and the prophet stress the two aspects of the same mysterious command, with the priest cherishing the mystery and the prophet proclaiming the command. The sage, advancing beyond the limits of the convenanted community, elaborates the claims of human reason. Yet he too feels the impact of the religious demand—"the beginning of wisdom in the fear of the Lord" (*Proverbs* 9, 10).

Thus, the Hebrew Bible, taken as a whole, represents the spirit of religious classicism. Every claim of our complex personality is allowed, but with measure and balance. A fixed tradition is set for the people; but prophets, we are told, will arise who will bring fresh insight indicating how the Torah should be interpreted and applied. The authority of prophets in their turn is dependent on the faith they inspire. The role of kings is circumscribed.

The individual faces God directly. Precisely because he is a son of God, he must avoid the excesses of piety such as mortification of the flesh. He is obligated to learn, to understand, to search. "Seek Me and live." This saying of Amos's is, according to a Talmudic sage, the central pillar upon which the entire edifice of Judaism is based. This teaching is echoed in the Book of Proverbs: "The soul of man is a lamp of the Lord, searching his inmost parts." (*Makkot 24a. Proverbs 20, 27.*)

Because the component of wisdom was specifically included within the sacred heritage, Judaism was stimulated by the Hellenic challenge instead of being overwhelmed by it.

The Jewish Sages discovered kindred spirits in the Greek philosophers. So was born the myth that Plato and Aristotle were disciples of the disciples of Jeremiah. It was a strangely powerful myth, enduring in the work of the ecclesiastical historian Eusebius, Bishop of Caesaria and counselor of Constantine. And this myth was supported by an even stranger legend asserting that Hellenes and Hebrews were brother-peoples, with Abraham as their common physical and spiritual father. (I Maccabees 12, 1-23) Here was a reflection of the inner unity of religious classicism. While the Hebrews developed the institutions of faith and the Hellenes the categories of philosophy, they were essentially engaged in the same task of clarifying man's nature and his destiny. The purpose of the Torah, according to Philo, was to make the Israelites cosmopolitans, citizens of the cosmos; and the Stoics regarded philosophy as the gateway to virtue and to the ideal of *humanitas*.

Yet it cannot be denied that the delicate balance of religious classicism is exceedingly fragile. The massive upheavals of history generate passions which burst through the boundaries set by calm reflection.

Alone in the wilderness, Moses communes with the God of true Being, whose Name is "I am that I am." But when he encounters the harried Hebrews, he is forced to utilize the familiar rhetoric of tradition, saying: "the God of your fathers has sent me to you." (*Exodus* 3, 15)

Moses aims to mold the entire people in his image, but he discovers that he has to put a veil upon his face when he addresses the populace. And here, the tragic failure of classicism becomes apparent—the philosopher-prophet cannot really feel the elemental passions of the people in all their terrible power. His very reasonableness and openness impel him to ignore the irrational impulses and the self-serving myths which drive the locomotives of history.

This failing becomes obvious in times of great upheaval. Then, the masses seek and find charismatic leaders, who respond to their anger and despair. They follow the pied pipers who give vent to their frustrations and hatreds. Occasionally, there appears a leader who is also a visionary, opening up new vistas of pride and glory. What if the promised heavens are only fantasies? They move people, and "turn them on." What else is there for those who have lost their way in life?

Religious classicism then appears to be lifeless and irrelevant. The new mood centers on the reality of sheer feeling, the "gut reaction." As Kierkegaard put it: "subjectivity is truth." Instead of seeing life as a whole, romanticism lights up a part; instead of an open faith, accessible to all people, it extols the uniqueness of its people's heritage, revelling in all that makes it "peculiar." The faith of nighttime, when our vision turns inward, supersedes the daytime faith of objectivity. The very style of exposition changes from prose to poetry.

People become impatient with the measured cadences of classical liturgies, and seek to "shout with joy"—to sing, to dance, to touch one another, so long as the embers of emotion continue to glow.

This type of faith and celebration may be called romantic religion. Its character is likely to be determined by the particular phase of anti-classical rebellion that has given birth to it. Essentially, religious classicism declines on account of one or several of the following events.

An historic catastrophe occurs, which shatters the confidence of the age. Life appears to be totally unreasonable and cruel. All human constructs appear to be as frail and vain as the huts of the peasants when a mighty volcano pours its devastating streams of lava down the mountainside. How idle it then seems for man to presume that his perception of right and wrong, true and false, coincides with those of the Master of the universe! Man can only surrender, admit the vanity of his achievements, and seek the guidance of a mystagogue, or guru, living or dead. Howsoever the rhythm of despair and existential faith is stimulated, it gathers force from the recitation of the failures of rationality on the bloody arena of history.

The emergence of an individual's feeling of anomie corresponds to the hurt of failure on the international scene. Anomie is the product of the clash of cultures, wherein the individual is torn between diverse patterns of value. He finds himself walking in a noisy marketplace of ideas, with no clear guidelines to find his way. Inevitably, he goes through a stage of perturbation in which his normal defenses and habits erode and crumble. If he is self-centered and ambitious, he possesses at least a firm fulcrum upon which to base his life. He becomes success-oriented, pragmatic, and tough. But, to the extent to which he has been captured by moral and esthetic refinement, he is caught between his inner need for uplifting ideals and his perception of the weaknesses of the diverse cultures around him. The tender-minded and the soft-hearted are the most bewildered. Like the "Suffering Servant," they have taken upon themselves the sins of the world. They have risen above Consciousness One, sheer egoism, and Consciousness Two, the crystallized ideals of the several establishments, to use the terms of Charles Reich; but Consciousness Three is still only a dream and a distant vision.

Classical religion does not appeal to them, since its very reasonableness leads them to regard other faiths as equally worthy. Furthermore, in their excited state, all that is classical is too staid, too slow, too much encumbered by the evils of the world.

Romantic religion responds to the two aspects of personal and historical despair. It calls upon the individual to intensify his sensibilities by narrowing their range and to accept his assertive passions as worthy and true. To counter the cold glare of rational objectivity, he is counseled to form a tightly knit community with other like-minded people, so that their feelings can be sustained and re-inforced. Such a group will then nurture its common insights and shield them from the gaze of the vulgar. The nuclear community, being the vanguard of the future, must be kept "unspotted" of the hopelessly corrupt external world.

The other source of romantic religion is a revived and glorified ethnicism. The source of all values is then no longer the individual, with all his existential ardor, but the historical community to which he belongs. The mystique of modern nationalism is certainly a most powerful religion, judged by any psychological and sociological standards. The individual is urged to merge his identity with that of the historic people, which is to him the only valid source of truth and value and happiness. To safeguard the cosmic worth of one's own tradition against the challenge of other groups, the nationalist mystique projects the concepts of uniqueness, or chosenness. Only this or that group is perceived as possessing the truth in its fullness; all others are considered corrupt, and victims of the veil of illusion. A mythical interpretation of life and history is gradually created in order to nurture these seeds of romantic religion.

In a beautiful essay on romantic religion, Leo Baeck maintains that religions fall into two classes, classical and romantic. He accepts Schlegel's definition of romanticism as the philosophy "which treats sentimental material in a phantasmic form" (Leo Baeck, *Judaism And Christianity*, Jewish Publication Society, Philadelphia, 1958, p. 189). Then he proceeds to identify romantic religion with Christianity, and classical religion with Judaism. He takes the involuted theology of Paul as the quintessence of Christianity, contrasting it with a sanitized and rationalized exposition of rabbinic thought. For Paul, the all-important fact was faith in "Christ Crucified," a faith which was based on neither logic nor tradition, but was a free gift of God. The Jew, with the Torah, and the Greek, with his culture, could prepare themselves for the reception of redeeming faith. But neither Torah nor logic could suffice by themselves to generate this healing faith, since the rational and moral faculties of man had been twisted out of shape by the cosmic catastrophe of original sin. Man could be saved only by the intervention of God.

Paul's faith makes room for ethics only as a consequence of the life of the elect; essentially, his concept of Divine Grace is arbitrary, "beyond good and evil." In Judaism, faith is the integration and conservation of man's self-transcending quest; in Christianity, faith is something other than man's values—a unique feeling, nourished and sustained by a blend of Jewish and pagan myths. In Judaism, the holy is conceived as a command, hence an obligation that falls into the order of this world, which is rational and ethical; in Christianity, the holy is essentially a mystery, hence, the "deposit of faith" is trans-worldly and trans-ethical.

I do not agree with this identification of Judaism as classicist in temper and Christianity as a romantic religion. While, like Baeck's, my own philosophy is definitely classical, I admit that Judaism contains romantic-mystical currents as well as a rationalist-humanistic stream. The classical philosophy has prevailed in Judaism at rare moments—in classical prophecy, in a Hillel, in a Philo, in a Rabbi Judah the Patriarch, in a Saadia, in a

Maimonides, in a Mendelssohn, and in a Krochmal. Leo Baeck was himself a fine example of classical Judaism. But the prophetizers were popular preachers in their day, and the prophets too lapsed into atavistic sentiments when they fell from their own highest standards and extolled the sacred mystery of Israel's election. The glorification of the seed of Israel, as distinct from the vocation of Israel, is a specific symptom of romanticism. In Halevi, sacred ethnicism is given its most elaborate formulation; and in the *Zohar*, ethnic sentiment is woven into a fantastic theosophy. The complexity and rigidity of Jewish Law could not be fully justified by the reasoning of a Maimonides. Nor could the mentality of martyrdom be rationalized on any classical principles. Hence, the reversion to the dark seclusion of Kabbalistic mythology in the long centuries of persecution and despair.

By the same token, Christianity had its classical as well as its romantic interpreters. Paul's philosophy was not understood, let alone accepted, by the early Patristic Fathers, who re-introduced the rationality of Hellenism and the moralism of Judaism into the teachings of Christianity. Similarly, the doctrine of the *Logos* and the teachings of Jesus in the Synoptic Gospels played decisive roles in the evolution of Christian doctrine.

The massive stream of Christian rationalistic scholasticism must be set over against those who affirmed their faith "because it was absurd." While in a comparison of their theological systems, Judaism was far more rational than Christianity, the Jews nonetheless displayed unequalled stubbornness and a degree of heroic self-sacrifice that no rationalistic system could justify. If Christian romanticism was chiefly of the individualistic sort, the modern world has seen the blend of ethnic pride with religion in the works of Schleiermacher and Dostoevsky, and in the racial theories of Renan, de Lagarde, and their imitators. In contrast, Jewish romanticism is largely of the ethnic type, with only an occasional sprinkling of individualistic, existential irrationalism.

As I see it, classicism and romanticism constitute a dialectical polarity within both Judaism and Christianity. The pendulum swings from one to the other in keeping with the temper of the age. In each case, a new swing of the pendulum does not simply bring back a previous philosophy. For in life, you never go back home. New facts, relationships, and ways of thinking modify the philosophy of every generation, leaving room for new intellectual leaders to fulfill their roles. But there is always an interaction between the philosopher and the spirit of the age, even if the philosopher conceives his task to be that of a critic and an adversary of his misguided contemporaries.

The eruption of Jewish romanticism in our day was an inevitable reaction to the cataclysmic events of the past four decades. The rise of Hitler in

Central Europe marked the end of the era of Emancipation. The hot pogroms and the cold ones, which dumped Jewish refugees like unwanted merchandise into a resisting international No Man's Land, turned Palestine into the only open haven of refuge. The subsequent holocaust and its aftermath deeply wounded the souls of Jews the world over. The rise of Israel, the Stalinist persecutions, the remarkable air-lift of distant communities, the rapid absorption of two-and-a-half-million Jews in the course of two decades—all these events turned Zionism from the philosophy of the few to the program of the many. As the economic and social successes of Israel were supplemented by brilliant military victories, Israel-centrism became well-nigh universal. And the distinctions between it and classical Zionism became academic.

The two sources of religious romanticism, an historic catastrophe and the glorification of ethnicism, were in the past generation supplemented by the third source: the individual's reaction to anomie. In the bitter after-taste of the Second World War, existentialism emerged first in intellectual and restrained forms. Sartre became the philosopher of the new generation, and Karl Barth its theologian, championing neo-orthodoxy; Franz Kafka became posthumously the novelist who best captured the absurdity of the human condition.

Popular existentialism in the fifties took the form of a return to religion. The individual, lost and despairing, can rediscover the meaning and purpose of life by recognizing the vanity of the world and preparing himself for an existential decision. Thus the effect of the war and the holocaust, coupled with the outburst of ethnic pride occasioned by the exploits of Israel, was reinforced by the growth and dominance of the existentialist approach.

The triumph of religious romanticism in the Jewish world did not completely shatter the position of religious classicism. Classical Reform was virtually abandoned. But, with due concession to the facts and value of ethnic diversity, the liberal tradition was reinforced by the victory over Fascism and Nazism. The dark forces of Antisemitism were completely discredited throughout the free world. The Emancipation was as truly successful in the Anglo-American and Western worlds as it was truly a failure in Central Europe. The post-War tide of liberalism revolutionized the universities of America, breaking down the barriers of class and race. The rationalistic spirit permeated the ranks of the Catholic Church, revived the interfaith movement, and projected the goals of ecumenism. The natural philosophy of Jews in the modern world was always that of a somewhat modified liberalism, amended by religious or ethnic emphasis. The liberal premises constituted the foundation for the freedom and equality of Jewish people in the Diaspora, while either religion or ethnic loyalty or both, in a variety of mixes, were needed to provide motivation for the continuity of a separate Jewish community.

The synthesis of religious classicism made the Jew feel at home in his native country, sharing its loyalties and ideals, while continuing to maintain his own religious culture, with all its ethnic overtones. In a romantic synthesis, the alienism of the Jew is likely to be expounded as the magisterial first principle, with life in the Diaspora being interpreted as inescapably problematical, even if temporarily desirable.

In recent years, the romantic temper and philosophy have predominated in the Jewish world, principally because the holocaust and the uncertain fortunes of Israel were the focus of attention. To be sure, the excesses of the youth movement have led to a revulsion against the wild weeds of popular romanticism—the gut-reaction, the exhibitionist wilderness of the spirit, or anomie, the fervent exaggerations, and the general myopia that is induced by mass-enthusiasm. But this reaction is still in its initial stages. And it is in this generation that the leaders of Diaspora Jewry may have to confront some very fateful decisions.

Some thoroughly pragmatic persons are now concerned with the character of Jewish identity. And for very good reason. At issue is the nature and destiny of the Jewish Diaspora. Should the Israeli view, which envisages the immigration of a minority to Israel and the assimilation of the rest, become the basis of communal planning? This view, for all its objective irrationality, appeals to the "pooled pride" of our people and to their latent fears. Because inner alienism generates outer rejection, this mood possesses the grave potential of becoming a self-fulfilling prophecy. It is not greatly ameliorated by any concessions to practicality granted by some cautious statesmen. For the real issue is one of vision and purpose. "Without vision, a people perishes" (*Proverbs* 29, 18).

The vision of Israel's destiny is seen differently by classicists than it is by romanticists. To the former, the essence of the Jewish heritage is a body of ideals, sentiments, mutual concerns, and aspirations; to the latter, it is peoplehood that matters, not in the ususal sense of the term but in the presumed incomparable peoplehood of the Jews—who are, in their own view, peculiar and unique, forever alienated from the sentiments and ways of thinking of the rest of the world. These elements of peculiarity and unique-ness are precisely the sentiments that the romanticists seek to foster, in order to keep the Jewish Diaspora from constituting itself as a normal component of the nations among whom Jews live. Strangely, it is the very philosophies of romantic and biological nationalism, which the European Antisemites developed, that now exert a special fascination for those Jews who exult in the thrills of "thinking with one's blood."

To the classicist, ideals and rational analysis constitute the decisive values of society. People are asked to transfer their loyalties from the ethnic divisions of the past to the cementing ideals of the state and humanity. While ethnic values and associations may be helpful in enhancing the vitality of a democratic society, they must not be allowed to distort the freedom of the individual and the role of the state. So, in America, the new ethnicism must be kept from affecting the state as a whole and the rights of the individual in the domain of economic and cultural opportunity. And in Israel, the Arab citizens must be accorded the same rights as the Jewish citizens. While to the romanticist the national component in the nation-state is pre-eminent, to the classicist, the statist or human component is predominant. Ever since the French Revolution, Jewish leaders have had to struggle against the dark reactionary passions of nationalist romanticism. Nazism and the Holocaust were the fearful consequences of a century of romanticist preaching of German peoplehood, *Volkstum*.

In order to confront the basic issues involved in a consistent affirmation of the Diaspora, our intellectual leaders have to rise above the immediate exigencies of our decade and see how our thinking has evolved in the past two centuries. Then we shall recognize the basic alternatives presented by the two world views that comprise our complex heritage. I have no doubt that, given the complete perspective of our times, most of our intellectuals will return to the classical philosophy, either in its religious or in its secular form.

# EXCEPTIONALISM AS META-MYTH

SOMETIME AGO the late Henry Hurwitz and I coined the term *meta-myth* to stand for the notion that the Jewish people are mysteriously and metaphysically different from the rest of humanity. This myth is of course deeply imbedded in the romantic and naive currents of ancient and medieval Judaism.

We called it a myth because in itself it is a vestige of ancient, pre-critical thought, though it is frequently associated in Judaism with the noblest ideals of self-sacrifice. Myths have a life and even a logic of their own, since they draw their power from the collective Unconscious. In mythology, the "will to believe" is directed toward concrete things—in this case, an empirical people of flesh and blood. Also, myths reflect the drive of instincts, which were developed in the struggle for survival, rather than the outreach of ideals—in this case, the hurt of injured pride and ethnic prejudice. Again, as Emile Durkheim and Lucien Levy-Brühl pointed out, primitive, pre-culture peoples worshipped "collective representations" of their own corporate being, in effect deifying the life of the tribe or the folk. In all its brute power, this kind of myth has been reincarnated in the "folkist" movements of our own day. And its power is not yet spent.

The meta-myth is not identical with the "Chosen People" concept, which could be interpreted in historical and rational terms—that is, as a fact of history, the Jews became the first bearers of monotheism. "My first-born Israel" (Exodus 4:22)—first in a family of many sons. This priority doubtless imposes upon Israel special obligations, in accordance with the famous "therefore" of Amos (Amos 3:2), But, apart from the initiative of God, the character of the Jewish people may not be different from that of other nations. Indeed, they may well be a "stiff-necked" people (Exodus 32:9). Furthermore, the Jews could be "chosen," in the sense of *example*, rather than *exception*; that is, the career of Israel dramatizes the turbulent love-affair between God and mankind. In its liberal interpretation, Israel represents

Originally published in *CCAR Journal*, 1979.

both the greatness and the littleness of humanity, according as it turns toward or away from God.

The meta-myth, on the contrary, stresses Jewish *exceptionalism*. It insinuates the nightmarish fog of mystery into the public image of the Jew of our day. It transfers the secret of the purpose of God, which was not revealed to any man, not even to Moses, to the mundane struggles of the market-place. A whole community is either chosen, or rejected, pre-determined for salvation or perdition. A fantastic theology becomes an invidious biology. Our so-called "uniqueness" is made to depend upon our blood. The Jews are "a people apart that is not counted among the nations" (Numbers 23:9). Halevi puts them in a unique domain, extending between humanity and the angels (Halevi, *The Kuzari*, I, 103). This mode of thinking became axiomatic in the vast literature of *Kabbalah*, and in the folk-imagination of our people. In the popular imagination, it drew immense power from the dispersion of the Jewish people—their "ghost-like" unity, in spite of their utter fragmentation.

The Christian religion took over the meta-myth, but changed its valence from plus to minus. The Chosen People, favored by divine fiat, were now the "rejected" people, living under a curse until the end of days. The pro-Semitic theologians labored hard to prove that Israel's fate was distinguished from that of mankind in two ways, a plus and minus, chosen, rejected, to be chosen again.[2] But even in the more favorable view, the Jew was not to be seen as just another human being, to be judged by the same standards, praised and condemned by the same lights. The historical categories of nationality and religion, cultural amalgamation and segregation, rationality and romantic fantasy do not apply to him. Superhuman and sub-human, he is accordingly in a class apart.

The historical consequences of the meta-myth were inevitable—about the Jews, the wildest charges were believable. After all, they were an enigmatic mystery, akin to that of the Incarnation; only unlike the latter, they incarnated, in the Christian view, God's Love turned into Wrath.

It is hardly necessary to pass in review the various expressions of the meta-myth in the long and dismal record of Christian Antisemitism. Jules Isaac has put us all in his debt by his collection of material from French Catholic sources. The Vatican Council had made a valiant effort to inhibit, if not to destroy completely, the dragon's seed of anti-Jewish mythology still rampant in the Christian world. The Christian task is far from completed, however. Christian writers still speak of the "rejection" of the Jewish people as a result of the Crucifixion—as if God had intervened in the course of history to put Jews, and only Jews, under His continuing "wrath." Even Augustin Cardinal Bea, who authored and defended the *Schema* calling on

Christians to desist from acting as "avengers of Christ," nevertheless claimed that a cosmic guilt somehow persisted within Jewry. *All* Jews must not be condemned for the crime of deicide (Augustine Cardinal Bea, *The Church and the Jewish People*, New York: Harper & Row, 1966, p. 69). However, the guilt "falls upon any one, who in some way *associates* himself with the 'perverse generation,' which is primarily guilty . . " (*ibid.*, p. 78). And "the refusal to believe in the Gospel and in Jesus is a factor in this judgment, and so, in one way or another, is a free decision to ally oneself with the 'perverse generation,' with the powers opposed to God" (*ibid.*, p. 85). Accordingly, Jews are left in an ambiguous position. Their "refusal" is *a* factor, not *the* factor. The meta-myth is suspended, not dissipated.

It is exceedingly difficult for an orthodox faith, claiming infallibility, to move clearly and unequivocally to a new position. Its protagonists have to back into the future obliquely, while protesting that they cling to an unchanged past. Nevertheless, I believe that in the contemporary Dialogue, the humanist position can be asserted and developed, in a way which will result eventually in the total repudiation of the meta-myth. This assurance is based upon the fact that the humanist outlook is itself part of the Judeo-Christian heritage. The very concept of Dialogue derives from the irresistible momentum of the humanist ideal within both Judaism and Christianity. In a meaningful Dialogue, this common heritage is likely to be reinforced in numberless and intangible ways.

However, this blessing will surely elude us, if our own ideologists continue to move within the shadowed underbrush of mythology. We live today in continuous interaction with our Christian neighbors, so that a Dialogue, implicit and many-sided, is constantly in progress. Indeed, we speak loudest when we think we speak to ourselves alone. Unfortunately, in recent years, the meta-myth in our tradition has gathered fresh force and a massive world-wide impetus. Within three decades, our generation was cast into the darkest depths and exalted to the loftiest heights. Such a fantastic chain of events fits better into the mold of mythology than within the compass of a reasonable world-view. But our destiny depends on the growing power of reason in human affairs. Say our Sages, "If a person devotes himself to understanding, it is as if the Holy Temple were built up in his day" (Sanhedrin 99a.).

By way of clarifying the general posture that an authentic life of Dialogue implies, I wish to call attention to the exchange of letters which took place in 1916 between Franz Rosenzweig and Eugen Rosenstock-Huessy. It illustrates vividly what a *Dialogue must not be*—since both parties were seized by the meta-myth, as by a *Dibbuk*.

This historic Dialogue is especially significant because of the stature of the two exponents. Rosenzweig continued to grow as a Jewish theologian, with his best insights appearing in his "minor essays" (*Kleinere Schriften*, Schocken, Berlin, 1937). Rosenstock-Heussy was a formidable philosopher, who, as a Jew, could not be accused of Antisemitism. He was converted at age sixteen, ten years or so before this debate. Nor, as his later life demonstrated, could he be accused of the perversion of "self-hate."

Alexander Altmann extols this Dialogue as an epoch-making event:

> . . . one of the most important religious documents of our age . . . Unlike the medieval disputations, in which dogma was arrayed against dogma, verse set against verse, this discussion is a true dialogue. It is indeed the most perfect example of a human approach to the Jewish-Christian problem. It is also an exemplification of what is called the "existential" attitude to theological problems . . . (*Judaism Despite Christianity*, Schocken Press, University of Alabama, 1969, pp. 26, 27).

Hans J. Schoeps also heaped extravagant praise upon the Dialogue. Schoeps and Altmann were enamored of this Dialogue because both participants were passionately "existentialist," repudiating the intellectual "common ground" of humanism and rationalism. Both disputants held fast to the myth that the Jew was metaphysically unique. Both had come to reject the kind of religion which was at that time best articulated in Adolf Harnack's *The Essence of Christianity*, an exposition of the Protestant faith in terms of three principles—the Kingdom of God, as an inner dedication to living in accord with the highest ideals, the awareness of God's Fatherhood as a living reality, and the task of striving for a "higher righteousness." These principles are clearly not in conflict with Judaism. A dialogue on this basis would be a friendly exchange of similar views differing only in nuance, and in historic associations with divergent patterns of rites and symbols.

But, according to both participants, such an approach would rob the Dialogue of the sharpness of confrontation. Both the Jewish Jew and the Christian Jew were eager to move the Jewish-Christian argument from the rational sphere to the domain of the trans-rational, the mysterious course of God's redemption within the flow of human history.

As Eugen phrased their common axioms fifty years later in his Epilogue:

> Franz and Eugen came to agree on the futility of the shilly-shallying academic shibboleths of their day—objectivity, humanism, and the so-called enlightenment. They agreed that real people can be Jews or Christians, but they may not play the roles of "Benjamin Franklin," or

"Thomas Paine," at least not for long, since there can be no common sense—certainly no good sense shared in common—among men who are content to be ciphers, dealing in generalities and platitudes (*Judaism Despite Christianity, op. cit.*, "Prologue-Epilogue," p. 75).

Strange, is it not, that "common sense" must be thrown overboard in order that one should rise above a cipher? Yet, Eugen describes this repudiation of "all positivists and pragmatists" as "a united front of Jews and Christians." By that time, Eugen had come to believe that God takes the initiative through the vision of Christ in opening the human soul to His call. He had written of "speech-thinking" and the "I-Thou" event long before Buber and Rosenzweig. "The soul must be called *Thou* before she can ever reply *I*, before she can ever speak of *us* and finally *it*. Through the four figures, *Thou, I, We, It*, the Word walks through us, the Word must call our name first . . ." (*ibid.*, p. 70).

Can one argue with the private revelations of latter-day prophets? Yes and no. If one pretends to live in the tradition of the Hebrew prophets, he must ask himself whether he is not one of the "prophetizers," from whom the prophets separated themselves. The distinguishing quality of the prophets, even if they did not always rise up to their own ideal, was to identify the Word of God with the moral-rational imperative. Whatever is contrary to this twofold demand cannot be divine. Yet, Eugen, presuming to rise far beyond "common sense," quickly sinks to the dark depths of mythology, which can hardly be distinguished from medieval superstition. Super-sophisticated as he was, he demonstrated the treacherous pitfalls that await those who depart from the well-lit highway of religious humanism. Their private "lights" turn out to be will of the wisps, leading to ancient prejudices. Consider the following phrases, which were interwoven into Eugen's dialectic:

(a) The Jews "always crucify again the one who came to make the word true."

(b) "With all the power of their being, they set themselves against their own promises."

(c) ". . . the image of Lucifer."

(d) Israel's "naive way of thinking that one has won inalienable rights in perpetuity against God."

(e) "You [the Jews] have no aptitude for theology, for the search for truth, any more than for beauty."

(f) The Jews strives too hard just to live.

(g) "The Jew dies for no country and no cause."

(h)    The reliance of the individual Jew is "on the number of his children."
       To sum up, "He is a paragraph of the Law, *C'est tout.*"

We all know that these and similar stereotypes come naturally to the
minds of traditional Christians. What is surprising in this Dialogue is that
Franz, at that time groping his way to authentic Judaism, sees virtually the
same picture. To him, the Jew is a mysterious, solitary wanderer, overladen
by a mountainous metaphysical burden, moving among hostile, uncompre-
hending people, resolutely rejecting their occasional friendly embraces and
steadfastly insulating himself from the world. One is reminded of Sartre's
image of the "authentic" Jew, choosing his own damnation from the hands of
his tormentors. Is this the meaning of the title the editor gave to this
exchange, as if Judaism finds its fulfillment in "spiting" Christianity?—Such
an empty, negative definition of the Jewish faith ignores the living kernel and
casts the spotlight exclusively on the outer husk of Judaism.

Franz, then in the early stages of his spiritual development, interprets
Antisemitism as a reflection of the Divine Will, as it were. Far from being
only a consequence of ignorance, envy and hate, it is a metaphysical
phenomenon, an expression of the deep wisdom of Providence, not to be
judged "by its vulgar and stupid expressions." It reflects a "theological idea,"
which both Jews and Christians sense, even if they do not understand; the
former articulate it in a peculiar "pride," the latter in an imperious hate,
which transcends the limits of understanding.

> This practical way, in which the theological idea of the stubbornness
> of the Jews works itself out, is *hatred of the Jews.* You know as well as I do
> that all its realistic arguments are only fashionable cloaks to hide the true
> metaphysical ground: that we will not make common cause with the
> world-conquering fiction of Christian dogma . . . and putting it in a
> popular way: that we have crucified Christ, and believe we would do it
> again every time . . . (*Ibid.*, p. 113).

Did we crucify Christ? Do we do it again, every time?—
For a century and a half, liberal Jewish thinkers have been proclaiming
that "the religion of Jesus" was fully within the compass of Judaism. It is "the
religion *about* Jesus" which emerged and developed within the Hellenistic
world that Jews refused to accept.

Not content with providing a metaphysical root for Antisemitism, the
young Franz, fired by the boundless fervor of a neophyte, maintains that the
"metaphysical basis" of the Jewish attitude to Christians consists of three
beliefs—1) "that we have the truth," 2) "that we are at the goal," 3) "that any

and every Jew feels in the depths of his soul that the Christian relation to God, and so in a sense, their religion is particularly and extremely pitiful, poverty-stricken and ceremonious; namely, that as a Christian one has to learn from someone else, whoever he may be, to call God 'our Father.' To the Jew, that God is our Father is the first and most self-evident fact—and what need is there for a third person between me and my Father in heaven? That is no discovery of modern apologetics but the simplest Jewish instinct, a mixture of failure to understand and pitying contempt" (*ibid.*, p. 113).

One can hardly believe that these words were written by a reverent disciple of Hermann Cohen, who was prone to identify the inner core of Christianity with what he called "prophetic Judaism." As he put it in a conversation with Prof. Lange: "What you call Christianity, I call prophetism" (H. Cohen, *Jüdische Schriften*, II, in his essay, *"Der Jude in der Christlichen Kultur,"* p. 194). By the same token, Rosenzweig was aware that the Christian includes the Old Testament in his heritage, hence also God's Fatherhood, though, to be sure, some radical Protestants in his day were prepared to follow Marcion and jettison the Hebrew Bible. We wonder, too, how he could possibly speak of a "Jewish instinct," prompting the individual's awareness of God's Fatherhood, in the second decade of the twentieth century, when atheism was rampant among Jews as much as among Gentiles and when the horrors of racism were becoming manifest.

Furthermore, as a Hegelian who saw the hand of God in the actual evolution of world-history, Franz Rosenzweig saw the Christian Church, and only the Church (excluding the faith of Islam), as the agency through which Judaism carried out its divine mission. We recall his image of the "star" of Judaism, with the rays of Christianity issuing from it to illumine the darkness of the universe. In the *Star of Redemption*, he wrote, "This existence of the Jew constantly subjects Christianity to the idea that it is not attaining the goal, the truth, that ever remains—on the way. That is the profoundest reason for the Christian hatred of the Jew, which is heir to the pagan hatred of the Jew. In the final analysis, it is only self-hate, directed to the objectionable mute admonisher, for all that he but admonishes by his existence . . ." (F. Rosenzweig, *The Star of Redemption*, English translation by W. W. Hallo, New York, 1971, p. 413).

We overlook for the moment this psychoanalysis of Antisemitism. A "metaphysical" phenomenon will harbor in its dialectic all kinds of fantasies. But, we note how readily such romantic, self-glorifying rhetoric quickly sours into the typical verbiage of Antisemitism itself. The Jew must serve as "a ferment on Christianity and through it on the world" (*Judaism Despite Christianity*, p. 136). Indeed, Antisemitism is now "metaphysically

grounded," for within the nations of Europe the Jew cannot but act as a
"parasite."

> For you may curse, you may swear, you may scratch yourself as
> much as you like, you won't get rid of us, we are the louse in your fur. We
> are the internal foe; don't mix us up with the external one! Our enmity
> may have to be bitterer than any enmity for the external foe, but all the
> same—we and you are within the same frontier, in the same kingdom
> (*ibid.*, p. 130).

If all this masochistic posturing were not bad enough, Franz does not
hesitate to draw the logical consequences of his self-image, as an incorrigible
outsider.

> I myself have written fully already of how our whole part in the life of
> the peoples can only be *clam, vi, precario* (secret, perforce, precarious). No
> doubt all we can do is hack's work; we must accept the verdict of what
> people think of us, and we cannot be our own judges (*ibid.*, p. 135).
> I myself, since you mention it, conduct myself merely dutifully
> toward the State; I do not take a post in one of its universities, and do not
> offer myself as a volunteer in the army, but go to the International Red
> Cross . . . (*ibid.*, p. 136).

It is left to Eugen, the Christian Jew, to remind Franz that the Emancipation was also part of history.

> Twist and turn as you like, the emancipation of the Jews is the process
> of the self-destruction of the European tradition, which has removed the
> dogma of the stubbornness of the Jews just as it blotted out that of the
> Christian Emperor (*ibid.*, p. 143).

We can forgive Franz Rosenzweig for his macabre vision of the Jewish
destiny, his racial mystique and his rebellion against the classical tradition.
In the Germany of his day only the Liberals and the Socialists could accept
the Jew fully as a citizen of the German nation-state. The traditional
Conservatives longed for a "Christian" state, and the rapidly rising cadre of
deracinated intellectuals sought greatness in the revival of ancient Teutonic
mythology. The Nazi ideology, built up steadily by Wagner, Nietzsche,
Moeller, Chamberlain and Spengler in diverse nuances, was rising fast and
furious on the horizon. A sensitive Jew, who for his own reasons rejected the
liberal philosophy, could not but seek refuge in the counter-myths of *Volk*

and *instinct*, the "decline of the West" and the resurgence of Teutonic fury, with the Jew retiring to live under the protective shadow of a *unique* Providence.

To get a feel of that age, we need only read the autobiography of Jakob Wasserman, a contemporary of the two young theologians, whose despair is summed up in these words:

> It is in vain to keep faith with them [Antisemites], be it as co-fighters or as citizens. They say—he [the Jew] is a Proteus, he can do everything.
> It is in vain to help them knock off the chains of slavery from their bodies. They say he will surely make profit out of the deal.
> It is in vain to counter any poisons; they brew it afresh.
> It is in vain to live for them and die for them; they say—he is a Jew.
> (Jakob Wassermann, *Mein Weg als Deutscher und Jude*, Berlin, 1922, p. 122)

To be understood and appreciated for his valid insights, Rosenzweig must be viewed within the context of his age. His mind was as a lambent flame which blended together many diverse fires. As we read his fervent prose, we can see him struggling to find a way in the treacherous minefield that was the German intellectual scene between the two World Wars. We have much to learn from Rosenzweig and Rosenstock, but we must recognize the "meta-myth" wherever we find it and know that its concentrated social venom is the invariant catalyst of mythological Antisemitism.

This awareness is a timely warning. For while the "meta-myth" in its Christian form has been allayed in recent years, it appears to have been born in a fresh guise in the Moslem world. Indeed as the Islamic nations see the dawn of a new Golden Age in their newly found oil-wealth, they are impelled by daily headlines to see the little state of Israel as their collective enemy. Naturally, the antagonist must be worthy of the steel of so mighty a horde; hence, the stature of Israel must be blown up to mythic proportions.

Even now, we see the ancient myth taking on an Islamic shape. Moslem writers see Israel as the body of a mythical octopus-like monster, with tentacles, visible and invisible, extending into the mighty capitals of the world, pulling the wires of the marionettes of parliaments and congresses. Soon enough, they will resurrect forgotten *Hadiths*, depicting the Jew as the inveterate minion of Satan. Hold on to your copies of *The Jewish Encyclopedias* and to the classic Jewish works on the Moslem faith, for in a little while we shall be inundated with tracts demonstrating that Islam was always and everywhere wedded to mythological Antisemitism! So, *ain beraira*, we never have an alternative.

In Greek legend, ghosts are reincarnated when they drink blood. Even now, this particular ghost has drawn blood and behold—it is materializing before our very eyes.

As Jews, we are all too prone to be fascinated and even intoxicated by the "meta-myth," with all its dark and heartwarming pathos. Only now, the myth is centered around the state of Israel, rather than about the widely scattered Diaspora. Everything about Israel is seen in an eerie light, so that it is either bathed in messianic, unearthly glory, or in the dark colors of pseudo-messianic despair. Overblown rhetoric resounds all about us, as if we were standing at the Eschaton.

In the past, we have prided ourselves on our capacity to reject the hold of myths upon our faith. Ezekiel Kaufman sought to demonstrate this thesis with an amazing display of erudition and brilliance. Reform thinkers in particular have been the stout champions of an anti-mythological mentality. The renowned philosopher, George Santayana, wrote in 1951, "Hebraism is a striking example of a religion tending to discard mythology and magic" (G. Santayana, *The Life of Reason*, condensed one-volume edition, p. 258).

But have not some of us turned ourselves into a myth, uprooted from humanity and endowed with a unique, mysterious sanctity? Have we allowed the momentum of this historic myth to seduce us to the worship of "blood and soil?" Have we joined in the chorus of the Israeli chant of despair, "the whole world is against us?" Has the messianic mood, in all its millennial depth, distorted our perception of reality, like a psychedelic drug? Have we lost the capacity to glory in the imageless Absolute, the source of the ideals of rationality and humanism? These are some of the questions that we should ponder, as the future rushes upon us with the speed of jets.

# OUR FAITH

# HOLISM AND THE JEWISH RELIGION

HOLISM IS the philosophy which regards the appearance of organisms or wholes in nature as the key to the understanding of the cosmos.

The data of evolution reveal the emergence of ever more complex wholes, embodying ever greater ranges of freedom. In an organism, the whole is more than the sum of its parts. An intelligence is manifestly at work that functions from the whole to its parts, forming a polar contrast to the mechanistic forces which operate in the inanimate world.

The organismic philosophies of Jan Smuts, Henri Bergson, Samuel Alexander, A. N. Whitehead and Charles Hartshorne elaborate the same holistic axiom, though they differ in details.

## Holism and the Jewish Religion

Holism is a modern world-view. Yet, in its essentials, it is the perennial philosophy of Judaism and the theistic religions stemming from it. The God of the Holy Scriptures is the "God of life, *elohim hayim*.[1] More specifically "the spirit of God " is identified as a primordial force, preceding the creation of the cosmos. We can read the biblical account of creation as a metaphor for the continuous creativity of God, in the realm of spirit. The Creator's "resting" on the Sabbath-day and blessing it symbolizes the transference of this concept from the laws of necessity governing nature to the domain of freedom and human society.

More to the point, in contrast to the glorification of sheer vitality in paganism, Scripture identifies God as revealed in the human spirit at its best. The divine work of creation continues in the free and fragile society of mankind, where the kingdom of God is emerging steadily, even if with agonizing slowness and occasional setbacks.

With this preamble, we proceed to indicate the characteristic mode of religious experience in Judaism.

35

The protean awareness of transcendence is generally shaped and structured by the continuing impetus of religious traditions. We absorb subliminally some basic postures and interpret our own experiences accordingly. We cannot altogether escape the momentum of our particular traditions, though by a sympathetic interpretation of other faiths, we may recognize the subjective character of some of our most fundamental perceptions.

In Judaism the thrust of revelation is perceived as a transcendent command—"Thou shalt" and "Thou shalt not." God's Will is apprehended as an ethical call. So, Abraham demands justice from the Almighty.[2] Jeremiah dares to indict the justice of Providence.[3] Isaiah declares, "the holy Lord is sanctified through righteousness."[4] The illustrations of this theme are numberless. A Jewish child is introduced to the requirement of *mizvot*, commandments, and he or she enters maturity as a son or daughter of the commandment (Bar or Bat Mizvah).[5] The word is in the singular, since the whole of Judaism is comprised in the sense of responding to the Divine imperative. The Torah as a whole is denoted as the *mizvah*, the Commandment.[6]

This emphasis on a transcendent ethical imperative does not exclude either the rationalistic or the esthetic categories. On the contrary, it implies both of these dimensions.

The divine command is not arbitrary but an invitation to join the Lord in completing the work of creation.[7] Man, as a free being, capable of cherishing the vision of a perfectly just and humane society is described as a partner of the Lord in the building of His Kingdom. We are most human precisely when we respond to the divine call. Hence, it is as free, autonomous beings that we structure the divine thrust as a command.

The divine Command is conceived in philosophical Judaism as primarily ethical, with all ritual precepts being interpreted as symbols and disciplines. So, Maimonides classifies the laws of Torah as being either of primary or of secondary intention, the former being ethical, the latter ritualistic.[8]

The Ten Commandments consist of seven purely ethical commands and three borderline precepts—belief in the One God, the injunction against the worship of images or of desecrating His Name, and the observance of the Sabbath. Since these three precepts were not binding upon non-Jews, the Sages spoke of "Seven Noachide precepts." Non-converted Gentiles were not enjoined from worshipping divine beings, in addition to the One God; the rabbis differed as to their obligation to sanctify His Name *(Kiddush hashem)*; they were not obliged to observe the Sabbath.[9]

Three of the Ten Commandments are therefore on the boundary between ethics and ritual. An ethical view of man implied belief in God, as the Infinite Spirit, partially reflected in the spirit of man. The first Commandment identifies God as the Source of human freedom. Already, Philo interpreted the concept of *imago dei, (tselem Elohim)*, as freedom, for the human mind "was shaped after the archetypal idea, the most sublime Logos."[10] The Sabbath is an implication of freedom, in both its social and ontological denotations. Man must be free from drudgery one day a week and celebrate His Kinship with the Creator, "resting" on the Sabbath.

The command to build God's Kingdom on earth involved the task of confronting the physical and social realities of life—i.e., to enter history as a creative force. Hence, the emphasis in Judaism on rationality and study. Reason is the reflection in our minds of the laws and principles governing the universe. The realm of necessity, that is, physical nature, is supplemented by the realm of freedom, which is man's collective effort to realize the *eschaton*, the attainment of the purpose of history. While the pagans saw the work of God chiefly in the rhythms of nature, the prophets and Sages of Judaism saw the works of God chiefly in the movement of human history toward the "kingdom of the Almighty". The *Heilsgeschichte* of the past was a symbolic articulation of the vision of the future. The Covenant of Sinai and its periodic renewals were anticipations of the prophetic hope for a Covenant written onto the tablets of the heart. The story of Creation, described in Genesis, is symbolic of the on-going creativity of the Supreme Being, "Who in His Goodness renews the works of creation day by day."[11] The *Eschaton* is not a particular day, fixed in the calendar of human affairs, but every day insofar as creative and redeeming events transpire within its duration.[12] So, the thrusts of the divine, in our experience, are essentially revelatory of the ethical imperative, but they imply also the duty of rational study and the civilizing, humanizing esthetic arts, which are so many aids to the celebration of the values revealed in human life, culminating in the worship of the Source of all values.

The widespread assumption that Judaism sees the divine revelation as sheer law is erroneous. Biblical-rabbinic theology recognizes the divine as an imperative, addressed to each individual as well as to the community as a whole. Even love, the love of God and of man, is commanded as a *mizvah*. Indeed, the Sages agreed with Jesus that these two commandments are at the apex of the hierarchy of commandments. While love as feeling cannot be ordered, love as a maxim of behavior can certainly be demanded. And feelings reflect deeds.

In view of divine creativity being continuous, the power of the Creator is immanent in creation; yet He is not enclosed within it; His word forms it. God is both immanent in the cosmos and transcendent to it. Our basic analogy is derived from the holistic hierarchy of being—from inanimate nature to one-celled plants, to multicellular organisms, to plants, to the ladder of evolution, culminating in man. Within human consciousness, spirit emerges as a structuring, ordering, orienting power. Spirit is a tri-dimensional reality—rational, ethical, esthetic. Holiness is the intense aware-ness of the transcendent source of the divine command. God is to spirit, as spirit is to man's formless consciousness of the "blooming confusion" that is the rush of raw data presented by the senses. God is revealed in momentary experiences, when His energizing and orientating powers are felt with varying degrees of intensity.

As I see it, the Jewish religion fosters a keen awareness of the distinction between animal vitality and the order of spiritual values. Hence, its funda-mental conviction does not claim that God is to the cosmos as the mind is to the body, but that God is to the cosmos as the mind is to consciousness.

I accept Hartshorne's assertion that God is di-polar-immanent and transcendent, abstract and concrete, being and becoming.

With the concept of a di-polar God, we focus attention on the polarity of mechanism vs. holism. The holistic dimension is seen in the hierarchy of living creatures and in the emergence of the human mind.

The building of wholes in freedom is the essence of the ethical task, beginning with the individual impelled to become an integrated whole, his creative potential realized and his faculties fully actualized. But, the whole-ness of the individual leads to his integration within the larger whole of the family. In its turn, the family must not remain self-enclosed. It must encourage its members to feel that they belong to the still larger wholes of nations, civilizations, religious communities and mankind as a whole. The advancement of human welfare requires that we remain open at all times to wider loyalties and refuse to venerate, much less worship finite wholes which claim to be self-sufficient. Our loyalty to the Infinite God implies that our loyalties to lesser wholes should be limited, balanced and harmonized by our loyalty to Him, whose "name is peace."

How do we encounter God?—Shunning the "dark speech" of mystics, we cannot speak of any encounters with God. But in our personal lives and in history we note occasions when the creative Will of God emerges with power, generating a vigorous awareness of a larger whole.

In the lives of individuals, we see this event in the moral imperative and in the esthetic imagination as well as in the objective application of criticism and self-criticism to everyday concerns. The command of God manifests itself in the sense of sin for offenses committed, or for the failure to act with compassion, or for the failure to use one's talents in their fullness.

In the lives of collectives, religious communities or nationalities, such failures are far more dangerous to the well-being of humanity and far more difficult to discern. The realization of limited wholes tends to close the minds and hearts of people to the more subtle calls of the divine imperative. At all times, the cutting edge of divine revelation is the point at which greater wholes in quality and quantity are straining to emerge. We encounter, not the being of God, but His command, to which we apply our rational understanding and our esthetic imagination. The blending of our ethical, esthetic and rational responses is felt by us as the sublime feeling of holiness.

## Revelation in a Holistic Universe

There are two contrasting views of revelation. The one sees in it a trans-natural breakthrough, which shatters the normal categories of human experience, depositing within us information or a protean feeling which is later concretized into certain beliefs or attitudes. The other regards it as a more intense apprehension of moral-rational-esthetic judgments. To the proponents of the first position, God's message is revealed in experiences, which are literally "out of this world"—invasions from the numinal realm, which cannot be contained within the causal nexus of the space-time continuum. To the proponents of the second position, God's Will resounds at all times within the recesses of the human conscience; but, it is not always heard with the same clarity, urgency and power. According to the theologians of the first group, the content of revelation is essentially non-rational and non-moral-*a mysterium tremendum et fascinas.*

The second group of theologians regards the content of revelation as the promptings of conscience or of the Categorical Imperative, *enhanced* by feelings of sublimity and the reference to a transcendent being.

The differences among theologians concerning revelation correspond to similar differences in relation to the evidences of the Supreme Being in nature. The first group sees the marks of the Divine in miracles, which transcend the laws of nature. The second sees "the hand of God" in the order and design which result from the operation of these laws of nature.

A clear awareness of this gulf allows us to recognize that the line of demarcation between order and wonder is in actual experience not always discernible. The sense of the sublime and the holy may be powerfully felt by a rationalist, while a believer in transcendence may find that moral action best expresses the import of the rhapsody of the sacred. But, to the extent that revelation is translated into beliefs, the difference between the two conceptions is unmistakable.

Since these differences usually cut so deep, it is necessary to state at the outset that philosophical Judaism concurs with the mind-set of the second group of theologians. In philosophical Judaism revelation is in essence an everyday phenomenon, the experience of objective worth and sanctity. As the rabbis of the *Mishnah* put it, "every day a voice comes out of Mount Horeb and proclaims—'woe to people who humiliate the Torah.' "[13] But, this normal phenomenon has its peaks and nadirs. At times, God's voice sounds so close, like "the hairs on our head"; at other times, it is a "still, small voice", which is virtually silenced by the noises of the street.

Is this difference in intensity entirely due to human subjective factors?— No one can question the importance of the subjective element. Our receptivity is conditioned by a thousand forces—psychological, intellectual, sociological and historical. But, we ask, must we rule out any objective variable altogether?—In a "holistic" universe, where God perpetually generates "novel" phenomena, may it not be that His "character" shines out with greater clarity at certain times and places than at others?—If things are really events, segments of processes, quanta of energies that pulsate in waves or rhythms, may not His encouragement of moral-rational advancement be similarly subject to a kind of rhythmic alternation?

To speak of a *Deus absconditus*, a God who "hides His face", withdrawing from this "vale of tears", is to indulge in mythical rhetoric, which is appropriate to the supernaturalist theologians. But, a God, who continues to supplement His creation by the "ingression" of "novel" phenomena, may vary His message in the dimensions of intensity, direction and clarity. The record of human experience reveals periods and times of such horrendous callousness that it is difficult to contradict such a conclusion.

What then is our conception of God?—My view is that God alone is Eternal Being as well as the holistic process in the various levels of creation. We cannot say anything specific about His character as Eternal Being. But all that we can and do say about His continuous creativity presupposes His Being. His reality implies a dimension of metaphysical depth that cannot be captured by our conceptual processes. The cosmos reveals processes which move in two opposite directions—those that build up greater wholes and those which disintegrate and degrade wholes. We consider that the former trend reveals the deeper meaning and intent of existence. We reject the notion of metaphysical dualism. God is the source of darkness as of light, of death as of life. But, it is light and life that express His purpose and will. As the Kabbalists put it, there is His Will (raava), reflected in the laws governing all experience, and then there is "the Will of wills", (raava diraavin) expressed in the bursts of love and compassion that illumine our lives.[14]

In another essay, I suggested that we think of God as "the projection on the canvas of infinity of the lines of growth of the human personality". But, this description tells of only one of the two poles of the Supreme Being—that of His nearness. We must still apply to His Being the medieval maxim—"the end of our knowledge is that we shall know that we don't know."

Processes and phenomena that we apprehend as being of supreme worth acquire a new range of meaning, when we recognize that they derive from one Source. At any one time, high and inherently true ideals may seem to conflict with one another. Such apparent contradictions, however, are due to failures in our own perception. Our "sinfulness" is the cause of the "Word of God" being fragmentized for us—"a command here, a command there, a line here and a line there", as Isaiah put it.[15] The Kabbalists speak of the physical universe as *alma diperuda*, a world of separations. We ascend toward God through the processes of *yihudim*, unifications.

Since we cannot have any knowledge of God as Eternal Being, is our assertion of His Reality purely arbitrary?—By no means. Here is where our faith in His Unity tips the scale. Faith is itself a "holistic" phenomenon, when it is the response of the soul to the divine thrust toward perfection, toward greater, more perfect wholes. Its object is not so much knowledge, but orientation toward ethical-spiritual goals and self-dedication toward their realization. It is not essentially "the will to believe", but the will to serve the greater ends of greater wholes and to seek the source of all unities. Faith, in the Jewish tradition is reflected more in the response of the Israelites at Sinai—"we shall do and we shall listen" than in the medieval formulation, "I believe with perfect faith . . ."

It is not the affirmation of a proposition, as Buber reminds us, but the resolve to act in trust. Faith is an expression of the depths of our own being, and is a legitimate affirmation only at the edge of our consciousness. A numinous apprehension may well be given the benefit of doubt at the point where reason and conscious experience cease to function, but we can lay no such claim in regard to specific beliefs, affirmations regarding events of long ago and sacred rituals generally.

Unity and uniqueness is all that we can affirm of God, but even this much we say out of an existential decision. So, the assertion, "Hear, O Israel, the Lord our God, the Lord is One" is immediately followed by the expression of our union with Him in love—"And thou shalt love the Lord, Thy God, with all thy heart and all thy soul, and all thy might".[16]

Moments of revelation occur when the sense of God's creative work in our personal and communal life is felt with supreme power. Such an apprehension evokes from us both a response of whole-souled dedication in love and an awareness of our limitations and sinfulness. Having glimpsed the Infinite task, we exclaim with the Psalmist, "What is man that thou art mindful of him?"[17]

Paradoxical as it may sound, the experience of the divine thrust toward a more perfect whole is as bewildering as it is orientating. The Talmud compares it to the sparks that fly in all direction when a hammer hits on an anvil.[18] All of life testifies to the inevitable war of all against all. Living beings feed on each other. The struggle for existence is relentless and cruel. Human history adds additional dimensions to the cruelties of sheer life. We are caught in a complex of contending wholes. To sense the divine thrust is to feel the compelling power of all these goals and their inevitable contradictions at any one moment. We have to make choices, but always, with a heavy heart, with "fear and trepidation".[19] It is not that the laws built into our personalities resist the law of God, as St. Paul complained, but that His Will, only partially revealed, transcends our comprehension.

We are pilgrims in the night, at break of dawn; the darkness is receding but the sun has not yet risen.

## Notes to Holism and the Jewish Religion

[1] Deuteronomy, 5, 23. 1 Sam. 17, 26, 36. Jer. 10, 10. Jer. 23, 36
[2] Genesis 18, 25
[3] Jer. 12, 1
[4] Isa. 5, 16
[5] The first sentence a Jewish child was taught was Deut. 33, 4.
[6] Deuter. 6, 25; 11, 22
[7] B. T. Shabbat 10a. Shabbat 119b. Bereshit Rabba 43, 8
[8] M. Maimonides, *Guide of the Perplexed*, III, 32.
[9] B. T. Sanhedrin 56a.
[10] On the Special Laws, III, 36, 207
[11] Standard Prayer Book, morning service.
[12] B. T. Sanhedrin 98a.
[13] Avot VI, 2.
[14] Zohar II, 239a.
[15] Isaiah 28, 10.
[16] Deuteronomy 6, 4-5.
[17] Psalms 8, 5
[18] Jeremiah 23, 29. B. T. Shabbat 88b.
[19] B. T. Berochot 22a.

# REVELATION AS QUEST—A CONTRIBUTION TO ECUMENICAL THOUGHT

The inter-faith trialogue between Judaism, Christianity and Islam cannot advance without a serious analysis of the concept of revelation. For each of the three faiths is ultimately based upon a belief that the Word of God had been revealed. In Judaism, the entire edifice of faith, like an inverted pyramid, is founded upon the one fulcrum of "the assembly at Mount Sinai." In Christianity, the revelations of "the Law and the prophets" are assumed and reinterpreted in the light of the Incarnation and the Holy Spirit. In Islam, the Quran is assumed to be the final revelation of the Word. Mohammed is described as "the seal of the prophets."

Those who interpret the essential content of revelation in simplistic, literal terms, can hardly engage in a meaningful dialogue with the members of other faiths. They look upon themselves as the possessors of final truth; all else is error, to a smaller or greater degree. On the other hand, rationalists who reduce the entire content of religion to so many ethical and metaphysical propositions have no need of dialogue; truth is the same, it is only the metaphors that differ.

The mediating position between rationalism and orthodoxy, represented best in our day by Tillich, pointed to the role of myth and symbolism in conveying the feeling of divine mystery. C. G. Jung and Mircea Eliade added to our understanding of the depths of the human mind and helped us to appreciate the functions of myth and symbolism. But, there is more to the divine-human encounter than the "mysterium tremendum" of holiness. There is also the call to action, a dedication to a lifelong search. Leo Baeck, in a famous essay, calls attention to the components of "Command" and "Mystery" in the highest moments of religious experience ("Judaism and Christianity" by Leo Baeck, J.P.S. Philadelphia, 1958 p. 171). While he goes on to describe Christianity as the religion of Mystery and Judaism as the religion of Command, I feel that such a rigid dichotomy is unjustified. We

Originally published in *Journal of Ecumenical Studies*, vol. 9, 1972.

must not elevate changes of emphasis into metaphysical categories. There are so many variations within each historic faith that even the best generalizations are only partially true.

Now, it is the component of Command that is the essence of the experience of revelation. It lies at the base of the three related faiths—Judaism, Christianity and Islam. Within each of these faiths, the essential content of revelation is like a thick rope, consisting of many and intertwined threads. At diverse times, different strands come to the forefront. It is the purpose of this essay to identify a major strand within the historic texture of Jewish thought, and to trace its implications. This elemental drive forming part of Christianity and Islam as well as Judaism is of the utmost importance in providing strength and substance to the ecumenical movement.

As objective students of religion, we should proceed to analyze the concepts of revelation within the three great traditions, as these concepts developed in response to various intellectual and social challenges. Yet, it is of the very nature of religion that it achieves its fullest reality within the domain of collective subjectivity. The living God addresses us through the actual life of our faith-community, not merely through the crystallized structures of concepts and institutions that are amenable to objective study. Indeed, the dialogue, or the trialogue, is indispensable, precisely because we deal with living phenomena. For this reason, my procedure is limited to Judaism, my own faith. I am certain that both Christians and Moslems will find in their own respective traditions ample illustrations and confirmations of the theses that are here presented. Their findings will be all the more meaningful if they reflect their own living convictions as well as the objective data.

I do not claim that the phase of endless search exhausts the meaning of the concept of revelation. On the contrary, our search is sustained, because it rests on a conviction of deep reassurance. We seek Him, Who has found us. The psychic moments of possession and privation imply one another. The symbols, myths and rites, reflecting the assurance of Divine Grace, are well known. But, all too often the elements of outreach were ignored in the past, and revelation was identified completely with the static elements of rite and belief. My point is that in a living faith deriving from the Judaic tradition, the component of an endless quest for the nearness of God is always present.

In this essay, I shall attempt to call attention to this aspect of the meaning of revelation within the historic heritage of Judaism. In religion, we always go back to the past in order to open new horizons for the future. Every renaissance in the life of faith partakes of qualities that appeared in previous periods of rebirth.

The discussion begins with the concept of God. The dialectical nature of revelation follows from the polarity embraced in the idea of God. Illustrations are then cited from "the law and the prophets." It is recalled that the elements of communal loyalty and universal wisdom are included within the biblical body of revelation. Rabbinic formulations of the essence of revelation at Sinai are cited, along with the development of these themes in medieval philosophy, and the counter-themes in *halachic* Judaism. The open horizons in Kabbalah and Hassidism are stressed, though in the view of this author, it is Maimonidean philosophy in the Middle Ages, and classical thought generally, that best reflect the genuine impetus of biblical-rabbinic Judaism. The implication of the dynamic phase of revelation for what may be called "a Jewish theology of non-Jewish faiths" is then presented and illustrated from the writings of pre-modern and modern Jewish theologians.

## The Concept of God

Our starting point is the biblical God, Who is Creator, Revealer and Redeemer. From the beginning, this awareness of God was as much a denial as it was an affirmation. While affirming in fear and love the saving Presence of God, the biblical authors were engaged in a perpetual battle against the idols of the nations. Later, the Sages were similarly engaged in countering the claims of the philosophers.

As against the pagan identification of the gods with the forces and rhythms of life, the Bible projects the idea of God as Spirit, the extension unto infinity of "the lines of growth" in the spirit of man. As against the impelling drive of philosophy for uni-dimensional consistency, the Jewish thinkers insisted that He was a living Reality, in personal life and in history, and that He was unknowable.[1] While the pagans stressed His immanence and the philosophers His transcendence, the biblical writers assert that He is both far and near at the same time, and in a way that we cannot know (Isaiah 66; 1, 2. J. Guttmann, "Philosophies of Judaism," Holt, Rinehart and Winston, N.Y., pp. 5–17).

So, in the course of Jewish thought, the philosophical quest of truth was maintained in an uneasy alliance with the religious assertion of His living Presence. The gentle skepticism of Wisdom literature was incorporated into the Canon. Philo effected a synthesis between Platonism and the Hebraic faith, stressing in particular the agreement of Moses and Plato in respect of the supreme goal of life, the idea of *imitatio dei*. (De Virtutes, 31, 168. The Talmudic sources of this doctrine are discussed in S. Schechter's "Some Aspects of Rabbinic Theology," p. 199.) Halevi assumed a dichotomy between the "God of the philosophers," capturing only some aspects of His Being, and "the God of Israel," who is an immediate Presence to the human soul. ("The Kuzari," Herschfield translation IV, 18) Pascal, as we may recall, echoed the same distinction. The God of Maimonides is consistent with Aristotelianism only in part; He stands beyond the cosmos as its Creator, and it is His Will that forms the underlying End of human history.

We may characterize the entire sweep of Jewish philosophy from the Bible to our own time as a dialectical reflection of an inherent polarity, an endeavor to hold on to the felt reality of the biblical God, on the one hand, and the unfettered quest of reason, on the other hand. This endeavor is sustained by the "moral certainty" that our yearnings for truth, goodness, purity and holiness are inwardly consistent, and that they derive from God, in whom these aspirations are fulfilled. We affirm His Unity as an unquestioned certainty, precisely because we are aware of the polarity of forces that inhere in Him, Who is the Ground of both Being and Value.[2]

Modern philosophies of religion tend to stress one or another aspect of the biblical God—in existentialism, His Presence; in idealism, His Wisdom; in evolutionism, His work in the cosmos and in history. Yet, underlying these differences in approach, there is an astonishing unity of conviction. A neo-Kantian, like Hermann Cohen, felt that God was most clearly revealed in the quest of truth, which, he declared, is an inner affirmation of the unity of the pathways of ethics and logic. A religious existentialist, like Martin Buber, elaborated a symphony of variations on the I-Thou relation, affirming the personal Presence of God as an immediate datum of experience. To a neo-Hegelian, like Franz Rosenzweig, God was revealed in the diverse transcendental thrusts that mark the history of Israel and the erratic advance of mankind. To a Mordecai Kaplan, it is in the bonds of communal dedication to a common vision of greatness that God is experienced as the Power that makes for salvation.[3] Yet, these varied emphases belong to one realm of discourse that is constituted by the polarity between the affirmation of the Divine Presence and the negation of any effort to delimit His Being, either by means of concrete symbols or through the use of philosophical abstractions. But this God, Who is beyond the grasp of any of our faculties, enters into communication with man, at least with some men.[3a] (Avery Dulles captures this paradox in a beautiful sentence, "Because God's revelation involves a personal approach to His creatures in finite forms, the God who speaks is more mysterious than the silent absent God." "Revelation and the Quest for Unity," Corpus Books, 1968, p. 61.)

## Polarity in Revelation

Revelation is self-revelation—hence, an awareness of His Presence, His truth and His creative thrust toward perfection. Psychologically, the glowing moment of revelation is not subject to analysis, but its felt effects may be articulated dialectically as a *Yes,* a *No,* and a quantum of psychic energy. The *Yes* is an affirmation of our highest self, an assurance of our acceptance in love, insofar as we truly, inwardly seek Him. We feel the wonder and the mysterious grandeur of our being embraced in His grand design. But, this *Yes* is inseparable from an equally categorical *No,* that intensifies our awareness of our littleness, our finitude; nothing that is ours is unblemished and perfect; the Absolute in all things and in all judgments escapes our grasp. We are left with a peculiar hunger, a restless drive to attain the unattainable—now, here, in this world. The Kabbalists speak of God's love as "direct light" and our love for Him as "reflected light," for our love is directed toward the building of His Kingdom on earth, through the employment of all our faculties.

These three categories are precisely what we, from our human stand-point, should expect to find in our encounter with the Infinite. We are part of His creative energy, but only when our higher self, the "image of God" within us, is truly in action; yet, all that is finite is "as naught" before Him. And the consequence of love, is the hunger for more love—yes, to be worthy of His love. It is in the realm of ideals that the seeds of love take root and expand. These three categories of revelation are likely to be found in all records of man's encounter with God. But, at diverse times, different aspects will be stressed. In Judaism, these categories are represented in the Cove-nant, the Fall and the Way.

The joyous shout of being chosen reverberates through all the halls of biblical and rabbinic Judaism. It proclaims the *Yes* of prophetic experience, as it was reconfirmed by the conscience of the people, generation after genera-tion.

But, the awareness of Covenant and Promise is counterbalanced by the melancholy refrain of failure. The fall of Adam, the sin of Moses, the Golden Calf, the trials of "the stiff-necked" in the wilderness—these tales furnish the prelude for the bitter denunciations of Isaiah and Jeremiah. Jerusalem, "The Holy City," is also "the city that kills its prophets." Whole epochs are described as dark nights of degradation; ending in the downfall of the Kingdom of Judah. The happy notes of consolation and promise are not lost altogether. For Israel was betrothed, yea married, unto the Lord. The Covenant is eternal.[4]

And the "Way of God," first mentioned as the vocation of Abraham and his descendants, is projected into infinity to culminate in "the end of days." This way is formulated in the laws of the Torah, and the Law is designated as *Halachah,* a way of walking. Articulated in laws, the way extends beyond the line of the law, *lifnim mishurat hadin,* embracing feelings and ideals "that are given to man's heart." Ideally, the Law is dynamic. "General principles were conveyed to Moses at Sinai"; presumably these principles would result in a dynamic process of adaptation of means to ends. If in practice the letter frequently triumphed over the spirit, the ideal of a progressive advance was not forgotten.[5] The Apostolic community, having experienced a mighty resurgence of the covenant-experience, describes itself also as a Way (Acts 9, 2; 19, 9; 22, 4; 24, 22). Nor did it lack the glow of a fresh Promise and the anguished feeling of the fall from grace, since its most loyal disciple was also the one who denied his master three times, before the cock crowed three times (Mark 14, 72).

The prophets and psalmists spoke of a divine restlessness, a hunger of the soul.

"Behold, the days are coming," says the Lord God
when I will send a famine on the land;
not a famine for bread, nor a thirst for water,
but of hearing the words of the Lord" (Amos 8, 11, R.S.V.).

"You will seek me and find me;
when you seek me with all of your heart" (Jeremiah 29, 13).

"As a hart longs
for flowing streams,
so longs my soul for Thee, O God.
My soul thirsts for God,
for the living God" (Psalms 42, 2-4).

O God, Thou art my God, I seek Thee,
my soul thirsts for Thee;
my flesh faints for Thee,
as in a dry and weary land where no water is (Psalms 63,1).

Hosea's metaphor is of a perpetual engagement (Hosea 2; 19, 20). Isaiah speaks of a marriage, an exchange of irrevocable vows (Isaiah 50, 1). In the Talmud, the whole of Judaism is summed up in Amos' admonition, "seek me, and live."[6]

## Communal Role of Prophecy

Is there any basic difference between revelation and inspiration? We interpret revelation from the human viewpoint, as an outreach of the self, not as an invasion from without. For be the numinous origin what it may, the human receptacle cannot but impose its categories and judgments. Yet, revelation is more than inspiration in three ways—in intensity, in God-centeredness and in respect of the socio-historic dimension. First, then, the term inspiration is so loosely used that it does not suggest the high serious-ness and deep pathos of revelation. Second, inspiration may well be experi-enced along one of the several lines of excellence—intellectual, esthetic or ethical. Revelation deepens and reinvigorates the feeling of holiness which embraces these ideals and directs them to God. Third, revelation is oriented to the life of a community, one that is already in existence, or one that it brings into being. Thus, the Talmud asserts that hundreds of thousands of Israelites experienced the ecstasy of prophecy, but only those prophecies which were significant for the life of the people were set down in writing. When the tannaitic Sages declared that prophecy had ceased, following the generation of Hagai, Zechariah and Malachi, they referred, not to the experience itself, but to its official function within Jewish life. In the life of a historic community, charisma normally turns into structure. Hillel, like certain other sages, "was worthy of the *Shechinah* resting upon him," in the sense of his becoming a messenger of God, but his generation was not worthy of this mark of grace.

There was no discontinuity between revelation and wisdom, according to the rabbis, providing the term wisdom is used in an all-embracing sense of human perfection, including moral concern, the esthetic arts and piety. "Without wisdom there is no piety, and without piety there is no wisdom." (Abot III, 21.) The Talmud suggests that wisdom may be superior to prophecy. In Maimonides' view, the first and most fundamental stage of prophecy is an accession of Divine energy in a person, making it possible for him to achieve a great social end.[7]

Is there any content in revelation? Manifestly, creative energy must be actualized in some concrete way. But, this actualization is conditioned by the character of the recipient. The Talmudic Sages were clearly aware of the distinction between the Divine intent and the human articulation. "All the prophets said the same thing, yet not two prophets prophesy in the same style" (Sanhedrin 89a.). Rabbi Simlai applied this thought to the command-ments of the Torah, which were presumed to be 613 in number—365 negative injunctions, corresponding to the days of the solar year and 248 positive ordinances, corresponding to the organs and parts of the human personality. Said he, only two Commandments were directly revealed to all Israelites, the first two of the Ten Commandments—"I am the Lord, thy God . . . " and "Thou shalt have no other gods besides Me . . ."; and the other commandments were formulated by Moses.[8]

In simpler language, only the fiery core of revelation, the *Yes* and the *No* of the Divine encounter, is directly experienced; the rest of Torah is the

endeavor of Moses and his successors to articulate revelation through legislation and exhortation.

## The Goal of Revelation

The goal of the quest is "the nearness of God," in personal life and in the
community. The psalmists speak of this goal.[9] Philo describes the life of
Abraham as that of the ideal man, who is rewarded by the "feeling of God's
Presence." "This is the defining mark of the people that is 'great,' to draw
nigh to God, or to be that 'to which God draws nigh' " (Philo, "DeMigrationi
Abrahami," ed. Loeb Classics, 59).

The tannaitic rabbis interpreted the goal of "cleaving unto the Lord" as
implying to walk in His ways . . . "as He is merciful, so be you merciful,
etc. . . . " (Sota 14a.). Unlike Philo, they were conscious of the great
difficulty of incorporating the goal of *imitatio dei* into the context of their non-
anthropomorphic faith. The tannaitic Midrash coins a special word to
account for the anthropomorphic expressions in Scripture—*Kevayochal*, "as it
were." Our intent points to God, but our forms of worship are only
direction-signs, pointing to Him. "Great is the [imaginative] power of the
prophets, who compared the form to its Creator." So, Maimonides in his
Code describes even the ethical attributes of God as deliberate projections
upon the Deity of the ideals that lead man to perfection (Hilchot Deot, I, 6).
These ideals arise out of repeated revelations, resulting in the massive
aspiration of a holy community for perfection.[10]

What is the relation between revelation and the secular world, or religion
and culture? Manifestly religion is to the diverse realms of culture as the
mind is to the senses, not as the senses are to one another. Revelation, as the
Divine thrust toward perfection generates two lines of endeavor—that of
individual salvation and that of communal advancement, both along the
"lines of growth," marked out by biology and history. The one quest or the
other may predominate at various times. The Torah suggests the possibility
of preferring Moses to all Israel (Numbers 14, 12). Isaiah was content with a
remnant (Isaiah 10, 21). But, the prevailing trend in Jewish literature is
communal and historical. To love God is to teach one's children and to
inscribe His teaching upon the door-posts of one's house and upon the gates
of the community.[11] The prophet is a "messenger" to the historical community; so is every gifted person. It is only as a "we" that we can heed the call of
"the eternal Thou," to use Buberian rhetoric. And Rosenzweig struck a deep
chord of the Jewish soul, when he wrote that the very word Jew evokes the
quality of the eternal. But, it is the eternity of the task, not of the ethnic

group—the task of joining in the building of the Kingdom of God.[12] Nor did the romantic nationalists differ on this point from the universalists. Judah Halevi, who believed that the seed of Abraham was a unique metaphysical creation, asserted nevertheless that the role of Israel could be fulfilled by even one person. For him, too, the task of the Covenant-People could be understood only in an all-human context. "Israel among the nations is like the heart to the other organs."[13] Through the restoration of its vigor, mankind will be saved.

As a quest, revelation points to an infinite goal—hence, the feeling of open-endedness, of a limitless horizon. In the biblical world, this feeling is reflected in the vision of "the end of days" and in the concept of the Kingdom of God. Since our imagination fails to prepare us for the infinite, we tend to bring it down within the confines of our own existence. We substitute for the infinite quest a finite possession, a law, a set of beliefs, a body of rituals or sacraments. These possessions reflect the feelings of reassurance and continuity that are reinforced in the glowing moments of revelation. We must not underestimate their authentic worth. But, the No of Faith is as real as the Yes, and it denies the sufficiency of all possessions. Pious smugness is one of the "Pharisaic plagues," condemned in the Talmud.[14]

Another way to undo the infinity of the task is to pretend that history had drawn to a close, and that we had arrived at the dawn of the eschatological age. It is the danger that confronts our generation with peculiar "relevance." The paradox is difficult to live with, but inescapable. We have to accept the infinite task as our own mission, realizable here and now; yet, know that it far surpasses our own reach. "It is not for you to finish the task."[15]

## The Quest in the Several Streams of Jewish Thought

The open-endedness of revelation is reflected in the three branches of learning, which continue the prophetic tradition—the process of *halachah*-legislation, the current of pietism and the stream of Jewish philosophy.

At first glance, it may seem that the Pharisaic scholars and their rabbinic successors were incapable of breaking out from their own tight, little world. Indeed, the threat of *rigor mortis* is an inescapable shadow of life itself. But the very nature of Torah-legislation as a way of actualizing the prophetic vision kept it from being congealed into lifeless laws. "The words of Torah procreate and multiply . . ." Indeed, a careful analysis of rabbinic legislation demonstrates that there were periods marked by the flexibility and fecundity of the halachic process, alternating with times when the dynamic impetus of *Halachah* was paralyzed by the fear of communal dissolution. The theologians of Reform, Conservatism and Reconstructionism are committed to variations of this concept. It is not unreasonable to expect that in modern Israel a new breed of Orthodox rabbis will recapture the spirit of a dynamic *Halachah*.[16]

*Halachah* fosters the feeling of obedience to the Divine Command. It embodies the affirmative phase of man's encounter with God—man's life is charged with cosmic significance. God has taken the initiative and has thrown out a rope, which floundering man may seize and thereby save himself from drowning in a sea of meaninglessness. Even one Commandment, performed with the fullness of devotion, brings man to God. But, the Law also fosters the awareness of limitation, even of sinfulness—the negative phase of piety.[17]

In pietism, the purpose of all the Commandments is to direct man's progress on the infinite road leading to holiness. Bahya Ibn Pakuda, the gentle philosophical pietist of the tenth century asserts that "the duties of the heart" are infinite in degree as well as in number. There is no upper limit to piety. Its demands are paradoxical, for every spiritual quality is bounded by other and conflicting ones. Furthermore, as one rises in acuity of feeling and perception, one's obligations increase proportionately. Hence, the infinity of the pilgrim's road.[18]

In Kabbalah, the personal motif of piety is to make oneself a fit "dwelling place for the Divine Presence" (ma-on lashechinah). This goal entails an endless process of purifying every expression of man's inner self. The communal motif in Kabbalah is "to uplift the Schechinah from the dust and redeem it from exile." This goal will be attained in "the days of Messiah." Hence, it is not really infinite, strictly speaking, but it is coterminous with human history as we know it.[19] In Hassidism, these two motifs were blended and deepened by the emphasis on the holiness of the common man. The Hassidim transformed the complex and esoteric ethic of Kabbalah into a popular pietistic movement, which stressed the basic virtues of humility, integrity, communalism and faithfulness. To be sure, *Hassidism* institutionalized the cosmic function of the *Zaddik*, who, in his turn, was to serve as a guide for his followers in the twisted paths of piety.

The founder of Hassidism aimed to revive the prophetic experience. "It was the intention of Moses that all Israelites should reach his level, when the Schechinah spoke out of his throat," and "every Israelite can indeed attain this level.[20]

In philosophical Judaism, the concept of revelation as an infinite quest was best expressed by Maimonides in his famous parable of the search for a glimpse of the king on his throne. This throne is situated in a huge, labyrinthine palace, which is surrounded by a primeval forest with very few paths that are marked. Many people are lured away from the palace; many others reach it and move round it in endless circles; some few penetrate into the palace itself. And only the rare person glimpses the King on his throne. It is not certain that Maimonides himself believed that he was one of the few who had reached their goal. In any case, he considered the Talmudic scholars to be among those who circle the palace, for they are prone to restrict the infinite quest within "the four ells of Halachah." At the same time, Gentile philosopher-saints may well be among those who have attained the beatific vision.[21]

In his exposition of the nature of prophecy, Maimonides defines the prophet as one who seeks the knowledge of God and prepares himself by an ethical life and an arduous mastery of the sciences for the attainment of the supreme moment, when his soul acquires the capacity to receive the "divine flow," which the Lord rarely withholds. Maimonides steers a middle course between the "philosophers" who describe the mystical climax as a human achievement and the dogmatists who think of prophecy as a gift that God might give arbitrarily to any one. In his view, the human quest of God, through an ethical life, a cultivation of imagination and of intellectual inquiry is basic; once the saintly philosopher has reached a high level of openness to "the divine flow," God is not likely to withhold His bounty. The decisive role of the imaginative faculty in the prophet's vision implies that its truth is relative, to be discerned by an imaginative effort. Also, the gift of imagination, characteristic as it is of statesmen as well as poets, is an intuitive awareness of the whole, a magnificent outreach of empathy. To be sure, Maimonides exempts the prophecy of Moses from the normal limitations of prophets. But, even the laws of the Torah have no other object than to promote the moral well-being of the community and of the individual. The content of revelation, then, consists of two parts—static laws and a dynamic drive. The laws provide guide-lines for the good life; the drive is directed toward the infinite goal of "imitatio dei," an ongoing quest of moral and spiritual perfection.[22]

In regard to the vision of the future, Maimonides also emphasized the openness and indefiniteness of revelation, insisting that it does not result in teachings that are clear-cut. We know that God will one day redeem us, but as to the means that He will employ or the real meaning of the various oracles, we have to wait for the scroll of human history to unfold. We shall know exactly what the prophets meant when the messianic age dawns. The *eschaton* will emerge out of the processes of history, without any suspension of the laws of nature. Living in the age of the Crusades, Maimonides suggested that the two rival faiths, Christianity and Islam, might have been intended by God to prepare the way for His Kingdom, since they teach about His sovereignty and disseminate the biblical view of life. If revelation is a thrust toward an endless adventure, then, there is ample work for all men and all faiths.[23]

## The Quest in Modern Judaism

Our modern age is history-minded, global-minded and sadly aware of human imperfection. We see all events in an all-human perspective and acknowledge that cultures and faiths interact. We recognize that, be the Absolute what it may, the human appropriation of truth is always fragmentary and in need of further supplementation. Our psyche is predisposed for infinite horizons, and we think of reality, not as static Being, but as a dynamic Becoming. In Spengler's rhetoric, ours is the "Faustian" soul.

Yet, we fear to view religion in the same light, lest we lose altogether the "Yes" of faith, the sense of our being anchored in eternity. Does not history-mindedness easily degenerate into an all-questioning and all-dissolving historicism? How can we guard against the dangers of moral relativism? The answer, it would seem, is the recognition that if revelation is open-ended, it is also a cumulative reassurance of "the lines of growth" in man and in society. I do not suggest that it is possible to formulate with precision the "common core" of religious faith. Each faith will add its own nuance to such a formulation. So, in the Talmud, the Seven Noachide Laws, which constitute the core of religion, were left undefined and vague, presumably for the reason that each faith may well formulate them in its own way.[24]

Formulations of "natural law," as if they were inferences of a diffuse, general revelation, are in keeping with a classical, rationalistic approach to revelation. This approach needs to be balanced by the evolutionary perspective in which the ethical is perceived as an act of cooperation with the growth of society. In that view, laws are only generalized norms of conduct, to be adjusted to specific situations and modified in accord with changing conditions. Manifestly, such issues as planned parenthood and Zero Population Growth hinge on whether we employ the rationalistic or the evolutionary standard. And the awareness of God's transcendence will keep us from upsetting the balance between these polar approaches in the belief that we truly know the mind of God.

The history-mindedness of biblical man was held in tension between the conviction that God works within history and the belief that His Will had already been revealed to Moses. Certainly, God's Will cannot be read out of the historical happenings as such, but only in so far as they are interpreted by prophets. Revelation provides the standards for assessing the course of redemptive history. But, is revelation itself a progressive phenomenon? If revelation is an ongoing adventure, there must be some progress in the comprehension of His Will. So, in spite of the impetus of dogmatism, the book of Deuteronomy allows that a prophet, like Moses, will arise in the future. The tannaitic rabbis noted that some of the great prophets abrogated certain Mosaic declarations. Following the disasters of the Great Rebellion and the Bar Kochba Revolt, the Sages assumed that humanity was going down-hill. The task of the loyal remnant of Israel was to preserve the body of revelation, not advance it. All that one could hope was that in the Messianic era all mankind will accept the Truth, which is already in the possession of true Israel.[25]

Nevertheless, the bold vision of a progressive revelation was not given up, even in the darkest periods of Jewish life. The Law (Halachah) itself was deemed to contain a dynamic thrust. The Lord Himself creates new *halachot* every day (Gen. R. 64, 4). The "Sons of Torah" were described as "builders," adding their mite to the heritage of the past. Room is left for the leaders of each generation to add their contributions in the realm of Law. And *Halachah* by itself did not preempt the Jewish mind. Whenever the influence of philosophy waned, the spirit of *Kabbalah* would generate a mighty yearning for fresh revelations. In Kabbalah, the revelation of fresh "secrets of the Torah" was charged with powerful redemptive overtones, for the *eschaton* will be preceded by a flood of mystical truths, substituting the flow from "the tree of life" for the time-conditioned principles of the Torah, which derive from "the tree of good and evil." In the early generations of Hassidism, the belief was general that the time was ripe for new incursions of the Holy Spirit and of prophecy.

As to the Torah of the Messiah, we encounter opinions that a "new Torah" or a "renewed Torah," will then be revealed. The Messiah, according to an anonymous Midrash, will be a more exalted being than Abraham, Moses and the ministering angels.[26]

## The Quest and Ecumenism

If the deposit of revelation is a quest, then each covenanted community cannot but welcome, and even seek the active cooperation of other groups, equally covenanted, for the achievement of the same goal. The way is infinite, and it consists of many twisted paths. It does not mean that "all religions are equally true," but that a peculiar truth is found in nearly every faith. And divine Truth is so rich and many-sided that only fragments are found in any one faith.

This insight is already articulated by the prophet Micah, who followed up the vision of the End of Days with the declaration—"For let all the peoples walk each one in the name of its god, but we shall walk in the name of the Lord our God, for ever and ever" (Micah 4, 5-J.P.S. Translation). The possibility of diverse, relatively true, revealed faiths coexisting at one time is contained in the ancient notion that the various nations are governed by angels—that is, by agents of the Divine Being, representing partial aspects of His Will. The Midrash allows that prophets as great and even greater than Moses, have arisen among the nations.

The attitude of Rabbi Gamliel at the trial of Peter and John was typical of the Pharisaic position, at least of its Hillelite faction. "For if this plan or this understanding is of men, it will fail; but if it is of God, you will not be able to overthrow them. You might even be found opposing God" (Acts 5, 39 R.S.V.). This position was repeated many years later at the trial of Paul, "what if a spirit or an angel spoke to him" (Acts 23, 9)? God draws people to Him in diverse ways: He might well choose to redeem many Gentiles through the agency of Christianity, without annulling His Covenant with Israel.

Christians were acknowledged as "spiritual proselytes" in a broad segment of Halachic literature.[27] Maimonides viewed both Christianity and Islam as divine agencies that help prepare the way for the Messiah. Of particular interest is the statement of an eighteenth century halachist who was a fanatical heresy-hunter and almost completely untouched by the Enlightenment. Commenting on the principle of Rabbi Yohanan Hasandlar, a second century Palestinian teacher, "every community that is for the sake of heaven, is destined to endure," Rabbi Jacob Emden points out that this principle applies to the Christian church as a whole.

"Certainly the Sage did not concern himself with communities that are not related to us, but with those new faiths and sects that derived from us. . . . Indeed, when we take account of the cults they supplanted, which worshipped stocks and stones, and did not know God as the Absolute Power, administering reward and punishment in the hereafter, their church may truly be called an 'ecclesia for the sake of heaven.' For they proclaim the Deity to distant nations. . . . They glorify the Lord, God of Israel and His Torah, even among people who have never heard about Him. Therefore, their good intentions cannot be in vain. The Compassionate seeks the heart. . . . Furthermore, Christian scholars are known for their love of truth. . . . By their researches into biblical history, many of them have added to its glory. . . ."[28]

In this judgment, Emden ranks the Christian polity as a divine institution. He views it in the light of its historic achievement, its dedication to the quest of truth and its love of God. Individual Christians are judged by their intentions.

It has been the fashion to trace the positive attitude of Judaism toward Christians and Christianity to the labors of Moses Mendelssohn, Lessing's model for "Nathan, the Wise." But, whereas Mendelssohn severely criticized the irrational elements in Christianity in the name of the normative "religion of reason," Emden, himself an irrationalist, was able to esteem the Church, with all its historic dogmas, as a divine agency. Mendelssohn took up Albo's argument that religious rituals are like medicines, which the Lord of history assigns to different peoples in accord with their respective needs. It follows that different and even opposing faiths may be divinely ordained for diverse groups.[29]

Solomon Formstecher suggested the image of the sun and its rays as analogous to the relation of Judaism and Christianity. Franz Rosenzweig regarded the Church as the missionizing agency of Judaism to the pagan world. "Without Judaism and Christianity, there is no salvation." Buber's views ran the gamut from his early opinion that Christianity was the authentic current of genuine Judaism to his later conviction that the Jewish faith was "belief in" God, while Christianity taught the doctrine of "belief about" God. Claude G. Montefiore sought to include portions of the New Testament in Jewish liturgy. The Reconstructionist movement points to the historic, ethnic base of both Judaism and Christianity; as a general rule, the feelings of communal fellowship must be spiritualized so that each nation might be refashioned after "the image of God."[30]

We need only add the emphasis on the individual, that is typical of the modern spirit, particularly in the countries of the New World. The biblical prophets asserted that each individual must be judged on his own merits, regardless of the qualities of the group. In the Talmud, the righteous Gentile is held up as an example of virtuous living. In recent Jewish theology, Buber and Cohen, writing from standpoints at the opposite ends of the existentialist-rationalist spectrum emphasized the sacred character of the individual.

Finally, there has been a revival of eschatological feeling in both Judaism and Christianity. In Judaism, the recent memories of Auschwitz have built up the dark mood of Armageddon, and the rise of Israel generated a vibrant sense of messianism. This apocalyptic consciousness, far from being confined to Jews, is shared by millions of young people in the western world. They see the horrors of the *eschaton* in the steady drift toward a nuclear holocaust and in the mindless pollution of the environment. The building of the Kingdom is not an immediate "either-or" decision for our generation. So,

Christians turn in hope to the second Advent and Jews to the coming of the Messiah. Both are joined in the certainty that there can be no salvation for any nation or faith save in the salvation of all mankind. Both can accept each other as partners in the task of preparing the way for His Kingdom. The task is so great that the contributions of all historic groups are indispensable. Hillel's dictum takes on fresh meaning for each historic faith—"If I am not for myself, who will be? but if I am for myself alone, what am I?—and if not now, when?"[31]

# Notes to Revelation as Quest

[1] In the creation-story of Genesis, only man is provided with the spirit of God. The image of God was already interpreted by Philo as the human mind. "Let no one represent the likeness as one to a bodily form; for neither is God in human form, nor is the human body God-like. No, it is in respect of the Mind, the sovereign element of the soul, that the word 'image' is used . . . ." (De Opificio Mundi, XXLII, 69; see also, Quaestioni in Genesis, I, 4).

Nothing so offended Jewish sensibilities as the worship of animals in Egyptian religion (Josephus, "Against Apion," I, 24). Of God's unknowability in Philo, an unphilosophical tenet, see H. A. Wolfson, "Philo" II, pp. 110-126. He demonstrates the thesis that Philo was in all essentials a defender of Judaism, employing the imagery and rhetoric current in his day.

[2] Deuteronomy, Rabbah 2, 31. A Marmorstein, "The Old Rabbinic Doctrine of God," reissued by K'tav, N.Y., 1968.

[3] A general description and bibliography of these thinkers will be found in J. Agus' "Modern Philosophies of Judaism," Behrman House, reissued in 1971. Also, in J. Guttmann's work, "Philosophies of Judaism," translated by David W. Silverman, (New York: Holt, Rinehart & Winston, 1964).

[3a] Avery Dulles captures this paradox in a beautiful sentence—"Because God's revelation involves a personal approach to His creatures in finite forms, the God who speaks is more mysterious than the silent, absent God." *Revelation and the Quest for Unity*, Corpus Books, 1968, p. 61.

[4] Matt. 23, 37. Rabbinic sources mention a similar complaint by Jeremiah. Pesikta Rabba 26 (129). Pal. Taanit 4, 69a. Babylonian T. Sanhedrin 104a. The eternity of the Covenant is asserted by Jeremiah 33.25, "Eternal covenant" in Isaiah 55, 3; Jeremiah 32, 40; 50, 5; Ezekiel 16, 60; 34, 25; 37, 26. Paul restates this conviction in Romans 11, 29.

[5] The realm of concern, beyond the Law, Berochot 7a, Baba Kama 99b. Things of the heart, Kiddushim 32b. That general principles of legislation and interpretation were given at Sinai, Genesis Rabba 4, 41. Of the "great principles" in Torah, Sifri, Aikev 52. The "way of God," Genesis 18, 19. Abot 2, 1.

[6] Makkot 24a., where other summations are also cited.

[7] Revelation as of historical role, Megillah 14a. Of end of prophecy and role of wisdom, Yoma 9b. Baba Bathra 12a. Maimonides, "Guide of the Perplexed," II, 45. Pines edition, p. 376. In Maimonides' view, prophecy remains a contemporary possibility. To Halevi, the renewal of prophecy is dependent upon the return of the Israelites to the Holy Land. The Jewish Christians of the First and Second Centuries regarded Jesus as a prophet, like unto Moses. See H. J. Schoeps, "Jewish Christianity," Philadelphia, 1969. The ideological battle against prophecy in the Christian Church is described in Jaroslav Pelican's "The Emergence of the Catholic Tradition," Chicago, 1971 p. 105.

[8] Sanhedrin 39b. Makkot 23b. (Maimonides regards these two principles as "knowable to human speculation," though the Israelites received them at Sinai. "Guide," Pines' translation, p. 364.)

[9] Psalms 69, 19; 73, 28. Isaiah 58, 2.

[10] Shabbat 133b. Kethubot 111a. On "Kevayochol," Aruch Hasholem, vol. IV, p. 130. Genesis Rabba, 27. "Guide of the Perplexed," II, 40.

[11] Sifri, Voet-hanan, 32 on Deuteronomy 6, 5. To love God is to bring people to love Him.

[12] F. Rosenzweig, "Der Stern der Erlösung," III, p. 48, Berlin, 1930.

[13] Judah Halevi, "The Kuzari," II, 36. Hirschfeld translation. The sentence on p. 110 should read, "If we are good, the Divine Influence is brought through us into the world." See also the Commentary of David Kimhi on Isaiah 53.

[14] Palestinian T. Berochot, 9, 5.

[15] Abot 2, 21.

[16] The conception of Torah as a living organism is discussed in G. Scholem's "On the Kabbalah and its Mysticism" N.Y., 1965, chapter 2. The concept of alternating periods of

expansion and contraction in the development of Halachah is elaborated in Chayim Cherno-witz's monumental studies, four vols. of "Toldot Ha-halachah" and three vols. of "Toldot Haposkim" (Hebrew).

[17] That even one Commandment may be a means to salvation is asserted against the opposite opinion, that one transgression may lead to hell, in several places in the Talmud. Maimonides in his commentary on the last Mishnah of Makkot declares this assertion to be a basic principle. Sanhedrin 81a. Midrash Tehillim, Bober edition, 15, 7 p. 40. The contrary opinion is stated in the New Testament, the letter of James (2, 10).

[18] Bahya Ibn Pakuda, "Duties of the Heart," Author's Introduction. S. Rosenblatt's translation, Yale U. Press, 1948.

[19] The ethics of Kabbalah were elaborated in this way by Moses Cordovero in "The Palm of Deborah," translated by Louis Jacobs and published by Vallentine, Mitchel, London. Moses Hayim Luzzato's manual of ethics was translated by M. M. Kaplan and published under the name, "The Path of the Righteous."

[20] "Zafnat Paneah," by Rabbi Jacob Joseph, Petrikof edition, pp. 25a. & 33a. "Tsavoat Horivosh," edited by B. Mintz, Talpiot, Jerusalem, 1961, p. 22. "Tanya," the classical work of Rabbi Sheneur Zalman was concerned with the vocation of "the average person."

[21] "Guide of the Perplexed," III, 51. A. J. Heschel raised the question whether Maimonides believed that he had attained the rank of prophecy. Some of the old commentators were so shocked by the implications of this chapter that they refused to acknowledge it was indeed written by Maimonides. Commentary of Shem Tov, Warsaw, 1930.

[22] "Guide of the Perplexed" II, 45; III, 23. "Hilchot Deot." I, 6.

[23] "Hilchot Melochim" chapter III. Maimonides' positive appreciation of Christianity and Islam for their historic role in preparing humanity for the Kingdom of God is found·in the uncensored Constantinople edition, Hilchot Melochim, X, 14.

[24] B. T. Sanhedrin 56a-60a. Among the so-called "seven commandments of the sons of Noah," positive commands are not taken into account. Noachides who devote themselves to the elaboration of their traditions are said to be like the High priest. Sanhedrin 59a. According to one version, there were thirty Noachide commands. B. T. Hullin 92a. According to some talmudic teachers, Noachides are obligated to "sanctify the Name"—a general principle which has wide implications. Sanhedrin 74b.

[25] B. T. Makkot 23a., on the negating of some Mosaic declarations. On the decline of the generations, see B. T. Shabbat 112b. On the acceptance of Torah by all nations, B. T. Avodah Zara 3b. Palest. T. Avodah Zara 2, 1.

[26] The comparison of the "secrets of Torah," to be revealed fully in the Messianic Era, to the Tree of Life, while the existing laws are of the Tree of Knowledge, is assumed in the Zohar. See Zohar I, 26b. This question is discussed in Mishnat Hazoar, vol. II pp. 388-398. Gershom G. Scholem, "On the Kabbalah and its Symbolism," N.Y., 1965, p. 68. On the Messiah and his "new Torah," Otiot di R. Akiba, Alef, Zayin. Zohar, Vayikra, 23. His high status, "Yalkut Shimeoni" on Isaiah, chapter 52.

[27] The term "spiritual proselytes" is better than the designation semi-converts for the so-called "fearers of the Lord." See discussion of H. A. Wolfson, "Philo" vol. II, p. 370. The status of Christians is discussed in the Tossafot on B. T. Avodah Zara, 2a. In the official Code of the Sixteenth Century, Shulhan Arukh, H.M. 525, 5, there is printed the gloss by Rabbi Moshe Rivkes, called Beair Hagolah, which declares, "But the peoples in whose shade, we, the people of Israel, are exiled and amongst whom we are dispersed do in fact believe in Creatio ex nihilo and in the Exodus and in the main principles of religion, and their whole aim and intent is to serve the Maker of heaven and earth, as the codifiers have written."

[28] Commentary on Pirke Abot by Jacob Emden, published under the name, Etz Abot in 1756.

[29] J. Albo refused to accord the Christian faith the status of an authentic divine faith. In his "Book of Principles," III, 25, translated by I. Husik and published by J.P.S., he argues that Christianity contains anti-rational dogmas, which reason cannot allow. This was also the position of Nahmanides in his famous debate. Revelation can be trans-rational but not contrary

to reason. At the same time, Albo allows the possibility of the co-existence of diverse true faiths for peoples who have been conditioned to different beliefs and practices.

[30] Solomon Formstecher, "Die Religion de Geistes," Franz Rosenzweig, "Stern d. Erlösung" (New York: Holt, Rinehart & Winston, 1968). Claude G. Montefiore, "Liberal Judaism," 1903 and his Jowett Lectures of 1910, "Some Elements of the Religious Teaching of Jesus."

[31] *Abot* I, 14. A review of "The Jewish-Christian Argument" through the centuries is found in Hans J. Schoeps' work under this name (New York: Holt, Rinehart and Winston, 1963). A historical-sociological approach to the same problem is offered in Jacob Katz's "Exclusiveness and Tolerance," (New York: Schocken, 1961). The first section of Jacob B. Agus' book, "Dialogue and Tradition" deals with this theme, especially the chapter, "Mutually Challenging, not Mutually Contradictory." (New York: Abelard-Schuman Ltd., 1971.) The philosophy of Herrmann Cohen is summarized in my previously mentioned work "Modern Philosophies of Judaism."

# THE COVENANT
# CONCEPT—PARTICULARISTIC,
# PLURALISTIC, OR FUTURISTIC?

IN A draft statement by a group of rabbis attending an interfaith seminar, the following sentence occured "It must be emphasized that the traditional Jew cannot conceive of God entering into a covenant with another special group of humans".

Since the statement was tentative, the authors asking that it "*not* be reproduced or printed", we do not here identify the source. But the harsh exclusiveness of this sentence is so painfully clear that it may well serve as an introduction to our theme.

Naturally, the term "the traditional Jew", can be taken in the sense of the average person, the man in the street. We can hardly expect to encounter theological sophistication at streetcorners. Still, the purpose of all theology is to affect the thought and feeling of the common man. In that sense, this assertion may not be fallacious. But if tradition be taken in its fullness, then this remark is as untrue as it is naive. What is the meaning of the covenant in traditional Judaism?—Is it as simplistic and exclusive as the quoted statement implies? Or does it allow for a pluralistic conception with the possibility being projected of several covenants valid simultanously, or does the very nature of a covenant with the Transcendent God exclude the presumption of knowing God's Will, in its fullness?—If so, other covenants with other peoples cannot be ruled out.

Our analysis will deal with the covenant concept in Judaism, but the implications of our study are manifestly ecumenical. In each of the three monotheistic faiths—Judaism, Christianity, Islam—the same dilemmas and problems, even if not the same solutions, will be found.

We begin with the covenant concept, as it appears in the Hebrew Scriptures. The biblical authors were searching for an apt metaphor of man's

Originally published in *Journal of Ecumenical Studies*, Spring 1981.

encounter with God. They thought of God as Creator of "heaven and earth"; they experienced God's "nearness" to their hearts and souls;[1] they were certain of His sustaining power—"underneath are the everlasting arms";[2] they despised the superstitions and abominations of the pagans, and by way of contrast knew themselves to be uniquely favored, exalted, chosen, loved; they yearned for a concrete practice or symbol that would serve as a perpetual reminder of the fleeting moments of exultant faith. While they were aware of the human impossibility of grasping the fullness of the Divine Will, they, humanly enough, sought to imprison the Infinite within the bounds of the finite. The concept of a universal emperor governing his far flung empire indirectly, through intermediaries, and covenanting with one people as objects of his special concern seemed to fit these experiences.

In essence, the golden moments of Revelation occur in the lives of all people. Deep crises and existential contradictions are followed by the reassertion of the familiar landmarks of the spirit. This rebound from anomie and despair is at times synthetic rather than a return to the status quo ante. Surges of reassurance in the value and truth of a transmitted tradition, serve to integrate newly perceived spiritual ideals with the practices of the past. An illumination suggestive of infinite horizons supervenes upon an intoxicating enthusiasm for a particular tradition, bounded by fixed dogmas and ethnocentric myths.

The prophetic experience of revelation is the general faith-event in our life, molded by an impassioned ethical concern and articulated poetically.[3] Faith is an event, a process, a pulsation, as are all things in an organismic universe. In this event, the Whole becomes an overwhelming reality to a person, in thought as truth, in feeling as love, in the resolve so to act as to repeat the experience. Love generates the yearning for more love and the determination to make oneself and society fit "dwelling places for the *Shechinah*."

The faith-event contains several polarities—God is transcendent, yet He is somehow "near to those who call upon Him in truth". He is the One God of all mankind, but He chooses certain persons, peoples, moments, to express His Will. He demands loyalty and faithfulness to all that is humane and ethical, but also loyalty and faithfulness to Himself.[4] He favors that which all good men everywhere feel is good and right, but He also demands specific sanctifying rituals, which are peculiar to His service—"be ye holy, for I am holy".[5] Above all, His Will is both clear and elusive—clear enough to be known by every person, in his "solitariness", or in his moments of "ultimate concern", but also He is so elusive that only when people are given a "new heart and new spirit" can they truly serve Him.[6]

In sum, in the moments of revelation, we experience three dimensions of feelings—each with its own Yea and Nay. *Reassurance*—the transcendent God is "near" to the pious, as protector and Redeemer; but also Far, with all our insights being feeble stabs in the dark—"the Lord is in His holy temple, let the whole world be silent before Him".[7] *Reorientation* to specific ideals and goals, along with an awareness of His concern for all men and the elusiveness of His Will. *Rededication* to the quest of His nearness, in the future, since in the present the bounds of finitude cannot encompass the Infinite. The negative awareness, that we can neither comprehend nor impose limits on either His Being or His Will or His Purpose, is as integral to the experience of revelation, as the affirmative grasp of some commands or symbols, which were associated with holiness, at a particular time and place.

Indeed, the knowledge that we do *not* know God's Will is as essential to the divine encounter in monotheism as the same affirmation in the philosophy of Socrates. The first two of the ten commandments "were spoken by the Power itself", we are told in the Talmud.[8] The other eight were pronounced by Moses. In other words, the divine encounter itself contains only a *Yea*—God is here as Revealer and as Redeemer, and a *Nay*—no words and no figures can represent Him fully. So, when Moses asked "to see His Glory", he was told that only fleeting memories of His having passed, metaphorically, "His back" could be apprehended.[9]

Biblical religion, we must remember, was unique, not in its affirmation of a revelation or a covenant, for these were common convictions in the pagan world. The uniqueness of the biblical faith lay in its Negation—the One God towers above and beyond any representation or any revelation. In dedicating the Holy Temple as "the dwelling place" of God, King Solomon stated, "The Lord has chosen to dwell in darkness".[10]

In view of the twofold cutting edge of revelation, we may well inquire whether the covenant concept can serve as an adequate metaphor for the experience of revelation. Manifestly, the concept itself varied greatly even in the earliest periods of the Hebrew Scriptures. There was the contract between equals, two friends, or man and wife. More typical of the ancient world was the contract between a godlike King and his vassals. The famed biblical scholar, Harry Orlinsky, maintains that the former experience was paradigmatic to the biblical authors.

"In the view of the biblical writers, God and Israel had entered voluntarily into a contract as equal partners to serve and further the interests of one another exclusively".[11]

While he allows that the biblical authors assumed the existence of a concurrent covenant with humanity, he does not provide for the sense of infinite horizons in any genuine religious experience. In a note, he disputes the validity of "the vassal type of covenant of ancient peoples".[12]

In our view, his interpretation fits some passages of the Bible. But, it is altogether inadequate for the understanding of the spectrum of meanings in the biblical covenant concept. The tensions and paradoxes within the concept ranged from the seemingly arbitrary Divine choice of and covenant with Abraham to the absence of a Divine commitment in the Faithful Agreement of Ezra and Nehemiah.[13] Abraham's call is described as a kind of exodus, the beginning of the destiny of Israel. And it is stated in terms of universality—"and all the nations of the earth will be blessed through you".[14] The dimension of "not yet" is echoed in the prediction of 400 years of slavery and torment for the children of Israel. The one note of "equality" is detectible in Abraham's bold outcry—"can it be that the judge of the entire earth will not do justice?"[15] But, even then Abraham acts as a spokesman for humanity, who is also a humble petitioner, not an equal partner.

The covenant of Ezra and Nehemiah is concluded not between God and men but between the leading men of Jerusalem themselves. There is no reference in the introductory prayer of Ezra and Nehemiah to the covenant of Moses either at Sinai or in the prairies of Moab. At Sinai God gave commands, true *Torot*, good *mizvot*.[16] God commands and the Jew obeys. Nehemiah's only reference to a covenant is to the one concluded with Abraham, "the father of a multitude of nations".

As we survey the various references to a covenant in the Hebrew Scriptures, we find that this notion is open-ended in several ways; it is counterbalanced by several other covenants—the covenant with mankind, represented by Adam and Eve, also by Noah and his descendants; with Abraham as the father of all who convert. Indeed the call for a renewal of the covenant in the future is integral to the awareness of a covenant in the past.

Moses himself felt the need of renewing the Covenant in the prairies of Moab; so did Joshua[17], Jehoioda[18], and king Josiah[19]. Special covenants were drawn up in order to achieve national reforms—to free the Hebrew slaves in Jerusalem[20] and to expel the foreign women[21]. In addition, special covenants were made with the children of Levi, of Aaron and of David.

The prophets were uncomfortable with the notion of setting conditions for and limitations upon God's Will. God's relations with Israel were due to His Goodness, His love, His compassion. The first Isaiah does not mention the word covenant. His call for Israel's loyalty draws upon the natural feelings of gratitude for special favors. Isaiah was keenly conscious of the transcendent majesty of the Lord—the "mysterium trememdum" of holiness. "High as are the heavens above the earth, so high are My thoughts to your thoughts".[22]Hosea accuses the people of transgressing the covenant, "like

Adam", referring possibly to generally human sins.[23] Amos speaks of Israel's singularity in "being known" to God, but he also affirms that "they (Israelites) are like the children of the Ethiopians unto me".[24]

In the later prophets, the notion of a covenant is referred to the future and its very meaning is spiritualized. Hosea describes the future covenant when war will be no more and Israel will be betrothed in steadfast love, in compassion and in faithfulness.[25] Jeremiah speaks of "putting the Torah in the hearts of the people" as a new covenant. Ezekiel predicts "a covenant of peace, an eternal covenant".[26] Deutero-Isaiah foretells in one of the "Servant" chapters a new creation of the people whereby they will be transformed "into a covenanted people, a light to the nations".[27] Malachi's "angel of the covenant" also belongs to the future and is apparently concerned with the purification of the ritual.[28]

Manifestly, many of the biblical authors were keenly aware of the dangers inherent in the notion of the Covenant—the narcissistic feeling of superiority, the legalistic tendency to reduce a living faith to so many fragmented practices;[29] the confining of the transcendent and eternal God within the narrow limits of a time-conditioned body of specifications. In sum, the Covenant-concept may easily be corrupted to the point of shutting out the openness of the faith-event, its dynamism, its infinite outreach. To counter the formalism inherent in the Covenant concept, the Bible frequently adds the words, *hesed*, steadfast love, or *shalom*, peace, to the word, *berit*, covenant.

The tensions within the Covenant concept became more marked during the Hellenistic period. It suffices to note that Philo hardly refers to any covenant. In his life of Abraham, he writes of the divine commands written in nature as well as in the Torah.[30] Abraham's migrations are symbolic of "the search for the true God". Abraham was "himself a law and an unwritten statute".[31] He stresses the humanistic purpose of the choice of Israel—"the nation dearest of all to God, which as I hold, received the gift of priesthood and prophecy on behalf of all mankind."[32]

As the latest edition of the Theological Dictionary of the New Testament summarizes the evolution of the Covenant idea in the Septuagint and Philo,

> "the divine will self-revealed in history and establishing religion—this is the religious concept of the *diathiki* in the LXX and it represents a significant development of the Hebrew term even while preserving its essential content".

> "Even in Philo the firmly developed religious concept shines through the enveloping imagery. The term is obviously a formula for the gracious will of God disclosed in history".[33]

Paul's development of Covenant theology by contrasting the covenant of Abraham with that of Moses and the covenant of spirit with that of the letter set the stage for a bitter polemic with the Jewish Sages.[34] Matthews' formulation of Jesus' saying at the Last Supper brought Paul's interpretation into the central life of the Church.[35]

The third century rabbis countered by asserting that "Abraham our father observed all the commandments of the Torah, even to the mixing of cooked food"[36] (a rabbinically-instituted ordinance, whereby one was permitted to prepare food on a holiday for the Sabbath). Both religions were dominated frequently by the champions of an exclusionist theology.

However, even in the ancient world, non-exclusionist voices were heard from time to time. The tannaitic sages affirmed the validity of the *Seven Laws of Noah*, that is, of the universal revelation of ethics and faith.[37] They also declared that true prophets arose among the Gentiles.[38] A prophet, as the rabbis taught, was a messenger sent to a particular people. In other words, more than one valid body of revealed laws is possible. We recall that while the Stoics believed in the universal dissemination of "seeds of reason", the Rabbis regarded Wisdom itself as deriving from the Supreme Being.[39] Indeed, for the Rabbis, Wisdom was a concomitant of Torah, inseparable from the Torah itself, the gift of revelation. "If there is no wisdom, there is no piety; if there is no piety, there is no wisdom".[40] In this spirit Rabban Gamliel defended Peter and the apostles, offering a pragmatic counsel—"Refrain from these men and let them alone, for if this counsel or this work be of men, it will come to naught, but if it be of God, ye cannot overthrow it; lest haply ye be found to fight even against God".[41] The head of the Pharisaic school allowed that there might be other versions of revelation than those entrusted to his care. Similarly, at the trial of Paul, when Gentile Christians were already a dominant factor, the Pharisees declared, "We find no evil in this man; but if a spirit or an angel hath spoken to him, let us not fight against God".[42]

These liberal opinions were echoed in *The Ethics of the Fathers*, where an Alexandrine Sage declares that "an ecclesia for the sake of heaven is certain to endure".[43] We can hardly doubt that he referred to the Christian church—it endures because it is inspired by the love of God. Another second century Sage asserted that a Gentile who sincerely engages in the study of Torah—either of the universal teachings of Noah or the law of Judaism—is like the High Priest, who enters the Holy of Holies.[44]

Such voices, however, were rare in the troubled centuries of the ancient world. The predominant atmosphere of the Talmud was zealously exclusive. The Gentiles, taken as a whole, were presumed to have violated the Noachide laws.[45] They were therefore utterly condemned. Satan's corruption had marred their judgment; their only chance is to convert to Judaism when the Messiah comes; in that case they will enter the dubious category of "unwilling converts" (gerim gerurim).[46] The Israelites, too, would not have accepted the Torah, if they had been free to follow their own inclinations. But the Lord lifted up the mountain-range of Sinai and held it over their heads, threatening to bury them if they did not consent to abide by the Torah. It was only in the time of Mordecai and Esther, a millenium or so after Moses, that the Israelites proved themselves to be willing martyrs for the sake of Torah.[47]

Did the biblical authors believe that God could not or would not conclude a Torah-like Covenant with other peoples?—There appears to be no warrant for any such belief. Isaiah looked forward to a triumvirate of the chosen—

"In that day Israel will be the third with Egypt and Assyria, a blessing in the midst of the earth, whom the Lord of hosts has blessed, saying 'Blessed be Egypt my people, and Assyria the work of my hands, and Israel my heritage' ".[48] The notion that all genuine worship is addressed to the One God is implied by Malachi.

"For from the rising of the sun to its setting my name is great among the nations, and in every place incense is offered to my name, and a pure offering; for my name is great among the nations, says the Lord of hosts".[49]

Zephania compares the diverse rituals of the various nations to a babel of languages, which will be turned into "pure speech", the worship of the One God.[50]

As to the Sages of the Talmud, we noted their ambivalence. We encounter references to an oath that God took not to *transfer* His covenant to other nations.[51] His faithfulness precluded any revocation of His relationship to Israel, as Paul argued in Romans 9-11, but it did not prevent Him from adding new persons to His people or contrariwise reducing His people to the barest minimum. No one questioned that the Messianic Age would witness the conversion of all nations to the true faith of Israel.[52] And the "light of the Messiah" might appear slowly and by degrees, like the dawn.[53] So, in the eschaton, all mankind will be included in God's plan of redemption.

To be sure, the Sages assert that the Lord consented to Moses' request not to allow His *Shechinah* to rest on nations other than Israel, but then this tradition reflects the opinion of the exclusionists, who were opposed by the moderates and the rationalists.[54]

Exclusive voices predominated, we may assume, in times of bitter polemic and persecution. "Lest you will say that another Moses will bring us another Torah from heaven . . . (we are assured) that no part of it was left in heaven".[55] Here, then, the negational phase of revelation, the humble acknowledgment of finitude is totally ignored. As a rule, the Sages were reluctant to set up categorical distinctions between the several non-Jewish faiths, exempting some, like the Christians and the Zoroastrians, from the general category of idolatry. They spoke of the Noachide principles in general, and in specific cases, a Sage could testify, "I know this or that Gentile is not an idol-worshipper".[56] They also observed that "the Gentiles outside the borders of the land of Israel are not idolators, but they are simply following the customs of their fathers".[57]

In respect of non-Jews, then, only God can tell whether they worshipped Him in truth.

If an entire nation embraced the Jewish faith, then they would feel that they were part of greater Israel. So in the letter of Joseph, the Khazar King, we read that he believed the descent of his people was from Japhet, Noah's son, and Togarmo, but that he trusted "the Lord, God of Israel will hasten our redemption, gather our exiles and our scattered ones . . ."[58] By joining the faith of Israel he and the Khazar nation became part of the larger people of Israel, sharing in its promise of earthly redemption.

Saadia calls the chapter in his book, dealing with the Sinaitic revelation, "Command and Admonition". All rational laws are obligatory for all men. But "in respect of non-rational laws . . . the Creator added them for us by way of command and admonition in order to multiply our reward and our prosperity on their account".[59]

In his view, the Covenant with Abraham, the father of all converts to monotheism, continues to be valid, even after the Torah of Moses was accepted by the Israelites.[60]

In his philosophic work, *The Guide of the Perplexed*, Maimonides does not even refer to the verse which tells of Moses concluding the covenant by the sprinkling of blood on the altar and the people.[61] In his interpretation, the authority of the Torah rests on its truth, as attested by the supreme prophetic genius of Moses, not on any contract, duly drawn up, signed and sealed. The very term, *berit*, covenant, hardly occurs in the "Guide of the Perplexed".

To be sure, in his ninth principle of faith, Maimonides speaks of the belief that the Torah will never be "exchanged" *(muhalefet)* and that there will never be "a different Torah" *(Torah aheret)* deriving from the Creator.[62] Maimonides did not intend to rule out change and adjustment within the life of Torah, as some Commentators imagined, but to assert that in its essence the Torah contains philosophic truth, and truth is immutable. Doubtless, he sought to reinforce Jewish resistance to the belligerent assertions of both Christians and Moslems that their revelations abolished the Torah of Moses. On the other hand, he recognized that the two daughter-faiths of Judaism served to prepare humanity for the messianic age by disseminating the ideas of monotheism and the scriptural ethic.[63] The philosopher-poet Judah Halevi suggested the metaphor of a tree with a broad stem and three branches. The fruit produced by the three branches will ultimately contain the same seeds, those planted by Abraham.[64]

The fourteenth century philosopher, Joseph Albo, who was called upon to represent Judaism in the famous disputation at Tortosa in 1413-1414 asserted "that it is possible for two divine Torot to be true simultaneously for two different communities".[65]

Albo argues that the Lord is a physician who may well prescribe different medicines to the same person at different times and to different people at the same time.[66]

But while the medieval rationalists allowed for plural covenants, the mystics and romantics thought otherwise. The oft quoted maxim, "the Holy One, blessed be He, the Torah and Israel are one", which the authors of the above mentioned draft take as their fundamental maxim, occurs in the Zohar and it reflects the mystical current of Judaism.[67]

Indeed, the mystical ideology taught that Jews were biologically distinguished from the rest of mankind, their souls being rooted in the highest realm of holiness. A very popular mystic wondered at the fact that Gentiles don't look so very different from Jews, though the souls of the latter derive their sustenance from the Divine Pleroma, while the souls of the former are rooted in the "other side", the demonic realm.[68] Here, then, was a Jewish counterpart to the Spanish infatuation with "limpieza", limiting posts of responsibility to pure-blooded descendants of "old Christians", on the ground the Jewish souls were corrupted by centuries of disbelief in Christian dogmas. Characteristic of the opposition between the ethnocentric-mystical interpretation of the Covenant and the humanist-rationalist view is the contrast in the two interpretations of the "priestly" function of Israel, —offered by Rashi and Seforno respectively. Rashi interprets "priests" as meaning princes, that is, the Israelites will become the governors of all other nations; Seforno asserts "this is the import of a 'Kingdom of priests,' to teach and to explain to all men the task of serving God together . . ."[69]

In the past two centuries, the rationalist-humanistic concept of revelation prevailed in Jewish thought of the western world.

Moses Mendelssohn, the champion of Enlightenment, wrote that the mark of a false religion is precisely its claim to exclusiveness.[70] Even the unbending defender of uncompromising Orthodoxy, Samson Raphael Hirsch, conceived of Jewish destiny in universal terms.

"Their (the Israelites) speedy removal from the Land (of Israel) brought about their spiritual and moral salvation . . . The State and Temple went to ruin, but the people . . . went out to assume the burdens of their great mission in the Dispersion".

Herrmann Cohen brought this rationalist-humanistic trend to its climax, as is evident from the following quotations:

"Man, not the people and not Moses; man, as rational being, is the correlate of the God of revelation".[71]

"The Covenant is the instrument of faithfulness. Therefore, God concludes a covenant with Noah, with Abraham and with Israel".[72]

"God does not love Israel more or differently than His love for men in general . . . In Israel, God loves Israel only as a model, a symbol of mankind, a mark of distinction within it, for only monotheism is able to establish the unity of the human race".[73]

In his magisterial work, *Jewish Theology*, Kaufmann Kohler, longtime President of the Hebrew Union College, considers the Jewish "trinity" to be not the unity of God, Israel and Torah, but God, Man and the Kingdom of God. He retained his humanistic vision, though he subscribed to some racistic ideas. Reflecting the preoccupation with race in the early decades of the Twentieth century, he wrote, "In fact, the soul of the Jewish people reveals a peculiar mingling of characteristics, a union of contrasts which make it especially fit for its providential mission in history".[74]

Martin Buber, as is well known is unclassifiable. At one time, a folkist, a mystic, an interpreter of *Hassidism*, he moved steadily toward a position "on the boundary", between romanticism and rationalism. In his description of the faith-event in Judaism as a personal "believing in", contrasted with a propositional "believing that", which he attributed to Christianity, he focused attention on the openness of revelation, its transcendence of all knowing. He rejected the legalistic phase of Judaism in order to keep himself open to fresh experiences. He was aware of the danger of reducing religion to a contract, duly signed and delivered. His admiration for *Hassidism* was due to his "idealization" of their movement, especially in its early phases. He identified with their presumed endeavor to transcend the boundaries of the Law.

Franz Rosenzweig, in keeping with his Hegelian orientation, interpreted the Covenant between God and Israel as a living tradition, rather than as a book or a series of books. The Divine Will is dynamic, consisting of thrusts of redeeming vitality. Revelation is a continuing phenomenon, with bursts of God's love eliciting new expressions of Israel's love. Rosenzweig regarded the Christian community as a providential instrument for the realization of the covenant with Israel. In his famous metaphor, the function of Christianity is to convert the world; that of Israel to be faithful to its ideal self. Like the sun, which is unthinkable without its rays, the Covenant is inconceivable without both Israel and the Church.

Mordecai M. Kaplan devoted his life to the formulation of a synthesis between Jewish nationalism and humanism. He called for the rejection of the dogma of the "Chosen People", in the sense of a people set apart and insulated from the life of humanity. To him, the notion of a special Covenant with Israel was abhorrent. All nations are called upon to apply to their own life the prophetic teaching of "ethical nationhood."

## Conclusion

We conclude from all the above that the proposition we quoted at the beginning of this essay reflects only one of the several strands composing the Jewish tradition. It articulates the judgment of the fundamentalists, romantics and mystics, certainly not the view of the prophetic-philosophical school, from Abraham to Rosenzweig and from Maimonides to Mordecai Kaplan. I need hardly add that I identify with the philosophical trend in Jewish thought, in the interpretation of the covenant concept. I take the paradigm of the covenant to be Abraham's rebellion against the practice of sacrificing children rather than "his passing between the pieces" of slaughtered animals. The former was then a revolutionary ideal, the latter was already an archaic way of formalizing a contract. The "Faithful Agreement" of Ezra and Nehemiah is to me a demonstration of the way the Jewish tradition took form—through a series of self-assumed ordinances, or *takkanot*. All that we do to express our love of God articulates the voice of God within us. So, the rabbis spoke of ordinances that they themselves formulated as "commandments" of the Lord. There were also survivals from the dim past, such as the system of sacrificial offerings. Such archaic practices should be consciously confined to the past, while their inner spirit is cherished as part of the sacred tradition. In this self-renewing and self-critical spirit, the Covenant concept remains valid even in our day.

I offer the following propositions as both a personal confession of faith and as a contemporary expression of the prophetic-philosophical school of thought:

1. A Covenant establishes a living tradition, whereby the piety of past generations is preserved as the heritage of succeeding generations. It is through the Jewish tradition that I grew up to feel the majesty and the message of God. But it is also the same tradition, that encouraged me to study and to appreciate the open horizons of philosophy and the ardor of

other faiths. The emphasis on God's transcendence in Judaism kept me from surrendering to the notion that God's Will, in its fullness, is reflected within my tradition exclusively.

2. A lifetime is needed to sense the import of a great historical faith and relate it to contemporary experience. Therefore, we cannot but live within the confines of one tradition. But, divine revelation in all its dimensions, is universal and all-human. Hence, we must learn to maintain a vital tension between our subjective feelings, rites and symbols and the objective world, as it is presented to our minds and hearts by the emergent world-wide culture of which we are part.

3. God is the source of all great and ennobling ideals. Our experience of holiness blends harmoniously all ideals and values, even as the mind synthesizes the impressions of the senses. So, revelation is an extension and harmonization of human values, not a rejection of them. If aught is not humanizing, it is not divine. The thrusts of revelation are not those which shatter the structures of human wisdom, but those which extend and enhance the slow and stumbling efforts of mankind. Just as the God we worship is revealed in the marvels of cosmic creation and the daily wonders of life and spirit, rather than in the so called "miracles" which impress the gullible, so the Word of God is revealed primarily in the common experience and tested wisdom of mankind, secondarily in particular cultures.

4. Particular revelations are vehicles of spiritual power, but their specific content is metaphorical. Our finite minds can reflect the Infinite mind only "through a glass, darkly", by the utilization of fragments of human experience. Not all metaphors are born equal. They can function as rungs on Jacob's ladder, but also as slippery steps toward the pit of self-righteous illusions. The metaphors of ritual and dogma, in my faith, as in other religious communities, are always more than action-symbols or figures of speech. They are freighted with the memories of the past and charged with the covenanted loyalty of a living community. As such, they are invaluable, providing we bear in mind their metaphorical character.

5. I repudiate the notion that God "contracted" His Will within the stated precepts of the Jewish tradition, in the same manner as He "contracted" His infinite being in order to create this finite universe. This Kabbalistic notion of "tsimtsum" (contraction) cannot be understood literally. In "contracting" Himself, it is He who does the contracting, at every point. There cannot be aught which escapes His Power, "The whole earth is full of His Glory". The description of His self-limitation in allowing room for human freedom is intended to suggest the existence of two levels of reality— as seen by man and as seen by God (*mitsidenu* and *mitsido*). "Self-contraction"

is meaningful only in a metaphorical sense, as "when a father reduces his mind to the level of a small child" when he tells a childish fable or plays childish games. The father's mind remains incomprehensible to the child, while the world of the child is make-believe to the father.

The doctrine of God's "self-contraction", or "withdrawal", or "eclipse," seems plausible when it is applied to the reality of human freedom. If humans are truly free, God must have limited His own Power. But, I contend that it is precisely in the free mind of man that God is most manifest. There are situations in life, where the Presence of God is hidden from our sight, and there are window-like areas, which are transparent to His radiance. In all cases, we can only speak of God's "absence" as a subjective feeling, not as an objective reality. God is everywhere, and He is manifest wherever the "things of God" are realized.

6. When we speak of "the Chosen People" in Judaism, I take the phrase to refer to the ideal Israel, the covenanted people, as in Isaiah's formulation, "to be a covenanted people, a light to the nations". We of Israel are called upon to act as an *example* to other individuals and nations, not as an *exception*. More is expected from those to whom more was given in history, through no merit of their own. At any one time, a particular person or people may have a treasure of spiritual gifts to share with others. But, no individual or people is permanently and in all ways separated from or uplifted above the rest of mankind.

I consider that the Golden Rule applies to communities as well as to individuals—no community should claim exclusive rights or privileges or a unique cosmic status. We should learn to "understand in love" other faiths as we expect others to understand us in love.

## Notes to *The Covenant Concept*

1 Deuteronomy 30, 14. Isaiah 50, 8. Psalms 34, 19. Psalms 145, 19. Psalms 73, 28.
2 Deuteronomy 33, 27.
3 J. B. Agus, *The Prophet in Modern Hebrew Literature*, in the Goldenson Lectures, 1955-1966, Hebrew Union College Press, Cincinnati, Ohio.
4 Micah 6, 8.
5 Leviticus 19, 2.
6 Ezekiel 36, 26; 11, 19; 18, 31.
7 Habakuk 2, 20.
8 B. T. Makkot 23b.
9 Exodus 33, 12-23; 34, 1-8.
10 1 Kings 8, 12
11 H. Orlinsky, *The Situational Ethics of Violence*, in *Violence and Defense in the Jewish Experience*, J.P.S., 1977, p. 58
12 Ibid, note 1, p. 45
13 Nehemiah 10, 1
14 Genesis 12, 3
15 Genesis 18, 25
16 Nehemiah 9, 13
17 Joshua 24, 25
18 2 Kings 11, 17
19 2 Kings 23, 2, 3
20 Jeremiah 24, 8
21 Ezra 10, 3
22 Isaiah 55, 9
23 Hosea 6, 17
24 Amos 3, 2; 9, 7
25 Hosea 2, 20-22
26 Ezekiel 34, 25. Jeremiah 31, 31
27 Isaiah 42, 6; 49, 8
28 Malachi 3, 1
29 Isaiah 28, 10, 13
30 Philo. *De Abrahamo*, XIII, 60. Ed. Loeb Classics
31 Ibid XLV, 275
32 Ibid XIX, 98
33 *Theological Dictionary of the New Testament*, ed. Kittel. Vol. II pp. 127, 128.
34 Galatians 3; 2 Corinthians 3, 6
35 Matt. 26, 28
36 B. T. Yoma 28b
37 B. T. Sanhedrin 56a. Hullin 92a.
38 B. T. Baba Bathra 15b.
39 B. T. Berochot 55a.
40 Avot 3, 14
41 Acts 5, 38, 39
42 Acts 23, 9
43 Abot 4, 11. It is believed *Hasandlor* means the Alexandrian.
44 B. T. Baba Kama 38a.
45 Hullin 92a. Baba Kama 38a.
46 B. T. Avoda Zara 3b.
47 B. T. Sabbat 88a.
48 Isaiah 19, 24
49 Malachi 1, 11

50 Zephaniah 3, 9

51 B. T. Gittin 57b

52 In Maimonides' formulation of this belief, it is not clear whether "the true faith" of the future will be Judaism or universal religion. *Hilchot Melochim*, XII.

53 Shohar Tov, Tehillim 18, Jerusalem Berochot 1, 1.

54 B. T. Baba Bathra 15b

55 Deuteronomy Rabba 8, 6

56 B. T. Avoda Zara 65a.

57 B. T. Hullin 13b.

58 Letter of Joseph, King of Khazaria, in introduction to Halevi's *Kuzari*.

59 Saadia, Emunot Vedeot, III, 1

60 Ibid, III, 7

61 Exodus 24, 8

62 Maimonides' introduction to the eleventh chapter of Sanhedrin, in his commentary to the *Mishnah*.

63 Maimonides' Code, *Hilchot Melochim*, S, 12, in the uncensored edition of Constantinople.

64 Judah Halevi, The Kuzari IV, 23

65 Joseph Albo, *The Book of Principles*, translated by I. Husik, published by J.P.S. Philadelphia, I, 25

66 Ibid, II, ch. 13-23. See the comments in Ch. 10 of Louis Jacobs' *Principles of the Jewish Faith* pp. 302-319, Basic Books, N.Y. 1964.

67 Zohar, Emor, III, 93b.

68 R. Isaiah Hurwitz, *Shenai Luhot Haberit*, Introduction.

69 Exodus, 19, 6

70 M. Mendelssohn, *Jerusalem*, part two.

71 H. Cohen, *Religion of Reason*, translated from the German by R. Hallo, p. 79

72 Ibid, p. 441

73 Ibid, p. 149

74 K. Kohler, *Jewish Theology*, 1968 edition p. 327

# THE "YES" AND THE "NO" OF REVELATION

THE PIVOTAL role of Socrates in the evolution of Western thought is unquestioned. He knew that he did not know; yet, he pursued relentlessly the quest for wisdom. His personality exemplified the two-sided edge of wisdom—its "yes" and its "no". In essence, he discovered the scientific method—the determined quest, the tentativeness of all formulations, the cooperative character of research and the test of all propositions by their consequences.

In the eyes of most Athenian citizens, the negation of Socrates loomed larger than his positive teaching. They blamed him for "corrupting" their youth, by his skepticism, his disregard of conventional truths, his biting sarcasm. In the history of thought Socrates is ensconced as the exemplary philosopher. His affirmation of the supreme value of the search for truth was balanced by his negation of superficial, convenient falsehoods. The two aspects of his personality were inseparable. Rigorous thinking in the field of morality as in physical science requires the scalpel of criticism as well as the endless mass of factual data. Thoughtfulness is a double-edged adventure—yes, values are real; no, we do not hold them in our grasp. In both its aspects, the search of wisdom is self-validating—"the unexamined life is not worth living".

Does "Socratic ignorance" form part of biblical religion, as it was slowly molded by prophets and sages?—It is generally assumed that the biblical authors allowed no room for doubt and questioning in their interpretation of the faith. "Thus spoke the Lord" they asserted. Who can question the Will of God?—The prophets are presumed to have been ecstatics, who aimed to educate a people of "true believers", eager followers obeying blindly "the laws and ordinances" of the ancestral faith. Revelation was, to the biblical

Originally published in *God and His Temple*, ed. by L. E. Frizzel (Dept. of Judeo-Christian Studies, Seton Hall University). South Orange, N.J. 1980.

authors, a clear and concise affair, a kind of speech, as unambiguous as "When a person speaks to his friend".

This view of biblical religion corresponds to the popular notion of faith, as a surrender of personal judgment, a clear cut decision to have done with doubts, a sacrifice of the intellect on the altar of piety.

In this essay, we propose to illustrate the fact that the negational component of revelation is as significant as the affirmative one in biblical-rabbinic religion and, by extension, in all faiths that are founded on the Jewish heritage. Clearly, the ecumenical movement would be greatly aided by the realization that absolutist dogmatism is simplistic and alien to the nature of a living faith.

Faith can be either placid or dynamic. If the teachings of the faith have become so much "knowledge", with no room left for the wonder of mystery, then faith is placid. The believer is then protected from the surging tides of opinion by the invisible walls of a sacred tradition. Whatever it means to be "saved" in any tradition, placid faith "saves" the believer from the turbulence of doubt and the dangerous quest of new horizons of wisdom.

Dynamic faith is an event, a temporary experience of the rhythmic pulsation of trust and doubt. Belief is experienced as a subjective decision;— "It is I who make the decision"; hence it is an act that is time-conditioned, culture-conditioned, a way-station on the infinite ascent to "the mountain of the Lord". In the faith-event, negation and affirmation are one, as in every act of becoming. Hence, "the ambivalence of the sacred". Mircea Eliade points out the widespread recognition of polarity within the holy.

" . . . that *sacer* can mean at the same time accursed and holy. Eustathius notes the same double meaning with *hagios*, which can express at once the notion "pure" and the notion "polluted". And we find this same ambivalence of the sacred appearing in the early Semitic world and among the Egyptians". (M. Eliade, *Patterns in Comparative Religion*, World Publishing, N.Y. 1963, p. 13.)

We may add that in Hebrew the roots, brch, kls, kdsh, mean respectively both blessing and cursing, worship and ridicule, the holy and the unholy. An awareness of the two-sidedness of religious belief, which distinguishes it from knowledge, is implicit in this linguistic phenomenon. The prophet Hosea lists the several stages of commitment, leading to the "knowledge of God"—loyalty forever, moral action, faith. (Hosea 2;21,22) In the Gospel of Mark, the father of the epileptic child cries out, "Lord, I believe; help thou my unbelief". (Mark 9,24) Here, faith is affirmed and negated at the same time.

"A consideration of faith in the Old Testament cannot overlook the astonishing fact that two basically different and even contradictory groups of meaning are used for man's relation to God, fear on the one side and trust on the other". (*Theological Dictionary of the Old Testament*, vol. VI, p.183) We may add that in many a Psalm, faith in the "nearness of God" and the feeling of having been abandoned by Him are expressed in contiguous sentences. (Psalms 30;40;44;73)

The revelation-experience of the literary prophets is but a more intense form of the faith-event that occurs to all or most people. At times, we are minded to sing of the Glory of God in our lives and then again we experience moments when our life appears to be devoid of meaning. We, who are ephemeral, confront an eternal reality; we are elated by this encounter and also downcast by its transience. We are touched by eternity, but it eludes our grasp.

The "word of God", in the mind of the prophet, imposes a mission, a task that would "save" the community from an impending disaster. In the faith-event, the divine imperative is the echo of an echo. There is the Affirmation—you are called to be of service; you embody a transcendent value, "the image of God"; you are invited to become "a partner in the work of creation". There is also the "Mysterium tremendum" the mystery of not knowing the specifics; the Negation which reminds us more and more insistently that the will of the Infinite cannot be compressed into so many words; that our task is part of an endless and collective adventure; that our horizons are open-ended.

"For my thoughts are not your thoughts
neither are your ways my ways, says the Lord
For as the heavens are higher than the earth,
so are my ways higher than your ways
And my thoughts than your thoughts". (Isaiah 55;8,9)

The faith-event is integrated into the value system of a society and its cultural expressions. In the biblical religion, it was structured within either the love of God or the Law of God.

In the former case, the faith-event is interpreted as an act of divine love and the human response as dedication to the love of God. The recognition of God's unity leads to the command, "thou shalt love the Lord, Thy God, with all thy heart, with all thy soul and with all thy might" . . . The command to love is itself an act of love, and the response to God's love (Deut.6;5) is to yearn for more of His love. In the rabbinic commentary to this verse (Sifri,32) this precept is interpreted to mean—"thou shalt cause Him to be

beloved by all men, as did Abraham . . ." Love is expansive both horizon-
tally and vertically. The love of God issues in the love of men and in the
longing for "the nearness of God". In turn, that longing is interpreted in
rabbinic commentaries as the task of rendering one's own self to be "a
dwelling place for the Divine Presence (Maon lashechinah)". The social
version of this ideal is to share in the building of the Kingdom of God, "to
improve the world by means of the Kingdom of the Almighty" (from prayer
attributed to Rav, third century Babylonian sage). The personal quest for
divine "nearness" is inseparable from the social ideal of seeking to prepare the
world for the Divine Presence.

In the latter case, the faith-event is viewed within the perspective of
lawfulness. All of creation is enchained by the bonds of law, which were
established by the Divine Will. Man is free to be either wayward or obedient.
He is called to fall in line with the laws of God, which are as irrevocable as
the laws of nature.

Thus says the Lord,
who gives the sun for light by day
and the fixed order of the moon and the stars for light by night
who stirs up the sea so that its waves roar
the Lord of hosts is his name.
If this fixed order departs
from before me, says the Lord,
Then shall the descendants of Israel cease
from being a nation before me forever.

The people of Israel consists of those who abide by that Law of God,
which will one day become the constitution of mankind as a whole. (Isaiah
2;2-4)

The presumed contrast between the Law and the Gospel has become a
theological cliché. The Law is as constitutive of rabbinic Judaism as Love is
of Christianity. Indeed, the basic difference is like a fork of the road. If the
perspective of love prevails, the growth of rituals will center round the
infinite grace of God, with metaphors of word and deed that stress God's
boundless mercy. In the perspective of lawfulness, the proliferation of rituals
will reflect the scrupulosity of divine law—our earthly law must reflect "the
higher law" of the Creator. "Torah is the earthly, lowly form of the higher
wisdom". (Genesis Rabba 44)

However, love for all its spontaneity is a quest as well as a possession. As
such, it will generate a dynamic restlessness, a yearning for higher levels of

perfection in the life of society as well as in the personality of the believer. The Protestant movement did not create the messianic ideal as a *creatio ex nihilo;* it merely liberated that drive. It is also natural for the pulsations of love to be structured in law, a dynamic, progressive law. Similarly, a system of laws aiming at the transmutation of the "natural" society into one living by the transnatural law of the Creator cannot do without the support of the love of God, trust in His infinite mercy and forgiveness and the messianic drive to build God's Kingdom on earth.

In both aspects of the faith-event, the sense of an infinite outreach will be expressed in a perpetual questioning as well as in a series of affirmations. In both communities, fixed forms for the feelings, thoughts and actions of their respective worshippers will be maintained, but there will also be a dynamic drive for the transcendence of these forms. The inner dialectic of faith may be temporarily halted by the reification of faith into rituals and dogmas. The transient and the concrete may be idolized as if they were themselves divine, not metaphors for the divine will. It is the function of the negational component of the faith-event to keep the processes of inner development and social advancement from grinding to a halt.

Biblical religion is an excellent illustration of the dynamics of faith. Von Rad, the great biblical scholar, defended the view that the Hebraic faith (Yahwism) was expounded by three concurrent interpreters (Jeremiah 18;18)—priests, prophets and sages. The priests taught the traditional ritual, the prophets addressed themselves to the issues of the day, the sages treasured the distilled wisdom of human experience and the revelation of God in nature. Of the three teachers, the prophets represented the cutting edge of progress. While the priesthood guarded the tradition, as it took shape in the distant past, and the sages nurtured the embers of nascent rational reflection, the prophets focused attention on the moral implications of contemporary issues and projected the vision of the redeemed human order of the future. The prophets said both "yes" and "no" to their tradition, preserving the ritualistic framework, while endowing their heritage with deep moral fervor and sensitivity. They became the sponsors of moral dynamism, by negating the absolute import of religious rituals and ethnocentric myths.

We can best appreciate the nature of the prophetic enterprise, when we view it historically as a continuous battle against pagan idolatry. The pagan priests sacralized both the varied forces of nature and the intricate structure of society, from the family to the tribe, to the nation, to the empire. The gods formed a hierarchy, with those of the highest rank and ultimate reality merging into the impersonal iron rule of fate. The gods to whom cults were dedicated were anthropomorphic and immanent in nearly all things. The sacred was reified and trivialized. In the pagan mentality, the "yes" of the faith-event was celebrated in a total sanctificatin of the here and now. The line between the human and the divine was blurred since there was hardly any gap in the "great chain of being" extending between heaven and earth. The "No" of faith, the transcendent dimension of the holy, was ignored in the public cults and left for the solitary meditation of philosophers.

The prophets recognized the dynamic interaction between the transcendent One God and His immanent Presence in the moral-spiritual intuition of man. Hence, while only the One God is worthy of worship, He must not be reified. He is not in material things, but His "image" is reflected in the human personality at its best. This paradox is stated most clearly by Deutero-Isaiah,

> Thus says the Lord:
> 'Heaven is my throne
> and the earth is my footstool;
> what is the house which you would build for me,
>     and what is the place of my rest?
> All these things my hand has made
>     and so all these things are mine,
>                    says the Lord.
> But this is the man to whom I will look,
> he that is humble and contrite in spirit,
> and trembles at my word.' (Isaiah 66;1,2)

God is beyond all limitations and even conceptualizations, but His "nearness" is best felt in compassion, in humility, in piety.

The prophet's objection to the building of a "house of God" was anticipated by Samuel, who stopped the practice of bringing the "Ark of the Lord" into the battlefield to insure victory. So, too, the prophet Nathan opposed the building of a Holy Temple by King David. (1 Samuel 7;5-17) The prophet Elijah does not seek God in the Temple of Jerusalem. Instead, he goes back to the wilderness and to Mount Horeb. The Lord appears to him not in the fire, not in the storm, not in the earthquake, but in "a still, small voice". (Kings 19;12) Isaiah rebukes the people for their naive trust in the efficacy of sacrifices and pilgrimages. Amos maintains that the word of the Lord reverberates in the hearts of all men and women. His confrontation with the High priest of Beth El is paradigmatic of the perennial conflict between those who hear the Word in their conscience as against those who enshrine it in rites and institutions. (Amos 3;8,7;10-17) Jeremiah carried the anti-Temple campaign to a fresh summit, when he exclaimed,

"Do not trust in these deceptive words: 'This is the Temple of the Lord, the temple of the Lord, the temple of the Lord' ".

"For in the day that I brought them out of the land of Egypt, I did not speak to your fathers or command them concerning burnt offerings and sacrifices". (Jeremiah 7;4,22)

The essence of God's Will is justice, love and humble trust. (Micah 6;8) Continuing this prophetic tradition, Jesus combatted the self-righteousness of *some* Pharisees, even as did the Pharisaic teachers themselves. (B. T. Sotah 22b. Berochot 9;5)

As champions of Hebraic monotheism, the prophets combatted the pagan mentality by saying in effect—"Yes, but". So, they acted in reference to the cosmos, the land, the people, the ritual and the shape of the future. Their negation was new, their affirmation was not.

In respect of the cosmos, the pagans postulated not only a diversity of gods, but also a state of incipient warfare among them. As they saw it, the gods created the world, but each god was limited to one aspect of creation. How else could they account for the natural disasters which afflicted mankind from time to time? The prophets assumed a unity of divine power—hence, an undergirding harmony and an invincible stability. "For underneath are the everlasting arms", (Deuteronomy 33;27) and "the gods who did not make the heavens and the earth shall perish from the earth and from under the heavens." (Jeremiah 10;11)

The cosmos is made by the divine power, but this Power is above and beyond the powers of nature. Hence, the holidays, which were originally related to seasonal changes, were reinterpreted as celebrations of the work of God in history.

The land is holy to a god—this was a common axiom. Centuries passed before the worship of the Baals was extirpated in Israel. The prophets agreed that the land of Israel was holy to the One God, the Master of the universe. But in their view, this quality of holiness could not be organic, an intimate bond between soil and divinity. It could only be conditioned on the behavior of the people living on it. The colonists settled by the Assyrians reflected the pagan ways of thought; they did not know "the custom of the god of the land", who afflicted them by means of lions. (2 Kings 17;25) The Israelites encountered the One God in the wilderness of Sinai. He was not bound to any particular soil. But His design embraced the land of Israel as the habitation of a holy people. So, the land was holy, yes, but not in itself, only as a mark of favor to a people.

In the pagan view, there was an intimate bond beween a god and his people. Again, the prophets interpreted this bond as a conditional relationship, which applies to all men and women. The Israelites are not holy, by nature, as a biological datum. They are called upon to become holy. (Leviticus 19;2) And all men and women are similarly called. One day, they will hear that call and come for instruction to the "mountain of the house of the Lord". The prophets fought against the natural narcissism of the Israelites. The "chosen people" is but a loyal "remnant". (Isaiah 10;20,21) Assyria and Egypt, Israel's neighbors and oppressors, will also be "God's people" and "the work of His hands". (Isaiah 19;21-25)

The "covenant" between God and the Israelites replaced the natural organic bond between a people and its deity. The covenant is conditioned on the loyal observance by the people of a specific ritual. But this covenant belongs to the temporal order. In time to come, the true Covenant will come into being, the one written on "the tablets of the heart". (Jeremiah 31;30-33) The prophetic vision of the future was the core of their message to their own contemporaries. The "new Covenant" of the future supplements the vision of a united and redeemed mankind, drawing its inspiration from the Torah of Zion. In every aspect of that vision, the negation of a pagan axiom provided the cutting edge of spiritual growth.

In the Near Eastern world, the King was the link between the gods and the people. With the rise of David to the throne of Israel, some of the same rhetoric is employed by the prophet Nathan. "I shall be to him as a father and he will be to Me as a son . . ." (2 Samuel 7;14) But, the prophet immediately sets conditions for the favor of God. In a sense, all Israelites are classed as "sons of God" by the Deuteronomist, but the son of David is more so.

Henri Frankfort contrasts the concept of Hebraic Kingship with that of the Near Eastern world, as follows:

"Kingship too, was not for the Hebrews anchored in the cosmos. Except by way of contrast, it has no place in a 'study of ancient Near Eastern religion as an integration of society and nature'. The Hebrew King, like every other Hebrew stood under the judgment of God in an alien world, which as the dying David knew (2 Samuel 23;3-4)—seems friendly only on those rare occasions when man proves not inadequate" (quoted in M. Konvitz's *Judaism and Human Rights*, p. 98).

The emphasis on divine transcendence is apparent in the revivalist efforts of Ezra and Nehemiah. They draft a "firm covenant", but they no longer dare to attribute their work to God. It is representative of *Halachah*, the system of ordinances which governed the life of the Jew. The "firm covenant" is a voluntary undertaking. God is in the background; His prophets are suspect. We sense the feeling of the leaders that their generation is not worthy to receive the direct Word of God through the agency of a prophet. In later literature, we encounter frequently the remark that so and so would have received the Holy Spirit, if only the age were worthy of it.

Yet, the immanence of God was not forgotten in the post-biblical world. In the Targums, this aspect of the Deity is almost but not quite hypostatized as the Presence of God (*Shechinah*), His Glory (*Yakra*), His Word (*Memra*). God in Himself is above and beyond the concepts drawn from our experience; yet, His power and presence are projected into our lives.

Philo attempts to explain this paradox. As a mystic, he felt the Divine Presence in the ideas that flowed into his mind as a rushing mountain stream. But as a philosopher, he asserted that God was "unknowable". Indeed, he brought the concept of the unknowability of God into the mainstream of religious philosophy. Both the "yes" and the "No" of revelation were well exemplified in Philo's thought.

We have argued in behalf of a concept of revelation, which recognizes the subjective component of belief and removes the aura of absolutism from particular bodies of rites and dogmas. This concept is manifestly consistent with the ecumenical outreach that is the most promising religious movement in our time. Religious communities are divided by their subjective traditions of faith and deed, but they are united in their arduous quest of the divine. We recognize the indispensability, the sanctity, even the uniqueness of the different traditions, but not their title to the exclusive possession of all truth. We affirm this proposition as men of faith, not as agnostics. We assert the sanctity of the humble quest of piety, even as we deny the absoluteness and the exclusiveness of any claim for the possession of the final goal.

What are the practical consequences of this concept? First, it guards against all tendencies to fill the vacuum left by the discredited vestiges of medieval theologies. In recent years, secular ideologies, at one end of the spectrum, and exotic cults at the other end have rushed to take the place of the historical faiths. The unity of faith and doubt was shattered by pervasive secularism, with the hunger for faith ready to be slaked by the "fast foods" of the cults. A dynamic concept of revelation puts all form of fanaticism under a question mark even as it nurtures man's hunger for "the nearness of God". By pointing to the infinite source of all ideals, the tendency to idolize fragmentary formulations is checked. In our contemporary world, ideologies have taken the place of the ancient idols. Such are the folk, as a mystical entity, or the Race, or the Class, or the State—all new.

Molochs, on whose altars millions of human beings may be rightfully sacrificed! For this reason, a dynamic faith performs the same function as the anti-idolatry crusade of the monotheistic faiths. Worship of the One God rejects the absolutization of partial truths as a sin and a prelude to disaster.

Second, the affirmative connotation of a dynamic faith is the assurance that all true ideals are mutually consistent. We need not sacrifice the logic of the mind for the logic of the heart, or freedom for security, or ethnic greatness for humanity, or the happiness of the present generation for the future of mankind, or visa versa in respect of any of these goals. All true ideals can be blended harmoniously. "Peace is the Name of God". (Leviticus R. 9, 9).

Third, the faith-event sets a supreme purpose for the life of each individual and supreme tasks for the historical religious communities. We are all part of one enterprise—"the improvement of the world through the Kingdom of the Almighty". The contribution of each person and each community is unique and irreplaceable. "Therefore, every person can say— 'for my sake the world was created' ". (B. T. Sanhedrin 37a.)

# RELIGIOUS ETHICS ON THE CONTEMPORARY SCENE

THROUGHOUT THE ages, the theory and practice of ethics was under the auspices of religion. Ever since the rise of the secular state and its concern for public education, the problems of ethics came to be shared by secular educators and religious authorities. This partnership was evident in the building up of Sunday Schools, afternoon religious classes and parochial schools. The role of the secular agencies in the education of the young increased constantly, yet, insofar as ethics is concerned, there was no corresponding increase in the teaching of ethics in the schools. Nor has there been an awareness on the part of philosophy departments of their obligation to take over this function in our society. Many departments of philosophy and the humanities generally have lost ground in the total program of our colleges. And for the most part philosophers have devoted themselves to problems of logic, language analysis, and the history of ideas. The task of examining ethical values and conveying them to the next generation is in danger of falling between two stools, between the diminishing role of religious education in our life today and the increasing emphasis on technology in our secular schools.

This paper is offered as a contribution to the task of distilling the social values of our religious tradition into the secular intellectual context of our day. While I shall be dealing with the contribution of Judaism, I feel that a similar approach from the Christian standpoint is equally valid.

## Nature of Law

A religious tradition is like a pyramid with a few general principles at the top and a massive social-cultural base. Hence, the task of interpreting and transferring ethical values has to be undertaken along several levels. When-

Originally published in *The Future of Ethics and Moral Theology*, Argus Comico, Chicago, Ill.

ever an ethical philosophy does function, it operates in depth, permeating the emotional life of the individual and the entire fabric of society.

Our analysis then, will begin with the surface values, then proceed to examine the basic tensions out of which they spring, then probe the types of personality that we aim to evolve.

Central to Jewish ethics, as we all know, is the desire to be guided by a divinely ordained, yet humanly formulated Law. We encounter, to begin with, this virtue of being law-abiding, but in an active, progressive sense. Not simply to obey the Law, because it was made by authority, and authority is from God. Such an attitude would amount to servility.

In Judaism, the Law was not ordained by the state; it was derived from the interaction of divine revelation and the life of a people; hence, obedience was also an act of *self-identification* with the "holy congregation" and with the Will of God.

Obedience to the law included the willingness to share in the making of laws. Consider the import of this maxim—"never did I transgress the words of my colleagues." It was said by Rabbi Akiba who, when he was incarcerated and given only a minimum of water, preferred to use it for the washing of his hands rather than for the slaking of his thirst. What authority do "the words of my colleagues" possess?—No more than a multiple of that authority which resides in myself. Yet, there would be no communal standards, if people were not taught to revere their laws. Socrates drank the hemlock, out of gratitude to laws which protected him for many years; Rabbi Akiba risked death out of identification with the law-making body in Jewish life.

The Law in Judaism was not an expression of divine fiat only, but also of divine goodness. Even those ceremonial ordinances which were manifestly irrational, were interpreted as being somehow designed for the elevation of human life—*letzaref bahen et haberiyot*. While its axioms were not to be questioned, its application to the changing facets of life was given over to the rabbis of every age. "The Torah is not in heaven—"it is for the living leaders to use their own judgment.

Hence, the Law was intermediate between *positive law*, resting upon delegated legislative power, and an ideal application of ethical principles.

To revere a law of this kind is a form of self-assertion as well as self-surrender; it is an expression of one's own recognition of the right—hence, it is antonomous at bottom, though heteronomous in form.

Reverence for the Law shifts the fulcrum of judgment from the self to God. One becomes habituated to asking not what do I want? or what am I? or even, how is my life to be fulfilled? The question that looms steadily before the worshipper comes in the impersonal form—what is it that *ought* to be done?

This change in formulation reflects a subtle change in motivation. There is an objective order to which it is right to conform. One must do the right because it is right—yet, not in a physical or mathematical sense, since the ultimate reality is the One God whose image dwells within us. "All that the Lord has created, He fashioned only for the sake of His Honor."

A sense of honor is the awareness of compatibility between an outer act and an inner reality. But, the essence of God is within us, and we too possess the sense of honor. It can be abused by association with a multitude of irrelevancies, but in essence it is the ultimate expression of our integrity.

To feel that the right and the true are expressions of our inner being—this is the ultimate meaning of reverence for the law.

Because the Law contains many precepts, it is possible to share in its life even in small ways. It is not necessary to put one's life always on the line, daily to tread on a razor's edge and perpetually enact the role of Hamlet. The little occasions of life provide the framework for an ethical career, not alone the great crises. So, for the unheroic routines of everyday life, ethics can and does have its message.

It is possible, say the rabbis, for a person to obtain a share in the World to Come by devoting himself to even one *mizvah*. Far from being an overwhelming yoke, a Jew could feel that he was given so many opportunities by which to share in the work of God. The quest of *mizvot*, opportunities to be of service, may result in the vulgarization of the self and its fragmentation. This is a danger that one must always bear in mind. But, at the same time this fragmentation of the ethical imperative made possible the sanctification of the mundane and the workaday activities, which constitute so large a part of the total economy of life.

Reverence for the law is of course the basis of an ordered community. In a secular society it is an ethical obligation to obey the law, even if in certain areas it is unjust. Our sense of honor demands it, for the values of the community inhere within ourselves as well as beyond us.

In rare instances, however, a high ethical principle may dictate a temporary deviation from the Law. We recall the example of healing on the Sabbath from the Gospels and the Talmudic maxim, "*piku-ah nefesh doha Shabbat*," "wherever there is danger to life, the Sabbath may be set aside." Such deviations are indirect affirmations of loyalty to the Law, since the exception proves the rule.

## *Religious Ethics in a Secular Setting*

Our theme calls for an understanding of the basic approach in Judaism toward ethical and social problems.

We are concerned more with the historical impetus of basic ideas than with their literary formulations. Beneath the familiar ideas and maxims, there is a psychic sub-structure, which is likely to be more enduring than the rhetoric of any one period. We may confidently expect that such basic structures of sentiment and aspiration will be effectively transposed into a changed religious context, or even into a purely secular world. If we grant that every principle and maxim of the sacred literature of a faith exerts a certain impact, we shall have to admit that the substructure of feeling and thought is that much more charged with the silent power of unconscious momentum. We can hardly doubt that the psychical makeup of the erstwhile Seminarian who became Joseph Stalin transmitted habits of thought from his youth into his years of maturity and even into the years of his paranoiac degeneration. Similarly, it is not difficult to detect the heavy hand of the Czar's bureaucracy in the presumably proletarian paradise.

In this era, we, the spokesmen of religion, have to become aware of this phenomenon of transference and not leave it to the mercies of the Unconscious. We face today the task of interpreting the values and drives of our philosophy of life to a secular world. In a real sense, we have to transpose one side of our being into the molds and ways of the other side, for the secular world is within us. While our relation to God cannot be exhaustively articulated in objective terms, its ethical implications must be so described, and carried over into a secular realm of discourse.

In any case, the effort must be made over and over again, for if faith is "the vision of things unseen," (Hebrews XI, 1) it is also the quest of truth and justice, that are objective in character. "He who has chosen to dwell in darkness" (I Kings VIII, 12) is the One "Who says to Wisdom, thou are My Sister" (Proverbs VII, 4). Ours is the age of the Dialogue; in a deeper sense, the Dialogue takes place not so much between spokesmen of different faiths as within the hearts and minds of all of us. And only if the inner dialogue is alive and vibrant can the inter-religious Dialogue be truly meaningful.

For this reason, I shall not attempt to describe the well-known principles of Jewish ethics and examine their relevance for the foreseeable future. Popular compendia of such sayings are available, and a detailed study is of interest to the specialist. However, at times, principles formulated in relation to an antiquated social context may acquire fresh relevance in our day. For example, in this great city of industrial unions, it may be of some value to examine the principles of Jewish labor law. Are the laws of contractual obligation applicable to laborers and must they therefore abide by the terms of their contracts?—The Talmudic principle is, "Po-el yo-chel la-hazor bo afilu ba-hazi ha-yom" (Baba Mezia, 10a.). "A worker may change his mind even in the middle of the day." This rule affirms that human freedom is so sacred, that a person cannot give it completely away. We can see immediately that this principle provides the answer to Hobbes' argument in the "Leviathan," an argument which might well bring the nightmare of "1984" into existence. A man cannot sell his birthright of freedom to another man or to the state as a whole. In regard to God, He is committed and covenanted, as a "son of Noah," if not as a son of Israel. He is free in regard to manmade laws, but his freedom is not an arbitrary fiat: it is rather an obedience to a higher law that he can hear in the depths of his being.

A similar principle is the one which affirms that "to help one individual to live is equivalent to the maintenance of a full world." (Sanhedrin 37a.) Here it is stated that human beings cannot be weighed and numbered as if they were so many finite entities. One cannot in conscience abide by the simplistic calculus of Bentham—"The greatest good for the greatest number." For infinities cannot be added mathematically—twice infinity is still infinity—and there is an infinite dimension to the human spirit.

Still, on the same level, we may cite an ancient rabbinic comment on the verse, "and thou shalt love thy neighbor as thyself." The comment is, "choose for him a beautiful death." (Sanhedrin 45a.) At first glance, it appears to be a ghoulish inference. But, the point of the rabbis is that man must never be dehumanized, not even when he is adjudged guilty of death. We are all too prone to limit the range of our human concern to those we like, or who resemble us, or who share our views. We are warned that even judicial murder must be human. Is not the threat of dehumanization precisely the menace that looms on the horizon of our day? Is it not possible that we and our opponents may be so beguiled by slogans that, in our quest of victory and triumph, we come to forget the human beings that breathe and travail beneath the mask of ideologies?

In the Judeo-Christian tradition, man's infinite worth derived from his capacity to mirror the Infinite, his ability to love God and to be loved by Him. Can this awareness of man's infinite potential be made meaningful in secular terms?—I think it can. Its implications are both negative and positive.

Even if one does not acknowledge the infinite depth of human nature, because of its roots in God, he must concede that the mystery of our being far transcends our ability to comprehend it. If the past century has taught us anything at all, it is the failure of the greatest minds to understand the nature of mind. Almost every generation saw the rise of a new psychology and of a social philosophy based upon it. Marx's economic determinism, Mill's rationalism, Comte's positivism, Nietzsche's "transvaluation of all values,"

Freud's discovery of the Unconscious, Bergson's intuitionism, Dewey's instrumentalism—each came with its own philosophy of freedom. While each movement, seen in retrospect, has added a mite to our understanding, each one in its day laid claim to finality. Let us not forget Mussolini and Hitler. They too were philosophers of sorts, having discovered that many, indeed most people, prefer the freedom of surrender to the freedom of individual self-assertion. Rather than confront the meanness of their own existence, they would prefer to don a uniform, march in step and breathe to the rhythm of conquest and glory.

Is not then the path of wisdom, for secularists as well as religionists, to admit that human nature is an enigma, wrapped in mystery?—Such an admission would serve as a "regulative principle," restraining the ardor of social planners and restoring a sense of perspective to all who would remake society along the lines of geometric perfection. I use the term "regulative principle" in Kant's sense, as a rule of action, rather than as an abstract proposition. This awareness would be a social equivalent of the Socratic principle—to know that one does not know. We need this awareness in the future, even more than in the past, for we are now entering the age of the computer. Up to now, we had to contend only with the narrow-minded specialist, whose activity was dangerous because it lacked the perspective of the whole of human life. A computer is the ultimate specialist.

To recognize the mystery of life, as a first principle of ethics, is to be perpetually biased in favor of individual freedom, freedom as against the presumed and calculated "greatest good for the greatest number."

But, freedom is not license. In the secular context, freedom is the effort to respond with the whole of one's being to a challenge. So, we come to the positive phase of the awareness of man's infinite potential. In religion, we say God loves all men, even the wicked, even the miserable, in ways that we cannot fully understand. Jewish law states that man is not allowed to mourn longer than the periods fixed by the tradition—the seven day period, the thirty day period and the eleven month period. And if one says, "but my love for the departed one was so great, it cannot be limited by days and even years." the *Shechinah* responds—"You did not love the departed one more than I." (Moed Kattan 27b)

The love of God for all men means that all can find fulfillment, and that the depths of the soul are not amenable to the methods of the statistician. Is not this a secular truth as well?—There is more to life than bread and cars and air-conditioned rooms. Perhaps, the peculiar malaise of our day is air-conditioned unhappiness—the staleness and the stuffiness of machine-made routines.

Ralph Waldo Emerson, in his famous essay on "The Principle of Compensation," produced an excellent secular version of the religious principle that God loves all his children. Everyone can find fulfillment in keeping with his gifts and his station in life. Are we not terribly in need of this wisdom in our day?—Having failed to convey to our people the truth that, as the biblical preacher put it, "the whole world hath He given into the hearts of the children of men," (Ecclesiates VII, 29) we find that our affluent society is being shaken to its foundation by massed envy and desperate frustrations. We stimulate desires for external goods and make it appear that happiness is measurable by this index; then, we wonder why those who are not so affluent, are so terribly embittered. "The poor will never disappear from the land," (Deuteronomy XV, 11) but these poor need the equivalent of the religious assurance that God loves them. "Near is the Lord to those who call upon Him, to all who call upon Him in truth." (Psalms CXIV, 18) This sentence is true, in a secular context, too, where God means the ultimate reality and the source of joy.

We cannot solve the problem posed by the "pooled envy" of the proletariat by simply expending ever greater sums for the War on Poverty. The explosion of expectancy will always outpace our achievements, and it already transcends the bare necessities of life. In physical terms, the rioters of today are far better off than the contented workers and farmers of yesterday. Yet, their sense of being deprived is real, all too real. Along with the physical tasks of reconstruction, there should be a spiritual effort of reclamation, pointing out that happiness derives from within. Needed is a secular equivalent of the human soul, in its confrontation with the loving God.

## Ethical Education

Actually, the secular meaning of the religious doctrine of man's infinite dimension can be stated easily enough. The real problem is one of education. How can the negative and positive implications of the mystery of human existence be conveyed to the people of our generation and of future generations? Where is the literature to teach it, the art to give it the feel of reality, the discipline and the training to make it work?

I submit that our society has not yet faced up to the need of providing an ethic for the large numbers of our people, who are no longer reached by the churches and the synagogues. In the Communist world, there are the Commissars and their endless meetings of indoctrination. We can see their limitations and their blind fanaticism, but we cannot deny that they do address themselves to a social need. We believe in emphasizing the worth of the individual rather than the supreme value of the state. But, the individual, to us, is not the self-serving consumer, but one who attains fulfillment through love and service. Do we now in our colleges and high-schools offer a secular ethic for the individual?

Without attempting to deal with the practical problems of ethical education, we return to our theme of the transposition of the religious principles of Jewish ethics into the idiom of the secular world. Now, we shall probe the deeper levels of principle, which underlie the ethical maxims of Jewish law.

Ethics was, in Judaism, inseparable from the structure of the faith. This statement, while true, does not dispose of the problem. For the realm of relations "between a man and his fellow" was always somewhat independent of the cult. The two tablets of stone, we recall, contained the two realms of relations, with men and with God, the command to honor one's parents being the connecting link between them. The greatest teachers of Judaism maintain that the entire purpose of the Torah was to foster "the ways of peace."

In terms of basic governing principles, Jewish ethics contains not simply the polarity of law and love, but two domains of law and two domains of love. And all four domains are focused in the central religious experience of Judaism—the events of the Covenant.

God made a Covenant with "the sons of Noah" and later with Abraham, still later with the children of Israel through the agency of Moses. The first Covenant consisted of general principles. Sometimes, these principles are subsumed under the category of "derech eretz," the ways of the world. This term reflects the Greek concept of "unwritten laws," that are binding upon both gods and men. At times, too, we can hear echoes of the reasoning of Roman jurists, who were engaged in elaborating the laws of "ius gentium." These laws were not spelled out in detail, since it was presumed that they might take many different forms. In any case, the primacy of these laws of religion and ethics was assumed in Holy Scriptures. All nations were to be punished for their infractions of these laws, since man qua man is aware of their validity. (Amos II, Isaiah XIII, 11-13) So, too, Paul reasons in the first chapter of his epistle to the Romans. The rabbis affirmed the primacy of this law in their own way—"by twenty-six generations, *derech eretz* preceded Torah." (Leviticus Rabba IX, 3) They assumed that what was prior in the Lord's timetable of creation was prior in value. For this reason "the Name of the Messiah" antedated the creation of heaven and earth, according to the Aggadists. (Pesahim 54b.)

The specific laws of the Torah were conceived as demanding a higher way of life from the sons of the Covenant. The charging of interest on loans was simply a matter of business for humanity in general, but within the community of Torah, loans were to be extended freely to those who needed them, and usury was prohibited. Even "the usury of words," that is for the borrower to flatter the lender, was strictly prohibited. In a similar way, the Torah-community attempted to put all business transactions on the basis of eliminating all forms of deception. It should not be necessary for the buyer to beware. Any deal where the price was unfair, to the extent of one-sixth, was declared to be invalid. Again, these restrictions applied only within the boundaries of the Torah-community. So, too, it was a *mizvah* to feed and take care of a neighbor's straying ox or donkey, until the owner is identified, but only within the bounds of the community. Outside the community, Israelites were simply to follow the prevailing laws of the state. "*Dina dimalchuto dina*—" (Gittin 10b.) the laws of the state are valid.

## Social Progress and Utopianism

Will the Torah-laws eventually bring all men to the Messianic era of perfection? Or will perfection be brought about by way of the break-through of another principle?—Here, we come to one of the areas of tension in Judaism.

The prevailing view of the Talmud held that the impetus of Torah-law would of its own momentum lead to the perfection of the messianic era. So, we are told in a famous passage that when the question was posed, "what is the name of the Messiah?" the disciples of each school gave the name of their teacher as the name of the Messiah. The disciples of *Yannai* said Yannai would be his name, of *Yohanan*, Yohanan, etc. So, too, Rav asserted that the Messiah would be someone like his teacher, R. Judah the Prince. (Sanhedrin 98a.) In other words, the pathway from Torah to the Messiah was direct and straight. The law itself leads to the Messiah. All that is needed is repentance.

On the other hand, we recall that both Jeremiah and Ezekiel spoke of a new law and a new Covenant, one that would be written on the tablets of the heart. (Jeremiah XXI, 31. Ezekiel XI, 19; XVIII, 31) This view was also echoed in midrashic literature, where the Messiah was supposed to inaugurate a new law and a new Covenant. (Genesis Rabba 98, 14. Tanna dibai Eliyahu Zutta, 20) The line of development from this mundane world to the utopian era of the future would have to be achieved through the incursion of love and grace. "middat horahmim," the policy of mercy, would take the place of "middat hadin," the policy of law. (Otiot di R. Akiba 1, 7) So, we come to the principle that supplemented and challenged the rule of law—namely, the ideal of love.

In respect of love, too, we find two coordinate realms in Judaism, love between the people of Israel and God, and love between the individual person and God. The Covenant with the people of Israel was believed to be a demonstration of God's unconditioned love for the people and for the patriarchs. At times, the people did indeed reciprocate this love, particularly in the wilderness of Sinai. But, even when they proved stubborn and unworthy, the love of God would remain true and sure. This love of God was not always easy to bear, since it imposed special obligations and demands. "You only have I known of all the families of the earth, therefore I shall visit upon you all your iniquities." (Amos III, 2) Yet, there are supreme compensations in the assurance of being beloved by God. When the final day of reckoning comes, there will be no doubt of this superlative blessedness. And in times of crisis, the people would pray to God, not merely as creatures who bear the Divine Image, but as "sons of the All-Present—" indeed, as "*Ahuvim*," His beloved. (Taanit 20a.)

Along with this collective principle of the love of God and its implications for conduct, there was the parallel motif of the love between the individual and God. Here, it is not the community as a whole, but the individual, every individual that can make of himself, "*ma-on lashechinah*," a dwelling place for the Divine Presence. (Genesis Rabba, 47) (Sota 17a.)

This bond of love is universal. In the book of Jonah, it is celebrated as compassion for the Assyrians who devastated the land of Israel. In the book of Job, it is affirmed in behalf of a non-Jewish saint and one who is afflicted. For there are *yissurim shel ahavah*, sufferings of love. (Berochot 5a) Not always, but occasionally we are purged and brought nearer to God through suffering.

It is in the Book of Psalms, that the individual's love of God attains its climax—"my soul thirsts for Thee, yes, my flesh yearns for Thee . . ." (Psalms XIII, 2) "And I, the nearness of God is for me good." (Psalm XXIII, 28) The obligation to love God with all one's heart, all one's soul and all one's might" becomes not a duty, but a supreme delight. And this joy of His "nearness" is open to all men. Said Rabbi Meir (ca. 150 c.e.), "even a Gentile who studies Torah is like the High Priest, who enters the Holy of Holies on the Day of Atonement." (Baba Kama 38a.) A later teacher asserted, "I bring heaven and earth to witness that whether Jew or Gentile, free or slave, everyone according to his deeds, the *Shechinah* rests upon him" (Tanaa dibai Eliyahu Rabba, 9).

This tension between two kinds of law and two forms of Divine love may be carried over into the secular world. We should, then, have one way of tracing the impact of religious ethics of Judaism upon the secular world of our day.

The first element would be confidence in the solution of problems through law. Ethics is not alone a body of sentiment and a cluster of ideals; it is a form of "practical reason"—hence, it can and ought to be expressed in laws. The Kingdom of God on earth can, according to this conviction, be established by means of legislation. While the logic of this principle is certainly one-sided, it does contain a large measure of truth. In our own generation we have witnessed the massive improvement of the situation of the Negro minority, first through the interpretation of the law by the Supreme Court, second, through the enactment of the fair employment, civil rights laws. We have proven that laws do change feelings and patterns of living. Instead of futile calls for an inner conversion to tolerance and brotherhood, the American nation has resorted to the machinery of law, and it has succeeded in setting the nation on the road leading to the goals of fraternity and unity. To be sure, there are limits to the efficacy, and even the justice of this method, as no one principle in any complex situation is ever completely valid. The line between equality and egalitarianism must be respected.

The second expression of the Law, the universal principles of the Noachide Covenant, can also be extremely fruitful in our day. For it would call for a common effort to work out a new code of international ethics and international law. Instead of consisting of conventions reflecting the inter-play of national interests and forces, international ethics and law should be worked out by conferences of intellectuals, clergymen and attorneys—somewhat after the pattern of the *Pacem in Terris* conferences. If it is not yet possible to enforce the decisions of the World Court, is it too early to form the body of ideas and to formulate the principles which would provide the climate for the functioning of the Court?

## Natural Law

At this point, a fresh examination of the philosophy of "natural law" is in order. The concept of "natural law," which existed in rabbinic, Roman and Christian thought, was framed against a static background of human reason and human history. With our deeper awareness of the flux of history and the evolving character of human reason, we are called upon to bring the concept up to date. We have to reject the two untenable extremes—one, that such laws can be formulated in detail and with finality, two, that such laws don't exist and that our sense of obligation is only the remnant of a conditioned reflex. The roots of the tree of "natural law" are set firmly within the nature of our mind, but the shape of its branches must be worked out by the people of any one generation in keeping with the best thought and the realities of their day. This conclusion follows from our double awareness as "children of God—" we sense the harmony that flows from His Being, and yet we know ourselves to be unable to comprehend it.

A Talmudic passage maintains that only the first two of the Ten Commandments were heard at Sinai by the Israelites, the rest having been spoken by Moses. (Makkot 23a.) The first Commandment, identifies God as the source of freedom, and man discovers this freedom in the three coordinates of spirit—the work of the mind, the voice of conscience and the creation of harmony. The second Commandment warns us against imagining that we possess His Word, and thereby fall into sin of idolatry. These two commandments can still be heard by secular men, even if they would formulate the first commandment in a non-theistic way—freedom is the mark of spirit and spirit consists in fidelity to an ongoing quest.

Thirdly, the concept of one people or one faith-community being the object of Divine love needs to be brought up to date. In Judaism, it is possible to recognize the tension between the two interpretations of this doctrine—Israel as "The Chosen People," in the sense of being set apart as an exception and Israel as the vanguard of humanity, called to serve as an example. When Israel is called "my eldest son," we recall that in Judaism all the sons of the family shared in the inheritance, the eldest one receiving only a larger share. On the other hand, there are passages in both Scripture and Talmud which appear to restrict the love and grace of God to the people of Israel. (Baba Bathra 15b. and 28a.)

Our age calls for a synthetic, creative fusion of Divine love for the individual with the divine love for nations. There are indeed collective forms of divine grace in the secular realm. Are not the endowments and advantages of the American people examples of the kind of love that God extends to a historic community? The western nations of today are "first born" sons, in technology, in democracy, in the arts of education and in the gifts of nature. This circumstance imposes upon us certain obligations, and we must remember that we are not better or nobler than others, let alone set apart as "touch me not" and "holier than thou" exceptions, but that we are representatives of mankind. If in history, some of us are more favored as nations, in life some of us are more favored as individuals.

We must acknowledge that nationalism is a form of divine grace, so long as it is not distorted by the vulgar identification of power with virtue. The sense of participation in the life of a great people, endows the individual with the strength of many. But, the national ideal must be tempered by that humanist approach, which lets us see the individual, who is the ultimate object of divine love.

Did the prophet Micah debase Isaiah's vision of the ultimate conversion of all nations to faith in The One God, when he added the sentence, "for all nations will walk, each in the name of its god, but we shall walk in the Name of the Lord, our God?" (Micah IV, 5) On the contrary, Micah converted an apocalyptic dream into an ideal of history. He pointed out that within every community developments could take place in the name of its respective god, which would lead toward a genuine monotheism. There would be unity in spirit, but diversity in pathway and in expression.

It would be a salutary development for mankind, if the United Nations Assembly were supplemented by a representative body of delegates representing humanity as a whole, elected on the basis of their personal reputation and endowed with an international citizenship that would guarantee them immunity from persecution everywhere in the world. Such a parliament of man would in the beginning have to be formed only out of the learned professions in each country. Whatever the procedure, the principle should be recognized that a society of nations must be balanced by a representative society of individuals.

## Revelation and Secularity

The one doctrine which separates the secular realm from the religious one is that of revelation. To the religious, certain teachings were given to man; to the secularist, all principles derive from the mind of man. But, we must not imagine that the concept of revelation was simplistic in the Judeo-Christian tradition. Actually, Jewish monotheism was existential, ethical and metaphysical, and a channel of revelation was associated with each of these facets. The One God did not dwell in isolation; on the contrary, he had taken the initiative in choosing the patriarchs, liberating the ancestors from slavery in Egypt and giving them His Laws. Every Jew coming to worship felt that he was already called, committed and seized by God at Sinai. The Divine Command called for an ethical orientation, for "clean hands and a pure heart," (Psalms XXIV, 4) in preparation for walking up "the mountain of the Lord." Also, some perception of the unity and inner harmony of the Cosmos was inherent in the ideas that God was the Creator and Lord of the universe. His Wisdom, His Logos, His Word or His Glory was postulated. We can say, therefore, that from the beginning, the priest, the prophet and the sage were agents of revelation—the priest standing for the existing hallowed tradition, the prophet for the living Word, the sage for the universal wisdom for the day. (Jeremiah XVIII, 18)

In our discussion, these three types of religious leadership are taken phenomenologically to represent the voices of authority in the life of people. Each of three functionaries considered that he was interpreting the mind of God. The priests were the guardians of Torah, the teaching, that derived from Moses, who was more than a prophet, indeed in a class by himself. (Numbers XII, 7) The classical prophets were unique personalities, in that they interpreted the Divine Word in accord with "the still, small voice" of conscience. In contrast to the "ecstatic" prophetizers, they did not allow emotional frenzy and popular prejudice to distort their perception of the Divine Will. And the Sages, too, believed that wisdom in general was derived from God. Also, their own insights were forms of revelation. Socrates had his demon, the debaters in Job were given glimpses of truth amidst the dark night of their meditations, and the sages of the Talmud were privileged to receive insights into the meaning of the sacred texts, which they interpreted as "small prophecies." (Berochot 55b.)

The three religious personalities of biblical religion correspond to the three ways, by means of which the human spirit seeks to relate itself to the mysteries of existence. It seeks the peace of absorption into the community, in nature and in the eternal Absolute. It seeks to enter the active stream of social life, becoming one with the emergent moral order of society. And it longs for the perception of truth and rational order. In a religious personality, these three quests are fused into the feeling of holiness, which contains these three dimensions. "Complete ye shall be with the Lord, your God." (Deuteronomy XVIII, 13) In the secular world, this dynamic unity is fragmented. There is no longer one focus for all three quests, no sense of the holy, no perception of the inner roots of unity of these apparently divergent, directions of the spirit.

If the age of Ideology has succeeded the age of Theology, the difference is not only the one between a theistic and a secularistic philosophy of life, but also between the dynamic unity of personality and a fractionized, disjointed, rootless self. While in theology, the persistent menace is the kind of unity that paralyzes thought and blinds people to the ever changing charade of reality, the danger in secular ideologies is the reduction of the Absolute to one or another fraction of the secular order. The sense of mystery and the feeling of participation in a transcendent order are transferred from the whole self and the whole of creation to one or another project, with a consequent loss of perspective and balance.

It has long been noted that ideologies are secular religions, but we wish to cast light on their nature, by discovering which components of religion they seek to embody. Is it the sanctification of the collective self? Is it the utopian equivalent of the apocalyptic vision?—Is it the calm but sad and sterile critique of all social efforts?

## Biblical Typology

To understand the impact of religious ethics upon the secularists of our day, we have to recognize the three-dimensional tension within the Judeo-Christian tradition.

While our analysis is confined to the Jewish stream within the mighty flow of western culture, it is possible to trace a similar line of development in Christianity. Both faiths are ultimately derived from the genius of the Hebrew Scriptures, which was the work of three religious personalities, contending against, yet embracing one another—namely, the priest, the prophet and the sage. We can cast some light on the frustrations of our post-ideological age, if we recognize their evolution from religious prototypes.

The tension between the three ideal personalities may be traced throughout the history of Judaism, down to the opening of the modern era. Generally, the sacramental and the rational ideals presented the basic polarity, which the prophetic approach sought to reconcile. The realm of ethics combines the feelings of love with the light of reason. The prophetic personality combines the critical wisdom of the sages with the sense of awesome mystery of the priests, evolving a fresh perception of ethical problems and keen ardor for dealing with them. In the prophet's mind and heart, the polarities of the social order converge and fuse into the synthesis of moral action.

How is God to be served?—The answer of the Sage would call for reflection and meditation, the love of learning and the search for purity and truth. The answer of the priest would be to obey the ritual laws, to share in the ceremonies of the cult and to be generous to the poor, the widow and the orphan. The prophet criticized the excessive emphasis on the cult, (Isaiah I, 11-17. Amos V, 4-15) stressed the service of the heart, (Isaiah XXIX, 13) called for "the Knowledge of God" (Hosea IV, 1) and demanded not merely the emotional spasms of charity but the creation of a systematic base of justice for the scaffolding of society. (Isaiah X, 1)

In respect of the feeling of community, the priests in all cultures catered to the popular feelings of ethnocentrism. The gods in ancient times represented the genius of the city or the state as well as of the varied forces of nature. It was the function of the priests to keep the peace between the people and their gods. On the other hand, the horizon of the Sage is much larger than that of the temple-bound priests. He is likely to be well-travelled, familiar with several languages and internationally minded. His concern is with humanity, its tragedy and destiny. In his teaching, he focuses attention on man in general, seeking to break down the barriers of provincialism and prejudice in the hearts of his countrymen. Again, the prophet is the seeker of the middle way. He appeals to the ethnic pride of his people, but he directs this pride into the channels of service to mankind as a whole. He employs the accents of nationalism, but he projects its aims and ambitions against an international canvass. Yes, Israel will triumph and conquer the world, but its triumph is that of the universal God and its conquest consists in Torah coming from Zion and the Word of the Lord from Jerusalem. (Isaiah II, 3)

How is one to find peace and surcease of sorrow?—The priest caters to this quest by directing the feelings of the worshippers to the Beyond. Heaven may be imagined in several different ways, and it is the vocation of priests to bring to people a foretaste of heaven and the assurance of being at peace with the mysterious powers of the hereafter. The Sage seeks peace in this world, by overcoming the fears and anxieties which bedevil mankind. He preaches imperturbability, or serenity, or the conquest of desire. Again, the prophet is the mediator. It is peace in this world that he projects, but not simply the inner peace of the Sage. He proclaims the ideal of peace for the future, an ideal which involves dedication to an ethical program of action here and now. His messianic hope involves the ultimate triumph of wisdom; yet, it can be sustained day by day only through the charm and potency of the priestly ritual. (Isaiah XI, XII)

In fact, it can be stated with little fear of contradiction that the literary prophets were most responsible for the distinctive grandeur of Judaism. For the priestly type is to be found everywhere, and the glory of wisdom is by its very nature universal. The prophets created a unique synthesis of mystery and wisdom, and directed its fervor toward the goals of moral action.

## Prophetic Ideal in Modern Judaism

At this point, one may ask, did not the institution of prophecy cease to be operative in Judaism?—According to tradition, Malachi whose real name was Ezra, was the last of the prophets. We know from Josephus that people who claimed to be prophets continued to function throughout the Second Commonwealth. (Wars VI, V, 3) Officially, however, the dignity of prophecy became so exalted that it could no longer be claimed by those who were reflective and self-critical. Accordingly, the unifying genius of prophecy was fragmented, with some of its facets being transferred to the Disciples of the Wise and others to the apocalyptic writers, to popular ecstatics, saints and mystics. The Talmud offers two versions of the identity of heirs of the prophets. According to one version, the Sages inherited the prophetic mantle; according to the other, the "fools" inherited it, that is those mystical enthusiasts who appear to be fools in the eyes of the world. (Baba Bathra 12a. Ibid.)

During the Middle Ages, the philosophic movement of which Maimonides was the climax represented one side of the prophetic synthesis, the aspect that is closest to the wisdom-tradition. The romantic movement which glorified the Jewish race was another fragmented version of prophecy, the aspect that succumbed to the lure of priestly sacramentalism. Halevi is the perfect epitome of this school. The Kabbalists, who cultivated their esoteric lore and trained themselves in mystical exercises represented still another facet of prophecy—the one closest to the cult-prophets, the bands of ecstatics who antedated the rise of classical prophecy. Out of these circles, a number of pseudo-messianic movements arose.

At the close of the Middle Ages, two titanic figures represent the two opposing fragments of the prophetic spirit—Benedict Spinoza and Sabbattai Zevi. In Spinoza, the prophetic mood was fused with the flame of wisdom to produce a philosophy of life in which the diverse quests of truth, of goodness and of peace became one grand passion. In Sabbattai Zevi and his followers, the frenzy of pseudo-messianism broke through the crust of the Law, which normally held it in check.

The majority of the Jews continued to cherish the Law and the prophets, allowing only a minimal place to the rising currents of universal European culture and secular wisdom. Save for a few pioneers here and there, the prophetic spirit was dormant.[1]

Two centuries ago, the prophetic spirit was revived in two centers of Jewish life, but in different ways. In western Europe, the Enlightenment brought modern Judaism into being. In Eastern Europe, Hassidism turned the mystical lore of Kabbalah into a mass-movement, which persists to the present day.

The modern movements in Judaism, Reform and Conservative, seek to recapture the total genius of biblical religion. To meet the scientific and nationalistic challenges of the modern era, Jewish savants rediscovered the dynamic balance which was so marvelously represented by the great prophets of Israel. Once again, they broadened the horizon of their people, leading them from the narrow confines of the ghetto to the broad fields of western civilization. Against a cosmopolitan background, they projected the concept of a "religious nation," a people that expresses its collective genius in the service of God and humanity. It was the "mission" of the Jews to represent the ideals of "ethical monotheism" in its communal life and to demonstrate to all mankind that national instincts can be sublimated into spiritual and international channels. Throughout the Nineteenth century, both the Reform and Conservative wings of modern Judaism were opposed to a revival of Jewish secular or political Zionism. Both movements sought inspiration in the biblical prophets and in the medieval philosophers, but the classical Reformers generally downgraded the Law, while the Conservative teachers sought to uncover "the positive-historical" values of the Law, in its evolution from the early Pharisees to their own time. On the whole, these modern movements reject the exclusiveness, even the dominance of the Law, favoring instead the components of Wisdom and Prophecy within the emergent patterns of Jewish life.

## Hassidism

The Hassidic movement began as a massive outburst of popular mysticism. It was led by saints, who believed that the Holy Spirit (Ruah Hakodesh) governed all their actions. It stressed the need of inwardness, the glory of enthusiasm, the virtues of simple piety, the power of unquestioning faith. It re-structured the Jewish community by means of the institution of pilgrimages to the "courts" of the great Zaddikim, whose decisions were obeyed blindly. Some Zaddikim were believed by their followers to possess a "spark" of the messianic soul, wielding great power on earth and in heaven. Their followers could feel that God was indeed near to them, being represented by one of His holy servants. As a result, the Hassidim were liberated from the deadening paralysis of antiquarianism. They were no longer awed by the past. In their own day and in the living moment, they could feel the call of the Divine. Hence, the premium on originality in worship and in teaching. Every Hassidic dynasty was encouraged to develop new and distinctive patterns of prayer and conduct. The movement remained bound to the letter of the Law and to every custom, no matter how trifling its significance. But, it lavished its genius of renewal on the realm beyond law, developing exercises in inwardness and mystical states for the elite as well as dances, songs and common meals for the masses.

On the whole, the Hassidic movement resisted all efforts to modernize any aspect of Jewish life. The antique garments which many of them still affect are intended to symbolize the resolute and total rejection of every incursion of the modern spirit into their life. So they combatted the new schools, the rise of modern Hebrew, the new emphasis on biblical studies and on secular culture.

At one time, the Hassidim were adamantly opposed to modern Zionism. The so called Satmarer Rabbe, asserted in a learned work, published only two years ago, that the great sin of our time was the conversion of the messianic hope into secular Zionism. ("Vayoel Moshe," by R. J. Taitelbaum) The vibrancy of the hope for the coming of the Messiah made them feel that any secular endeavor to secure the establishment of a Jewish state was a grievous sin, tantamount to the rejection of God's sovereignty. Some Hassidim who reside in Israel have refused resolutely to participate in elections to the Keneset.

However, the majority of Hassidim have adjusted to the new reality of Israel. Perhaps, it is God's Will to usher in the Messianic era by degrees. Indeed, some rabbis of the third century have taught that the messianic era would not burst out suddenly, like a stroke of lightning in the dark, but that it would rise like the dawn in the eastern sky, heralding the rise of the sun. (Jerusalem T. Berochot I, 1)

We have presented an analysis of Jewish ethics in terms of the basic orientations of the religious personality, rather than by way of discrete principles and collections of maxims. Does our exposition cast any light on the play of forces and ideals in Judaism today?—We believe it does. So enduring and vital is the momentum of a historical community that even radical changes do no more than provide new directions for ancient drives.

The most fundamental changes that the past century has wrought are seen in the emergence of a conscious and aggressive secularism. At times, the facade of religion is retained for reasons of utility or appearance, but in a deep and real way, perhaps half of western Jewry is thoroughly secular even if not consciously secularist. But, the secularist Jew is likely to retain and carry over into new domains the historical elan and mental bent of his religious tradition. Even when he employs the categories of the general secular culture, he is likely to infuse them with the passion and drive of his heritage.

In the nineteenth century, the priestly component of the Jewish tradition was largely rejected by the secularists. This component sets the seal of sanctity on the ritual law and on the collective survival of the community. The role of sanctified ethnism in the priestly mentality was not yet understood, a century ago. It was left to the French sociological school of Levy-Brühl and Emile Durkheim to point out that priestly religion is as much a celebration of the clan as it is a response to the mystery of nature. Be that as it may, the initial effort of Jewish secularists was to repudiate the priestly component of their heritage, and to do so with zeal and determination. They sought to enter into the Great Society that was already then in the throes of birth—or so, it seemed. And the ritual laws and ceremonies stood in their way.

As a result, Jewish secularists were thrown off balance. The quest of sanctity and the yearning for the seal of the Absolute were diverted from the domain of ritual to the various fields of secular culture. Jews became the greatest enthusiasts of the emergent literature, art and science of the modern world. In Germany, and in Austria, Jewish ladies provided the literary salons for the rising lights of emancipated literature. Goethe and Schiller and Heine became the new objects of adulation. In general, the Jews of western Europe were the most impassioned worshippers at the shrines of the new secular culture.

With the priestly element silenced and diverted into new channels, Jews were now divided between the prophetic and the rationalistic orientations to their society. After a period of confusion and vacillation, the prophetic mentality developed into the neo-messianism of socialism, while the wisdom-current turned into the ideology and temper of liberalism. Both movements, whatever their worth or validity, were endowed with the sacramental aura of the Absolute, which was diverted from the channels of ritual.

## Socialism and Liberalism

Socialism is by no means a Jewish movement. Certainly, the racial heritage of Karl Marx or Ferdinand Lassalle is not important, though both of them were probably influenced by the fact that as descendants of Jews, they were "outsiders" in their culture—hence, disposed to recognize its weakness and to project their own solutions for its "contradictions."

Of abiding significance is the fact that socialism was embraced as virtually a new secular faith by many millions, among whom Jewish secularists played a leading role. Many more Jews were swept up by the mass enthusiasm of the new faith than one would expect from their numerical proportions to the general population. This was true in Russia, in Germany and France, and in the United States. For a while, communism exhibited the typical stigmata of pseudo-messianic frenzy. It contained a new dualism, with only one Satan and one Savior; it foresaw a universal Armageddon, with all of history moving relentlessly toward the ultimate holocaust; it identified the Messiah with the corporate personality of the suffering ser-vants; above all, it asserted that the mind of the Messiah had already been revealed and the paraclete had already appeared. From then on, the elect saints knew they were elect, enclosed within a circular dialectic that no outsider could penetrate. The new revelation was folly to the unconverted and a stumbling block to the capitalists, who were impervious to all argu-ment. Words must now be used as bullets, with which to shock the opponents into line. Such is even now the mood and temper of radical communism, or Bolshevism.

The vast majority of western secular Jews rejected the lure of socialism and identified themselves with the liberal movement. To some extent, they could not help but choose the liberal parties, since the conservative circles were as a rule closed to them. As a converted Jew, Disraeli was exceptional; even so, he evolved a liberal version of the conservative doctrine.

By liberalism we mean basically the self-sufficiency of reason. Its general assumption is that all ills can be cured by the magical wand of rationality. While folly and contingency played their nefarious roles in the making of the varied institutions of our communal life, it is necessary to restructure all things in accord with the rule of reason. The state and the educational system should be freed from the impact of religion. Nothing that is irrational should be allowed to interfere with the political life of the country. And religion itself should be purged of archaic sentiments and illogical dogmas. The ideal religion is a rationalistic humanism, "the religion of reason."[2] The liberals were driven by an intuition almost as super-rational as the historical doctrines they attacked.

Does it not require the faith of a super-saint to imagine that people can be governed by reason and learn to reject all that is irrational?

The greatest secular Jews of the past generation were indeed super-saints. Freud believed that the neurotic ills of mankind were due to the repression of childish desires in the dark dungeons of the Subconscious. If only one could expose them to the light of day, how quickly they would fade away! Einstein could prove with geometric exactitude that only a world-government would prevent a third world war and he dedicated all his social influence to that end. Bergson was far more subtle and profound, for in his thinking, the tension between wisdom and prophecy was recreated. He looked forward to a society that would be transformed by new upsurges of mysticism as well as by the dominion of reason. He stood amidst the despair of the Second World War as the prophet of the new era, in which religion would become truly universal, embracing mystery, ethical action and rational knowledge in a new dynamic equilibrium.[3]

## Tensions in Jewish Nationalism

Before we deal with the current ideological situation, we have to take account of the resurgence of Jewish nationalism. The "we" feeling of an ethnic or historical community was brought to the fore in the past century, as a consequence of the growth of democracy. The people have the right to govern themselves, but, the people have been fashioned by their history into a natural kinship community. The priestly mentality is prone "to magnify and sanctify" the self-image of the ethnic community. This is particularly true in Judaism, where the national consciousness must go back to the Bible for its literary source. Jewish secularists, rejecting the law of the priests, the revelation of the prophet and the universalism of the sages, can still clothe their ideology in the rhetoric of the Bible. Just as the "false prophets" flattered and glorified popular feeling by the use of the same slogans that the prophets employed to rebuke and judge them, so the secularists of the priestly kind can and do use the majestic phrases of Scripture to glorify their ethnocentric ambitions.

But, alongside the neo-tribalism of the priestly nationalists, there were also the voices of prophetic nationalism. A'had Ha'am, Magnes and Buber worked out a philosophy of Jewish nationalism that was permeated with social idealism and conceived in the spirit of humanism. A'had Ha'am maintained that the dynamic essence of the Jewish soul, as it was hammered out on the anvil of history, was the resolve to establish a society that was perfectly in accord with the precepts of an absolute, objective ethics. He called for a return to the spirit of an Amos, for whom life without the quest of justice and truth was not worth living. To establish a Jewish commonwealth meant to him the endeavor to make a new beginning in the building of a society after the fashion shown to the prophets in their visions. A'had Ha'am was a secular ideologist; yet, he thought of ethical values as rooted in the structure of the cosmos. He transferred the Absolute from the realm of mystical faith to that of moral action, and he was convinced that Jews could not but devote their collective elan to the demands of prophetic justice and compassion.

Buber, too, assumed that the biblical mentality could be brought back to life, without that cluster of beliefs about Torah, which is the vital center of Scriptural thought. Buber interpreted the Hassidic world to our generation as a community in which the I-Thou relation predominates, and trust in God takes the place of belief about God. In his numerous essays, he formulated a deeply ethical ideology of Zionism—namely, the Jewish state is to be built in association with the Arabs, as a social laboratory for the prophetic ideals of human dignity and in the service of mankind.

The *Kibbutzim* in Israel represent an ideology that resulted from the fusion of socialist thought and Zionist-prophetic idealism. The *Kibbutz* eliminates greed and selfish competition. It substitutes the drive of collective welfare for the impulse of egoistic ambition. And it works.

It also seeks to cultivate the sense of human dignity and to provide spiritual landmarks for men and women by which to gauge their success. A new hero-image emerged out of Kibbutz-life—a young man in overalls, with the squint of the scholar and the callouses of the worker, who labors by day in the field and the chicken-coop, engaging in the evenings in cultural pursuits. He finds his fulfillment in the company of his peers, with little time for his wife and an hour or so of play-time with his children. His one goal is to serve the Jewish nation, and perhaps through it, the world. He scorns the corrosive luxury of the city and the exploitation of the workers and, in his own way, he regards himself and his tight little group as "the chosen ones" of history, if not the favored ones of the God of history.

A. D. Gordon's essays reflect the mood and temper of this unique product of religious ethics, socialist atheism and European romantic nature-mysticism.[4]

The acid-test of Jewish nationalists in Israel was the attitude to the Arabs around them. It cannot be said that they passed this test with flying colors. The separatism of the East European Jew was matched by the suspicious fear of the Oriental. The result was a gulf that could have been bridged only by a mighty effort, in the most favorable circumstances. As it happened, the political and later the military rivalry between the two communities made any kind of rapprochement unthinkable. Yet, to the credit of A'had Ha'am, Buber, Magnes and some socialist leaders, it can be said that they never ceased to try for 'Ihud,' the peaceful partnership of the two kindred peoples.

In the Diaspora, Jewish nationalism is now a powerful reality. It is the ersatz-religion of Jewish secularists, and in a religious setting, it is far more likely to be reinforced by priestly self-sanctification than to be molded by the prophetic mentality or restrained by the universal outlook of humanism. Torah-centered orthodoxy and folk-centered pseudo-religion are struggling for supremacy, and the outcome is not yet in sight.

## Toward a New Synthesis

What is the import of our survey of Jewish ethics for our contemporary situation?—We have seen the dire consequences of the fragmentation of the prophetic ideal. In western civilization, as a whole, the tale is far more tragic and instructive. Ours is a predominantly secular age, with the transfer of priestly faith from God to the social order or to one's historic community. A person's true God is the One for whom he is prepared to kill and die. The "little god" of most people today is either the nation or the social ideology—

Anti-Communism, or Communism, or nationalism. Our function as religious teachers is to reinstitute the living word of the prophetic personality as the arbiter between the modern forms of priestly loyalties and approved wisdom.

We have to transcend the contending ideologies and to fuse them in a new approach that safeguards the wholeness and the holiness of personality. We have to detach the Absolute from the mundane, keeping the prophetic ideal from turning into the frenzy of pseudo-messianism and the liberal vision from succumbing to the temptation of the social engineer.

Each one of the three religious personalities has its caricature, the priest in the magician, the prophet in the ecstatic or in the pseudo-messianist, the Sage in the withdrawn philosopher or in the pedantic scribe. Transposed into the secular domain, the same perversions appear. The social order or the nation is turned into a god, which is then glorified and sanctified ad infinitum. Freedom in itself is not an antidote, since people want to believe and, for the most part, to believe uncritically. The prophetic personality turns into an impassioned ideologist, willing to trample upon the rights of the living for the sake of realizing the ideal vision in his mind. And the philosopher turns into the alienated intellectual, or into a self-enclosed specialist. In all three cases, the creative vision of the mysterious unity of Love, Truth and Harmony is lost. The spell of the holy is either forgotten, or else it is relegated to the domain of "the wholly other."

The first task of the prophet is to say, No to all the attempts to introduce the Absolute into social ideologies. Our wisdom is faulty, our loyalties to the State and to the nation cannot be absolute, since they must be balanced by other loyalties. And Satan is not the monopoly of the enemy. He dwells within our hearts, even as he functions in the lives of our opponents. How the illusion of *monosatanism* has captured the minds of so many who cannot appreciate the truth of *monotheism*! Indeed, it is our peculiar form of Gnosticism, for which all evil was rolled and wrapped in one package. So, for many of our countrymen, Evil is personified and it wears the shape of whoever carries the banner of Communism. In any international situation, we ask only one question, is it bad for Communists?—As if they were all of one mind, and whatever is bad for them is good for us. To many a citizen, it must appear as if the world was tranquil before 1917, with only Indians being shot and only natives ground into the dust.

Precisely because the desire to sink into the everlasting arms is as strong today as it ever was, we must continue to point out that this longing should be directed to the transcendent God, not to any immanent ideology.

And if we say *No* to every ideology, we must learn to say *yes* to all that is true, wheresoever we find it. For this reason, the now unfolding Dialogue-movement is so precious; it provides an action-symbol for the quest of seeds of truth in the camps of those who differ from us.

In a deeper sense, the Yes-saying of an Amos or a Socrates is to the effect that there are indeed central truths for us to discover. We may be mistaken, in part or in whole, but our quest is not in vain. Here, faith as trust bursts forth out of the depths of our being. Any one formulation of the Divine will may be distorted by our human frailty. But, the Will is there, as firm as the rocks and the hills. It is expressed in our religious intuitions as well as in our rational reflections, though the two sources of truth cannot be fully harmonized.

So, we say "yes" to our fractional ideals and our changing vision of the good, but also "no," insofar as they would usurp the place of the whole. And we say "yes" to the self, as a whole, insofar as it seeks unity within itself and unity with the transcendent other, but also "no," insofar as it imagines it has found those unities. With this rhythm of impulse and inhibition, the self of man is driven forward, as the thrusts of the piston drive the wheels of the locomotive.

## Notes to Religious Ethics on the Contemporary Scene

[1] The entire development is traced in the author's *The Evolution of Jewish Thought*, published by Abelard-Schuman Ltd. N.Y. 1959. Also, in the essay, *The Prophet in Modern Hebrew Literature*, in Hebrew Union College Annual, 1957.

[2] H. Cohen's, *Die Religiond es Vernunfts aus den Quellen des Judentums*, Berlin, 1917.

[3] Henri Bergson, *Two Sources of Morality and Religion*.

[4] Buber's, Gordon's and A'had Ha'am's contributions to the Kibbutz-ideal are discussed in this writer's volume, *The Vision and the Way*, published by F. Ungar, N.Y. 1966.

# A JEWISH VIEW OF THE WORLD COMMUNITY

THE IDEAL of uniting all mankind in one society is today gaining ever wider acceptance. When many millions of people see on their television screens our "cool, green earth," as it appears to the astronauts, who can doubt that we are all passengers on one ship, condemned to the same fate?

Whatever happens on one part of the globe affects all of mankind, for good or ill. If the threat of a nuclear war hangs over the heads of all men, the promise of the good life gives hope to the most wretched on our blood-stained planet.

Yet, even if the vision of "one world" should be embraced most ardently by all men, there is no assurance that it will be realized. So long as people adhere to their present scale of values, all advances toward the goal of unification are likely to be frustrated. Zechariah counselled his people to love truth and peace, putting truth ahead of peace (8,19). To attain universal peace, we need a high degree of sophistication in soul-searching, utilizing all the resources of our religious traditions, along with the insights and institutions of the behavioral sciences. We have to recognize the areas of ambiguity in our noblest ideals, the shadows and penumbras that appear, whenever a lamp is lit in the dark.

This essay is a contribution toward this end. It consists of two parts, a brief historical review of religious humanism in the Jewish tradition and an analytical study of the theological concepts bearing upon this theme.

## I

The unity of mankind is a central theme of the Hebrew Scriptures, from cover to cover. All men and women are derived from one couple, Adam and Eve. Only one language was spoken prior to the building of the tower of Babel. In the end of time, mankind will again be one, walking together "in the light of God", abandoning the implements of war for the arts of peace,

Originally published in *Standing Before God*, ed. by A. Finkel and Lawrence Frizzel (New York: KTAV, 1981).

and basking together in the heavenly radiance of redemption (Isa 2, 2-4; Mic 4, 1-5).

However, the consummation of this hope is dependent upon the acceptance by all men of monotheism, in some form (Zeph 3,9; Zech 14,16; Isa 49, 1-6; 56 6-8). The pristine unity of mankind was due to a kind of pre-Abrahamite monotheism which, according to Jewish tradition, lasted until "the generation of Enosh," when idolatry became the fashion of the day. (Maimonides, Introduction to his Code, *Mishnah Torah*). Similarly, the redeemed, all-embracing society of the end of history will be marked by a universal acceptance of the sovereignty of God—"on that day the Lord will be One, and his Name One" (Zeph 3,9). This change in theological nomenclature will mark a deep transmutation of the human spirit—"and the earth shall be filled with the knowledge of the Lord as the waters cover the sea" (Isa 11,9). It is the universal acknowledgement of the Fatherhood of God, in heart and soul, that will make possible a genuine sense of brotherhood. Any advance in the horizontal expansion of the ideal society is dependent upon growth in the vertical dimension of life, the realm of ideals that leads from man to God. The prophets were not interested in mere formalistic successes, external patterns of organization that do not reflect genuine values of the spirit. Hence, their insistence that the social-political unity of mankind is dependent on its spiritual unity.

In order to serve as the spiritual vanguard of humanity, Abraham and his "seed" were selected and charged with special obligations—"that all the families of the earth will be blessed in thee" (Gen 12, 1-3). In the Mosaic polity, the people Israel are designated as "the first-born son" of the human family, or as "a kingdom of priests and a holy nation" (Exod 4,22; 19,6). It is the task of priests to bring laymen to the service of God; they must not dwell apart, in cloistered solitude, but teach all men to serve God together" (Commentary of Seforno on Exod 19,6). Thus, from the beginning, Israel was regarded as "the people of God," or as God's "treasure-people," in this special priestly sense.

The literary prophets recognized the tension between the ideal, holy community and the empirical people of Israel, but they insisted that Israel could not but remain forever the nuclear community of the future, since it was constituted by an "eternal covenant" (Isa 55,3; Jer 33,25). They foresaw two processes whereby the empirical people will be made suitable for its role—first, only a "remnant" of Israel will truly "return" to the Lord; second, some non-Israelites will "associate" themselves with the holy community (Isa 10, 21; 66, 21; Jer 16,19; Zech 2,15). With these reservations, the prophets regarded the living Israelites of their day as the heirs of the Promise and the "heartland" of the future Kingdom of God.

In the exilic period, the winds of assimilation swept away the marginal Israelites. The thin ranks of "the loyal remnant" were, however, inspired by a holy zeal to cherish every aspect of the tradition. Ezra and Nehemiah drew up a "sure covenant" (Neh 10,1) and considered only those who adhered to it members of the holy community. Their loyal followers separated themselves from "the uncleanliness of the nations of the land" (Ezra 6,21). No effort was made to convert the Gentile wives of Jewish spouses, or their offspring. It appears that at that time, the *halakhah* of conversion had not yet been formulated.[1] Also, the loyalists were scornful of the piety of the common people, "the people of the land" (*am ha'ares*) (Ezra 4,4; Neh 13, 14-22). In the book of Daniel, written during the early days of the Maccabean uprising against the Syrian government and its allied Jewish "Hellenizers," the author speaks of the Kingdom being reserved for "the saints of the most High" (Dan 7,22). Thus, the biblical canon contains a minimal as well as a maximal definition of "the people of God."

In pre-rabbinic literature, we encounter a wide spectrum of attitudes ranging from the total rejection of all but a few "elect" to the inclusion of all who shun idolatry and abide by the principles of ethics. The Qumran sectarians maintained that only those who belonged to their own society were "children of light." All others were doomed to destruction. In the "Wisdom of Solomon," the righteous saints are elevated to the status of the "sons of God" (2, 16.17). The author of the "Psalms of Solomon" was probably a quietistic Pharisee, who looked forward to the imminent arrival of the Messiah. He foresaw "sanctified nations" surrounding the House of Israel (17,40). The narrowest and most pessimistic view was probably the one held by the author of IV Ezra, who witnessed the destruction of the second Temple. Sirach speaks of every nation being governed by an angelic prince with Israel, the "first born" in the family of nations, being ruled by the Lord Himself (17,17). This widely held view is asserted also by the author of the Book of Jubilees, who in a fit of malice, adds that these national angels were instructed to mislead their human charges (15,31).

When we come to Philo, we encounter a bright and generous spirit. He speaks of a category of *gerim*, sojourners or proselytes in spirit, who belong to God, though they are not "sons of the Covenant."

" . . . the sojourner is one who circumcizes not his uncircumcision, but his desires and sensual pleasures and the other passions of the soul. For in Egypt, the Hebrew nation was not circumcized. . . . But what is the mind of the stranger, if not alienation from belief in many gods and familiarity with honoring the One God and Father of all?" (*Quaest. in Exod.* II,2., commentary on Exod 22,21).

In describing every day as a possible holiday dedicated to God, Philo speaks of "the blameless life of righteous men, who follow nature and her ordinances . . . All who practice wisdom, either in Grecian or barbaric lands, and lead a blameless and irreproachable life . . . as behooves true 'cosmopolitans' . . ." *(De Specialibus Legibus,* II, 12,42).

In his essay on Moses, Philo describes the prophet as addressing a message of repentance to all men. Of those who respond by renouncing idolatry, he writes, "They have shown the godliness of heart which above all leads to friendship and affinity, and we must rejoice with them . . ." *(De Virtutibus,* XXIII, 175). In the Testaments of the Twelve Patriarchs, forgiveness is exalted as an absolute ideal and the redemption of the Gentiles is predicated as a direct consequence of Israel's redemption.[2] Jewish propaganda for the Gentiles to give up idolatry, sexual offenses and other moral sins, lest they be destroyed by an eschatological catastrophe, is reflected in the Sybilline Oracles.[3]

If we take a survey of the world-community from the standpoint of a Hillelite Pharisee in the year 65c.e., it would be about as follows:

(a)  The righteous Israelites, who are destined for heaven and the resurrection, and the World to Come. These include the "righteous proselytes," *gere ḥaṣedeq.*

(b)  The "middle people," i.e. Israelites, who are neither saintly nor wicked. Here, the Hillelites differed from the Shammaites who asserted that such people must traverse through hell, even if only for a moment, in order to obtain forgiveness (Rosh Hashanah 16b). The Hillelites maintained that God forgives "the middle people," his Grace being offered freely to those who make some effort to win favor in His sight.

(c)  The "wicked" Israelites, *posh'ey yisrael,* who may be consigned to hell for a maximum of 12 months. We are not quite certain of the contemporary reference of that designation (Rosh Hashanah 17a).[4]

(d)  The malicious heretics, for whom there is no hope, particularly if they cause others to stumble. The Hillelites, prior to the destruction of Jerusalem, did not include the Jewish Christians, much less the Gentile Christians in this category, as is evident in the book of Acts (5,34 and 23:9).

(e)  The sectarian groups, Samaritans, Essenes, Zealots, Jewish-Christians, Gnostics, who are judged individually. (No *minim* among the nations; Hullin 13b. Aruch Hashalem V, 169).

(f)  The Gentiles who have taken the first steps on the way to conversion, refraining from the final step, on account of one reservation or another. This type of semi-convert is probably the subject of the stories, dramatizing the difference between Hillel and Shammai (Shabbat 30b).

Hillel's policy was to promote conversion by proceeding from the love of man, to the observance of the commands of Torah, and thence to the love of God—"Love mankind and bring them closer to Torah" (Abot I, 12); also, after stating the Golden Rule to the would-be-convert, Hillel said, "the rest is commentary; go and learn." (Shabbat 31a). Those Gentiles who accepted certain practices, like the Sabbath-laws, were apparently looked upon with favor by Josephus (*Apion* II,39), but with distinct dislike by the Talmud (Sanhedrin 58b).

(g)   The "pious among the nations of the world," who share in the World to Come and may even provide the norms of piety, whereby Israel is to be judged (Test. of Benjamin 10,10; Tos. Sanhedrin, 13). "Any one who denies idolatry is called a Jew" (Megillah 13a).

(h)   Gentiles who undertake to abide by the Seven Laws of Noah belong to the invisible congregation of the Lord, but Israelites are not obligated to include them among the beneficiaries of their philanthropy. But, if they avow their acceptance of these laws, before a court of three learned men *(ḥaberim)*, then they become part of the fellowship of Israel, in respect of all types of communal charity (Aboda Zara 64b; Tossafot *ad hoc*).

(i)   Gentiles who continue to practice the rites of idolatry for a variety of external reasons, but whose hearts are not in it, are not really guilty of idolatry, for "God looks to the heart" (Hullin 13b). This recognition of an inner reality that no man can judge was frequently quoted by the medieval rabbis, who might condemn certain rites as idolatrous and certain beliefs as false, without stigmatizing as idolatrous the people who practice those rites or hold those opinions. (See the letter of Moses Maimonides to Rabbi Hisdai the Sephardi).

(j)   Gentiles who cherish Wisdom and preoccupy themselves with the demands of their particular inherited faith, providing that faith incorporates the Noachide principles; also, those who entertain no creedal principles whatever and yet make their contributions to the various arts of civilization; all such men may well reach the highest levels of holiness, "like the High Priest," even if they have never heard of the God of Israel (Sanhedrin 59a).

(k)   Masses of people, who fall in no particular category, and who are judged individually on the principle that "the Lord does not spoil the reward of any of his creatures" (Baba Kama 38b).

(l)   The heathen idolators, who are willfully guilty of moral perversions, and sin against the laws which the Lord implanted in creation (Rosh Hashanah 17a).

These twelve categories include virtually all the people with whom the Hillelite Pharisees were acquainted. There is a great deal of vagueness in regard to all the Gentiles of categories (f) to (l). Perhaps, this was intentional, since the Jewish Sages did not presume to judge the nations. In contrast to Paul and his disciples, we find in the Talmudic apocalypse that the Lord himself judges all nations (Aboda Zara 2a). Rabbi Akiba was rebuked for his suggestion that the Messiah will share in judging the nations (Hagigah 14a).

Of particular interest are the so-called "fearers of the Lord" in the New Testament and Greco-Roman literature, (*phoboumenoi ton theon* or *sebomenoi*) and the category of a semi-proselyte, *ger toshav* or *ger hasha'ar*.[5] In the Talmud, the category of *ger toshav* was said to consist of those who in the presence of three Associates, undertook to abide by the Noachide principles (Aboda Zara 64b). But, the question is discussed by second century rabbis in a manner which shows that they were debating only a theoretical issue. The status of one who was baptized, without undergoing circumcision, or who was circumcised without being baptized, was debated by rabbis at the beginning of the second century (Yebamot 46a). The assumption in the Talmud appears to be that the status of *ger toshav* applied only when the Jubilee year was observed. Hence, it existed only before the destruction of the Kingdom of Israel. (This is the opinion of Rashi, Gittin 36a. The Tossafot disagree.)

Schürer suggests that baptism may have been required even of those who did not undergo full conversion (*History*, 1891 Eng. ed. IV, p. 323). G. F. Moore argues that there was no valid category of "semiproselytes" in rabbinic law. Yet, the widespread phenomenon of 'fearers of the Lord' in the Roman world is well attested. Prof. H. A. Wolfson speaks of so-called "spiritual proselytes."[6] The local authorities of the various Synagogues in the Diaspora must have set their own standards to regulate the admission of interested worshipers to this marginal status; such authorities were accustomed to act of their own accord in the areas where the Palestinian rabbis were deliberately vague. Prof. Salo W. Baron concludes, "There is little doubt that Diaspora Jewry went farther than the Palestinian Sages in the reinterpretation of the biblical provisions to fit the exigencies of their own environment."[7]

We note also the category in the Talmud of "attached converts," *gerim gerurim*, or "converts en masse," as Moore defines it. Rashi's interpretation that they are self-converted converts, who had not been accepted by a Jewish court, appears to be more correct (Aboda Zara 3b). That it was indeed a supreme *miṣwah* to bring people "under the wings of the *Shekhinah*" can scarcely be disputed. Well-known is the teaching that the Israelites were exiled in order that converts might be added unto them (Pesahim 87b). The sacrifices of the unconverted Gentiles were accepted in the Holy Temple, while those of Jews who have offered oblations to idols, or who have violated the Sabbath in public, were not accepted (Shabbat 69b).

In theory, the Jews clung to the vision of the unity of mankind in time to come. While they were accused of "hatred of the gods" and "hatred of the human race," they demonstrated in Rome under the slogan, "Oh, heavens, aren't we brothers, the sons of one father and mother. In what do we differ from every other nation and tongue?" (Ta'anit 18a). To be sure, there were times, when contemporary hostilities produced some bitter outbursts of hatred and contempt. Naḥman Krochmal, in *Moreh Nebukhai Hazeman*, chapter 14, cites many authorities for the proposition that some unworthy *aggadot* were inserted into the Talmud by copyists. But, on the whole, such lapses in faith and love, were rare. In normal times, the tannaitic Sages insisted that all acts of charity, from feeding the hungry to visiting the sick to burying the dead, must be extended to all men equally in order to multiply the ways of peace (Gittin 61a; Tosefta, Gittin, Ch. 3; Tossafot on Shabbat 19a; Berakhot 17a). Under stress, the community tended to polarize. While some Jews withdrew into a shell, shutting out of sight the world that was so harsh to them, others kept alive the outgoing, universalist orientation of prophetic Judaism.

The standard Prayer Book, which attained its final form in the Gaonic period, kept alive the hope for the universal society. In the prayer of *"Aleinu,"* which concludes each of the three daily services, the first paragraph extols the unique privilege of the Jew as the servant of "the supreme King of Kings, the Holy One, blessed be he." The second paragraph of the same prayer articulates the hope for the establishment of God's Kingdom on earth, "when the world will be perfected under the reign of the Almighty, and all mankind will call upon Thy name, and all the wicked of the earth will be turned to thee." The two paragraphs constitute one prayer, since it is the role of Israel to serve as a "light to the nations," the vanguard of redeemed humanity.

Of all the festivals of the year, it is the High Holidays in particular that celebrate the advance of mankind toward this goal. Rosh Hashanah, the beginning of the year, marks the anniversary of the birth of Adam and Eve, the parents of all men and women, and Yom Kippur is the day of forgiveness for all sins. The liturgy on these Days of Awe reaffirms the undying hope of Israel.

"And therefore, O Lord our God, let Thine awe be manifest in all Thy works, and a reverence for Thee fill all that Thou hast created, so that all Thy creatures may know Thee, and all mankind bow down to acknowledge Thee. May all Thy children unite in one fellowship to do Thy Will, with a perfect heart . . ." (Silverman edition, *High Holiday Prayer Book*, 1939, p. 152).

This consummation is conjoined with the hope for the vindication of Israel's destiny—"and therefore, O Lord, grant honor to thy people who serve thee. . . ." The particular "hope of Israel" was inseparable from the universal hope for the conversion of all men. Even in the ideal future, historic groups will preserve their identities, as in the vision of Isaiah—"Blessed be Egypt, my people, and Assyria, the work of my hands, and Israel, mine inheritance" (Isa 19,25).

During the medieval period, Jewish thought moved along three parallel streams—rationalistic, romantic and mystical. Each of these currents contributed to the enrichment of the ideal of a world-community.

Rationalistic Judaism transferred the focus of religious life from the inscrutable Will of God to the well-being and spiritual greatness of humanity. The purpose of the prescribed commandments was to train the individual in the disciplines of the good life and to promote an ideal society. Many of the rituals were historically conditioned—that is, they were designed to protest against certain idolatrous practices (Maimonides, *Guide for the Perplexed*, III, 32). In the course of time, and without any supernatural breakthrough, the messianic age will arrive, and all mankind will be converted to "the religion of truth" (Maimonides, *Hilkhot Melakhim*, XI).

Even now, the service of God is open to all men, with the "philosopher-saints" of all faiths coming closer to the vision of God than those who are simply loyal to the rites of the Talmud (Maimonides, *Guide*, III, 51). And the ultimate test of religious experience is a life of "steadfast love, justice and righteousness" (with reference to Jer. 9,23; *Guide*, III, 54). Maimonides' ideas were applied in Jewish law *(halakhah)*, by the much quoted legalist, Menahem Hameiri as follows—"But everyone who belongs to 'the nations disciplined by religion' *(umoth hagedurot bedat)* . . . is not included in this (the laws against idolators), and is to be regarded as a full Jew in respect of all this."[8]

Romantic Judaism, which operated with biological categories, conceived of all of humanity as one living organism, with Israel as its living heart. As the heart supplies all the organs with fresh blood, so it is Israel's task to inspire all nations with the love of God.[9]

The mystical current added the notion of the scattering of Holy Sparks throughout the world and the consequent need of redeeming these sparks. The purpose of prayer was "to uplift the *Shekhinah* from the dust" and thereby bring about the salvation of Israel and of mankind.

The doctrine of "Holy Sparks" scattered in all creation implied that God could be served even in so-called "secular" ways, an implication that Israel Baal Shem Tov converted into the core of the mystical mass-movement of Hassidism. And Martin Buber revealed the contemporary relevance of this doctrine in his "I-Thou" philosophy of interpersonal relations—namely, we address "the Eternal Thou," when we turn in love to every "Thou" that we encounter in life.

With the secularization of the messianic hope in modern times, the vision of a world-community was pursued along two different lines. The classical Reform theologians taught that mankind will be united through a process of religious enlightenment. Indeed, it was the special "mission" of the Jewish people to lead in the conversion of all men to a pure, rational form of "ethical monotheism." This advance in the ethical-spiritual domain will make possible the ultimate fulfillment of Isaiah's vision. And the role of the Jew, by virtue of his history as well as his faith, is to teach men to overcome ethnic bias and theological exclusiveness. Modern humanism, with its stress on rational and esthetic values, is itself a divine thrust in the direction of the Kingdom. God works through history, His wonders to perform, and in the nineteenth century, who could doubt the reality, the certainty, yea the inevitability of progress?[10]

After two world wars, the Holocaust and the Vietnam disaster, the easy optimism of the nineteenth century is all but gone. But, the nuclear umbrella has turned the humanist utopia into an indispensable instrument for the sheer survival of the human race.

The Zionist movement was similarly moved by the messianic ideal. But, while the Reform theologians identified Jewry as a religious community, the Zionists, in keeping with the European nationalist awakening, conceived of world-Jewry as a people *(Volk)*, or a nation. The Jewish faith is indeed inseparable from the life of the Jewish people, but the substance of Jewish loyalty, previously framed in religious terms, was now identified with the feeling of belonging to the historic community of Israel. In the Zionist view, the Jewish people can regain its vitality and creativity only in its own ancient homeland. When it is no longer threatened by the twin-headed hydra of annihilation and assimilation, the Jewish people will regain its ethical-spiritual genius, and will bring its own peculiar contribution to the treasure-house of mankind's culture. The nature of Israel's mission is conceived differently among Zionist Socialists (Hess, Boruchov), Zionist liberals (Aḥad Ha'am), and the Orthodox (A. I. Kuk). In any case, Israel's rejuvenation is conceived in Zionism, as in classical Reform, within the context of dedication to the building of the world-community.

In the second part of this essay, we proceed to describe the theological concepts underlying the prophetic vision of a world-community.

# II

God loves all men; yet, in all generations, there are those who may be designated "people of God," in a special and meaningful way. I do not refer to the exalted role or an *'Ish-Elohim*, a prophet like Elijah or Elisha, but to the more widespread and limited meaning that Abraham had in mind when he explained his fear that *yire'ath Elohim*, the fear of God, might be lacking in Egypt. In the large company of "people of God," there would be embraced all who advance the various causes that are calculated to bring into being the Kingdom of Heaven, *malkhut Shamayim*. It comprises therefore in the last resort an invisible company of men and women, whose genuine worth only God can tell. (The command to sanctify the Holy Name is incumbent upon Noachides as well as Israelites. Sanhedrin 74b). But, it would also include organizations and historic communities, insofar as these groups are truly dedicated to the task of forming the vanguard of mankind's advance toward the perfection of the messianic age. This general description in itself is far too simplistic to serve a useful purpose; indeed, it is loaded with many booby-traps, as an examination of the optimistic philosophies of the past will amply demonstrate.

The crucial task is to distinguish between syncretism and spiritual openness. The ancient Romans used to invite the gods of the cities that they set out to conquer to take up residence in their Pantheon. This practice was typical of the syncretistic mentality of the pagan world. In contrast, our Scripture condemns King Solomon for allowing his wives to build altars in Jerusalem to their respective gods (1 Kgs 11:4-9). In the Greco-Roman world, the Jews refused to join their neighbors in the amalgamation of gods and rituals. But, they opened their hearts and minds to the philosophic endeavors of their age. Syncretism is the cheap way of achieving unity by mingling the outer symbols of faith; it transpires on the outer, ceremonial plane; it robs each faith of depth, flattening religion out into a meaningless mumbo-jumbo. The emergent compromise is like a babel of tongues, loud, vulgar and devoid of the power to grip the imagination of mankind.

Shunning the attractions of syncretism, our Sages sought "to gather the Holy Sparks" that God had scattered among all peoples and faiths. According to the Kabbalists, it is for this purpose that Providence had scattered our people among the nations.[11] The "sparks" are gathered through an intensification of our own strivings for holiness. In the nineteenth century Krochmal interpreted the uniqueness of Jewish history in terms of this dedication of our people to the worship of the all-embracing totality of Spirit—an ambition that can ever be approached, but never entirely fulfilled.[12] In history, the world is unredeemed, and all of us are called to "prepare the way" for redemption.

In what follows, the implications of this position are outlined.

It is in three ways that the Divine Power enters into the human world, namely—Creation, Revelation and Redemption. In the biblical view, the history of mankind which begins with an act of Divine creation, will culminate in the attainment of complete redemption, this process being directed and accelerated through the gifts of revelation. In creation, God's Power is manifested; in revelation his will; in redemption, the Divine thrust to help man transcend his own personality and the pattern of values in his social order. Each of these phases of divine activity is continuous. Of creation, the Prayer Book describes God as "renewing in his Goodness daily the works of creation" (*Daily Prayer Book* ed. Hertz., p. 109. Psalms 104 and 24); of revelation, we learn of God as ordaining fresh laws daily (Genesis Rabba 64, 4); he is addressed in prayer as "the Redeemer," in the present sense, performing wonders "every day, morning, evenings and afternoons." (Present tense is used in the Amida, seventh benediction, Hertz *Prayer Book*, p. 140. Based on Pesahim 117b.) In Jewish theology, this threefold interpretation of the essence of faith was adumbrated in the teaching that there were three essential principles of faith—belief in God, in Torah, and in Providence (J. Albo, *The Book of Principles*, trans. J. Husik and S. Duran, *Sefer Magen Avot*). Franz Rosenzweig speaks of the three currents of metaphysical reality—Creation, Revelation, Redemption, with creation taking place between God and the world, revelation between God and man, and redemption between man and the world.[13] This brilliant schematization is certainly helpful, but we must remember that every divine impulse partakes of all three categories. God's Will is revealed in creation as well as in revelation, and to perceive his Will is to take the decisive step on the highway of redemption. Yet, these phases of the divine are sufficiently distinctive for us to be able to discuss them separately and to analyze their implications for the concept of the nuclear community of "people of God."

We take up the doctrine of revelation first, since it provides a clue to the twofold nature of God's activity—his universality and particularity. In the sphere of revelation, his will was manifested in a general way through the gifts of intelligence and conscience which he has implanted in the hearts of all men. We have referred previously to the Noachide principles. A more inclusive characterization of universal revelation would be the category of wisdom *hokhmah*. And in ancient times, wisdom included ethical and even religious values. Aristotle and Plato insisted on a distinction between shrewdness, or cleverness, and genuine wisdom. And the book of Proverbs asserts, "the beginning of wisdom is the fear of the Lord" (Prov 9, 10. Prov 1, 7 *da'at* is translated as "knowledge" in J.P.S. and R.S.V. A better rendering is "understanding"). In contemporary terms, we would say an existential commitment to ethical values or an intuitive perception of their validity is the first principle of wisdom. Manifestly, the category of wisdom is a universal possession of mankind.

We note that Torah and Wisdom share in this quality of "the fear of the Lord" *(Yire'at Adonai).* It is the "beginning" of Wisdom and the "end" of Torah (Deut 10, 12). Rabbi Akiba said: "Man knows that he is made in the image of God." Indeed, this awareness is the spontaneous expression of man's true being for, as another Sage put it, "all is in the power of heaven, except the fear of heaven" (Berakhot 33b).

The notion that the content of revelation is law is one of those half-truths, which confounded scholars since Paul. While law is the detailed articulation of revelation, as it unfolded through the ages in the minds of prophets, priests and sages and in the life of the people, the dynamic intent of the law is the training of people in the ways of holiness—to fear God, to love him and to walk in his ways (Deut 10, 12). So, a third century Palestinian rabbi asserts that only the first two Commandments were directly revealed by God—i.e. the essence of revelation is God's self-revelation in human freedom and in the shunning of all that is less than God, or idolatry (Makkot 23b). Maimonides defines the purpose of the Law as being the cultivation of an ethical life for the individual and an ethical order for society *(Guide* III, 28). At the same time, the Law is designed to foster the love of God and the fear of God (ibid, III 29 & 52). Both purposes are one, since man fulfills himself only in the highest moments of holiness. Revelation takes place at the cutting edge of man's quest of truth; it is a confirmation of previously revealed values and an aspiration for His "nearness;" it is the source of the hunger for truth, goodness and wisdom.

In our Holy Scriptures, wisdom was regarded as a divine gift, akin to the inspiration and fervor of prophecy. Wisdom dwells with God; it is the principle of creation (Prov 8, 22-31). Sirach extols it as the indwelling harmony that holds all things in thrall (Sir 24, 1-34). Philo maintains that it is an illusion for man to imagine that he himself is the source of his thoughts. All noble thoughts flow from God, and man's part consists in rendering his mind receptive to divine inspiration.[14] For this reason, the Hellenistic Jews believed that Greek wisdom was divine in origin; they speculated that Pythagoras, Plato and Aristotle may have been disciples of the Hebrew prophets (Josephus, *Apion.* I, 22). In the Talmud, the Sage is regarded as the latter-day successor of the prophet (Shabbat 119b). The thought is even projected that a sage, *ḥakham,* is better than a prophet (Baba Bathra 12a).

The Talmudic sages recognized that wisdom is a universal category, while Torah is the special possession of the Jewish people (Lamentations Rabba, 2). On seeing a Gentile sage, a Jew is obligated to thank the Lord for his sharing His wisdom with a creature of flesh and blood (Berakhot 58a). The true Sage learns from all men (Abot 4, 1). On the other hand, Torah is not

124     Jacob B. Agus

found among the nations (Lamentations Rabba, 2). Reacting against the claims of the early Christians that they alone understood the true meaning of the Pentateuch, some of the Sages insisted on the unity of Israel and Torah with hyperbolic rhetoric—to wit, Israel and the Torah are wedded, and a Gentile who studies Torah is committing adultery, as it were (Pesahim 49b; Sanhedrin 59a).

What is the relation of Torah to Wisdom? While in the several streams of Jewish thought, this relationship was conceived in different ways, the assumption is well-nigh universal that Torah and wisdom cannot be mutually contradictory (Abot 3, 21—no piety without wisdom). While Torah is trans-rational, deriving from divine inspiration, it is never anti-rational.[15] Indeed, Torah itself is "a lower representation of the wisdom that is above" (Genesis Rabba 17, 5). Hence, the ideal scholar should be learned in all forms of wisdom as well as in Torah. The members of the Sanhedrin, we are told, were supposed to be familiar with "the seventy languages," and even with the arts of witchcraft, though the practice of witchcraft was strictly forbidden (Sanhedrin 17a, 68a).

In medieval Jewish philosophy, the rationalists, beginning with Saadia, maintained that the principles of Torah and speculative wisdom were virtually identical. Torah presents us with conclusions, which reason would reach only through a long and arduous effort.[16] For Maimonides, all passages in Torah which do not accord with the dictates of reason must be interpreted figuratively.[17] Still, he recognized certain "necessary beliefs" for the masses of the people.[18] He believed in *creatio ex nihilo*, because this question could not be determined by reason; when the scales are balanced, we have to allow the nisus toward perfection within us to tip the scales in favor of the doctrine of creation—a doctrine "which makes Torah possible."[19]

A neo-Platonist, like Gabirol, did indeed set will above reason. A romanticist like Judah Halevi maintained that Torah brings the Israelite to a state of responsiveness to the "Divine Quality" that is far superior to any level of insight available to philosophers.[20] But, even Halevi insisted that God could not command us to believe aught that is contrary to reason (*The Kuzari* I, 89). The Kabbalists did affirm the existence of a realm of Divine Being, where all was paradoxical—infinity and finitude were commingled, limits were reached and not reached. Powers were divided and undivided—the principle of "the excluded middle" being honored in the breach almost consistently. That supernal realm was conveyed to chosen souls by means of revelation, and it could be conveyed from master to disciple only through the magic of personal charisma, "like one who lights a candle by a candle, without the first candle being diminished in the slightest."[21]

Yet, even Naḥmanides, one of the greatest luminaries of Kabbalah, asserted that man must not believe anything that is contrary to reason. In summing up his explanation why Jews could not accept the Christian faith, he pointed to the irrationality of Christian theology, as he saw it. "The core of the true dispute among us is not the concept of the Messiah . . . but the crux of the issue and the reason for the argument between Jews and Christians is the fact that you impute to the Deity things which are exceedingly repugnant . . . For what you state, and this is the essence of your faith, reason cannot accept, nature does not permit, and the prophets never implied. Also, the belief in miracles cannot be extended to cover such a phenomenon . . . The thought of a Jew and a man cannot tolerate such a belief, hence you argue for naught and your words are wasted, for this is the essence of our disputes" (*Sefer Havikuah Leharamban*, 12).

Naḥmanides had in mind the popular conception of Incarnation in the Church of his day; yet, he also laid down a general principle that "the thought of a Jew and man" sets limits to the content of faith.

In a book written by another participant in a disputation that took place a century and a half later, the author agreed that two different religions may coexist at one time, and be equally true (J. Albo, *Book of Principles* vol. 1, ch. 25). Yet, he refused to accord this concession to Christianity, on the ground that its teachings contradicted the clear principles of reason (ibid, vol. III, ch. 25).

In the age of Enlightenment, Moses Mendelssohn identified Judaism with "the religion of reason" and in a well-known letter he suggested that convergence between Judaism and Christianity would be possible only after the Christian faith had been reinterpreted along rationalistic lines.[22] Today, we know that there is much more to religion than reason can fathom.

As Pascal put it: The heart has its reasons that are too big for the mind, while the logic of the mind is too small for the heart.

Yet, it remains true that Torah and wisdom must advance hand in hand. Even a non-philosophical Talmudist, like Elijah Gaon of Vilna, had asserted "that Torah and wisdom derive from one source, and for every measure of wisdom that we lack, we miss ten measures of Torah" (quoted in *Aliyot Eliyahu*). God comes at us from several different directions at once, and we must take account of every form of revelation in our effort to seek His nearness. This synthetic adventure is possible because neither the body of revelation we possess nor the insights of wisdom available to us are closed and complete. To the modern mind, history is a very present reality. We see revelation as being an ongoing quest, as well as a possession. We seek "the nearness of God," but we can move ahead only so far. Our goal is to understand the Absolute and feel his Presence in our bones, as it were, but we cannot possess the Absolute.

What is the relevance of these reflections to our vision of the world-community? It is the distinction between the terms, "people of God" and "people of the Covenant." In the Talmud, a faithful Israelite is designated as a "son of the Covenant" *(ben berit)*. While the recipients of wisdom share in divine guidance, they do not necessarily belong to the people of the Covenant. Through the special obligations that a historic people or a newly constituted *ecclesia* assumes, it establishes private signs and symbols that become charged with holy significance for their members. People need houses as well as the great outdoors in order to feel at home in the universe; when a house is built, the outside universe is shut out, but only for certain times and seasons. And it is an act of Divine revelation that prompts us to build homes of the spirit for our collective existence.

In the biblical period, Covenants were made by patriarchs and kings, in the Name of God and for His sake. Joshua renewed the Covenant, so did kings Hezekiah and Josiah, and Ezra instituted the "sure Covenant" (Josh 24, 24; 2 Chr 29, 10; 2 Chr 34, 31; Ezra 10, 3; Neh 10, 1). The account of Ezra's reforms does not speak of a fresh theophany; yet, there was a clear awareness in rabbinic literature that Ezra was a second Moses, as it were (Rosh Hashanah 19b; Sanhedrin 21b; Koheleth Rabba 1, 8). For what we do for God, is in essence of God. In the Talmudic period, whatever legislation the Sages enacted, the people were supposed to regard as a divine commandment. So, the reading of the *Megillah* on Purim and the lighting of candles on Hanukkah are preceded by a benediction in which we thank God "for hallowing us by his Commandments and enjoining us to perform these rites."[23] Similarly, all benedictions recited prior to tasting food were formulated by the Sages; yet, we are told that any one who partakes of food, without reciting the prescribed benediction, "robs the Holy One, blessed be he, and the congregation of Israel" (Berakhot 55b; Tosefta Berakhot, 4). The sages allowed that "the pious among the nations shared in the World to Come," but they insisted that new proselytes could not set conditions or eliminate some items from the Covenant (Tosefta Sanhedrin, 13, 2; Sifra, Kedoshim, 8).

Now, the Covenant-principle can be generalized. An *ecclesia*, or any historic community, that is dedicated to God is a covenant-community. It becomes an instrument of God who works in history through communities as well as through individuals. The mark of his revelation in both cases is a hunger for "the knowledge of God" and a thirst for His nearness. But while the individual's quest of God is spontaneous and open-ended, that of the historic community is articulated in institutions and rites, in a so-called covenant.[24]

While the designation "people of God" became problematic and invisible, the meaning of a covenanted people remained concrete and empirical. Already, the prophets assumed that the Israelites will truly become God's people only at a future date. While the talmudic Sages were certain that the Israelites were God's children, in a special sense, they interpreted this relationship in a non-biological sense. The same Rabbi Akiba who glorified Israel "for their being called sons of the Place" asserted that the Ten Tribes were cut off entirely from the body of Israel. Is not this attempt to dissipate the aura of the archetypal image of the Twelve Tribes a bold affirmation of the rabbinic understanding of the meaning of Israel? Since the exiled northern tribes did not submit to the Torah, which interprets the meaning of the Covenant, they did not belong to *Kenesset Yisrael*, the congregation of Israel. As a matter of fact, the cold realism of the Sages did not calm the messianic expectations of the popular imagination. In the folk-legends of redemption, the Twelve Tribes continued to play a central role.

The Jewish individual could not assume that he was numbered among "the people of God." For no man is proof against sin. So, King David, pictured as a saint in the Talmud, was wont to say, "I know that God rewards the righteous in the World to Come, but I cannot tell whether I shall be among them." Jacob too was ever anxious lest sin cause him to lose the favor of God (Berakhot 4a). If these super-saints could not be certain of belonging to "the people of God," how could ordinary mortals arrogate such a title to themselves? The Talmud stigmatizes the smug Pharisee, who imagines he has fulfilled every Commandment, quite as bitterly as the Gospel of Luke. To be human is to be potentially wicked or saintly, for one's intention makes the difference. So, if a person says the wedding-formula to a girl, "on condition that he is a perfect saint", she is married to him, since he might have repented fully. Similarly, if his condition be "that he is thoroughly wicked", she is married to him, since he might have meditated an act of idolatry. A person must think of himself as being neither wicked, nor saintly, but somewhere in the middle, with the next act being decisive. Rabbi Judah the Patriarch was wont to weep over this uncertainty of man's status—"it is possible for man to acquire his world in one hour". We walk before God on a razor's edge. "Do not trust yourself until the day of your death," said Hillel. (Abot 2, 5) Even Moses could not depend upon his merit; he had to plead for the free act of God's grace.

On the other hand, every person, Jew or Gentile, can bring nearer the

Divine Presence by an act of *ḥesed*, steadfast love, and the Kingdom of God is established when the *Shekhinah* dwells securely on earth. A late Midrash portrays Elijah as asserting dramatically—"I bring heaven and earth to witness that whether a person be free or slave, man or woman, Jew or Gentile—according to his deeds the Holy Spirit rests upon him." The same idea is presented in a tannaitic source, in the name of Rabban Yoḥanan ben Zakkai. Rebuking the zealotry of his young disciples, he taught that while it is righteousness that uplifts Israel, the nations obtain forgiveness through deeds of steadfast love. Israel is bound by a covenant, with detailed specifications, while the nations can join the ranks of the favored through free acts of love. (Baba Bathra 10 b.)

The *miṣwot*-mentality of the Pharisees has been frequently abused, as if these progenitors of the latter-day merchants already conceived of heaven in cash-register terms.[25] To be sure, the Pharisees had to guard constantly against reducing religion to a cluster of external actions. And the best among them were always on guard. But, their emphasis on individual actions liberated the religious imagination from the temptation to play the role of God. They did not need to ask, "am I among the saved?" "am I and my people among His Children, or His Saints, or His Kingdom? "The Compassionate One seeks the heart" of His worshipers. All that we can do is to concentrate on the next decision in our lives. We should ask, "what is my *miṣwah* at this moment?" For this reason, the Talmudic rabbis allowed the feeling of belonging to "the people of God" to fade into the background, while they focused attention on seemingly trivial questions, the choices that one must make in his daily life.

This emphasis did not turn them into a closed fellowship, though at various times the danger of such a fixation loomed large on the horizon. Of particular interest is the report of a discussion between Rabban Gamliel of Yavneh and the young Rabbi Akiba. The old patriarch expressed his anxiety that one could not be saved by the law, since even the slightest transgression might lead one to perdition. (This fear, of course, is echoed in the letters of Paul and in the letter of James.) Rabbi Akiba argues in behalf of the contrary thesis, that the performance of even one *miṣwah* assures a person of sharing in the world to come (Sanhedrin 81a; Midrash Tehillim 15, 7).

The emphasis on redemptive deeds balances the concept of a nuclear core of redeemed persons. The polarization between the "chosen" and the rejected is softened. We come to think of the Kingdom of God as a free and open society, which people enter and leave in accordance with the quality of their ethical life, day by day. For the protean, emergent Kingdom is composed of deeds, not of people. "There is no man who does not have his hour, and no thing that does not have its place" (Abot 4,3). A rabbi who impulsively exclaimed, "how ugly is this man!" underwent a long penance, until he learned that there were no "ugly men," just ugly deeds (Taanit 20b). Every good deed, the rabbinic Sages declare, creates a good angel, and every evil deed a demon—i.e. a divine law operates in the cosmos, which is akin to the Newtonian principles of momentum and the conservation of energy (Abot 4,11). Sometimes, the consequences of an action may not be felt for centuries. When King Solomon took Pharaoh's daughter to wife, the angel Gabriel put an obstacle in the river Tiber around which silt began to gather, forming the foundation for the city of Rome (Shabbat 56b). On the other hand, "the merit of the patriarchs" saved Israel from trouble again and again. In respect of great *miṣwot*, a person enjoys their fruit in his lifetime, while their healing essence endures until the world to come. While the messianic End is certain to arrive in any case, the time of the advent can be hastened by the multiplication of deeds of love.

In Augustine's "Civitas Dei," the world is divided between persons, the "city of God," comprising those who love God to the point of total selflessness and "the city of man," consisting of those who love themselves to the exclusion of God. People are categorized and polarized. And he does not make clear whether the former are an invisible congregation, transcending sectarian bounds, or simply a glorified characterization of the Catholic church. In Judaism, the living nucleus of the Kingdon of God is both the empirical people of Israel and the company of angels generated by the *miṣwot* of the past and the present. The Sages were certain that the living people of Israel was the heart of the emergent society of redeemed mankind, even while in theory they agreed that the pious of the nations shared in the world to come. They saw terrestrial history as an acting out of a scenario composed in the meta-historical realm, where angels arise daily to sing unto the Lord and then to sink into a river of fire, flowing from the divine throne; yet, two angels, Gabriel and Michael, stand above this flux, and Michael is the "prince" of Israel (Hagigah 14a).

This view that the Kingdom is being built by the deeds of the righteous was supplemented by the belief in the inexhaustible power of repentance. In this way, the rabbis guarded against the danger of externalization that threatened to alienate man from his own actions. Repentance is an inner transformation, a reorientation of man, in his deepest inwardness. So Maimonides defines the goal of repentance as follows—"that He who knows all secrets may testify about the penitent that were he exposed to the same temptation, he would not commit the sin of which he is guilty." Such a transformation is possible, because of man's rootedness in the Divine Being.

The human soul cannot be completely cut off from its source and if one truly turns to God, all his sins vanish and he comes closer to God than the righteous, who have not sinned. Indeed, his very sins are turned into *miṣwot* (Yoma 86b). There is an infinite dimension to the human personality, since it embodies the "image of God;" hence every person is commanded to say, "for my sake was the world created" (M. Sanhedrin IV, 5). Because of this outreach beyond all finite limits, the human potential for self-transcendence is incalculable. A beautiful legend tells of King Menasseh's repentance. The angels surrounded the divine throne, intent on preventing the penitential prayers of the renegade from reaching the Presence, but the Holy One dug a hole in his heaven and put his hand through it to receive the petition of the penitent and to reinstate him in his favor (Sanhedrin 103a).

Apart from the performance of so many *miṣwot*, faithfulness was the keynote of the religious personality. As Martin Buber pointed out, faithfulness or trust is the central motif in Judaism—not the propositional "belief that," but the existential "belief in." The first paragraph of the *Shema*, in which one undertakes to love God, with all one's heart amounts to "an acceptance of the yoke of the Kingdom of heaven." So, dedication to the building of the kingdom is re-affirmed twice daily. The vision of the future is not merely re-kindled on the High Holidays, when it forms the central theme of the liturgy, but it is echoed in everyday life. Before partaking of food or drink, the prescribed benediction *(beshem umalkhut)* includes a reference to the Kingship of God, a consummation that belongs to the messianic era. Rashi interprets the *Shema* itself as an affirmation of this hope—"the Lord, who is now our God, will become the One God of all men" (ad loc. Deut 6:4). The Sages interpret the meaning of loving God as being "to cause him to be beloved by all people" (Sifre to Deut 6:5). Here is a general formulation of the goal of all missionary enterprise—it is not to teach so many doctrines, but to live the kind of life and build the kind of world which might result in God's being loved by more and more men. But, love is inseparable from faith and hope. Hence, the exaltation of the power of faith, in one of the earliest tannaitic works (Mechilta, Beshallah, 6).

Instructive for our purpose is the comment of an eighteenth century rabbi, Jacob Emden, who was a contemporary of Moses Mendelssohn, but who was so remote from the mood of the Enlightenment that he doubted whether the pious Maimonides could have composed so skeptical a work as the "Guide for the Perplexed." Commenting on the statement of the second century Palestinian Sage, Rabbi Yohanan the Shoemaker, "every community that is organized for the sake of heaven will endure and every community that is not for the sake of heaven will not endure" (Abot 4,14), Rabbi Emden wrote as follows:

"Certainly the Sage did not concern himself with communities that are not related to us, but with those new faiths and sects that derived from us . . . Indeed when we take account of the cults they (the Christians) supplanted, which worshipped stocks and stones and did not know God as the Absolute Power, administering reward and punishment in the hereafter, their (the Christian) church may truly be called an *ecclesia* for the sake of heaven. For they proclaim God to distant nations . . . They glorify the Lord, God of Israel and his Torah, even among people who have never heard about him. Therefore, their good intentions cannot be in vain. The Compassionate seeks the heart . . . Furthermore, Christian scholars are known for their dedication to research into the meaning of Holy Scriptures. By their studies in biblical history, many of them have added to its glory . . ."[26]

In this judgment, Emden ranks the Christian polity as a divine institution. It is dedicated to the Glory of God; it stresses purity of heart; it promotes the quest of truth and justice. Its capacity to endure and its role in history demonstrate that the God of history had assigned it a crucial role; it is indeed "a community for the sake of heaven". Yet, Emden would have been horrified at the suggestion that the establishment of the Christian polity had annulled the covenant of the Jewish people. For Jews, to forsake their own covenant is an act of apostasy; but, they must remember that they are not the only "people of God"; other historic communities, as well as other individuals, share in this honor and in its concomitant responsibilities.

Emden's judgment of the Christian church ties in with Gamliel's opinion, at the trial of Peter and John (Acts 5,38.39) and the view of the Pharisees at the trial of Paul (Acts 23,9) as well as Maimonides' judgment of the redemptive role played by Christianity and Islam in the history of the world.[27] Halevi too regarded Islam and Christianity as playing a redemptive, messianic role (*Kuzari* 4,23) though as an ethnic romanticist he asserted that the least son of Torah attains a higher level of piety than any non-Israelite (*Kuzari* 5,19).

It is interesting to note that the neo-Orthodox theologians of the nineteenth century, Bernais and Hirsch, spoke of a general revelation in the hearts of men, as well as of the specific Sinaitic revelation. "The quest of truth and justice within you is the primary revelation of God within you." The latter theologian, for all his uncompromising extremism, regarded the French Revolution of 1789 as "one of the hours in which God entered history," in spite of the fact that at that time, as on so many other occasions, "the light of God in the hearts of men" was quickly fragmentized and perverted.[28]

In sum, insofar as revelation is a divine activity, it comes to us in three ways—primarily, through our own convenanted community, secondarily

through the general revelation of human wisdom and thirdly as a challenge
and a spur of reflection, through the work of other convenanted communities.
We live within our own historic covenant, but we learn from the other two
sources as well as from our own. In each case, our insights unfold in the
course of history. It is particularly in the nature of wisdom to evolve and
expand. The role of history in the growth of wisdom may be acknowledged
without falling into the trap of an all-doubting historicism. We have to
maintain the living tension between the different covenanted communities
and the universal sphere of wisdom, which provides their common meeting
ground. Said Rabbi Judah the Patriarch, "which is the right road that a man
should choose?—That which is beautiful and good in his own eyes and
beautiful and good to mankind" (Abot 2;1. The term "beautiful and good" is
in Hebrew, *tifereth*, in Greek probably *kalos*). The very letters of the Hebrew
word for truth, *emet*, according to the Talmud, suggest that genuine knowledge derives from the conjunction of several viewpoints, for it consists of the
first letter of the alphabet, the last letter and the middle one, suggesting that
most issues in life need to be viewed from an affirmative, a negative and a
synthetic standpoint (Shabbat 104a; Rashi ad loc).

## Creation

Man was designed by the Lord to be a "partner of the Holy One, blessed
be he, in the works of creation" (in promoting justice, Shabbat 10a; in
observance of Sabbath, Shabbat 119b). His industry and inventiveness are
God-given powers, for the promotion of the settlement of the earth, that it
might be a paradise, not a wasteland. (A covenant was made regarding man's
productive work: Abot d. R. Nathan, 11; Isa 45, 18; Gittin 41b). In contrast
to the Greek legend concerning Prometheus and the fire he stole from the
gods, the Talmud ascribes the discovery of fire to a special act of Divine
favor. (God inspired the thought of rubbing two stones together in the mind
of Adam. Pesahim 54a). Abraham is represented in the Book of Jubilees as an
inventor of the plough (Jubilees, Charles' edition, 11,23). The secular art of
medicine was praised by Sirach as being fully in keeping with the Will of
God (Sirach, Charles' edition, 38,4). This attitude was contrary to the plain
meaning of 2Chr 16,12. Both attitudes were preserved in the medieval era.
(See Ibn Ezra's comment on Exod 21,19). It is a sin to idle away one's time
and refrain from doing one's part in "the settlement of the world" *(yishuvo shel
olam)*. For this reason, gamblers are not considered worthy of serving as
witnesses in a law-court (Sanhedrin 24b.) Some would limit the law to
professional gamblers. The talmudic sages were in many cases artisans, and
they taught that the *Shekhinah* dwells only where good and loving craftman-

ship is at work (Abot 2; Abot d. R. Nathan 11). In modern parlance we should say, religion and culture go hand in hand.

In this area, as in revelation, the polarity of pluralism prevails. There is the particularistic culture of the Israelites and an emergent, universal culture. The Sages were acquainted with Hellenistic and Roman cultures, which laid claim to universalism. Some of the *tannaitic* Sages were willing to acknowledge Rome as a Power enthroned by God in order to introduce the arts of civilization and lawful order to the world (Sabbat 33b. Tanhuma, Tazria, 11). Those who disputed this judgment questioned the motives of the Roman governors, not the worth of their achievements. A third century rabbi who visited the imperial city marvelled at the wonderful care which the Romans lavished on their marble statues, but he criticized their order of priorities when he saw the hunger and nakedness of the poor in that metropolis (Genesis Rabba 33,1; Tanhuma, Emor).

The range and character of universal culture was set over against the particular Hebrew culture that was so intimately interwoven with the Jewish faith (Rome and Jerusalem were seen as a polarity. Shabbat 56b). The "settlement of the land of Israel" *(yishuv Haʾareṣ)* was a supreme Command in Judaism, and the rabbis enacted many laws in order to promote that goal (Baba Bathra 101a; Gittin 8b; Kethubot 110b; Makkot 7a). So intimate was the bond between the Holy Land and the Torah that some modern scholars refused to acknowledge the universal dimension of the Jewish religion.[29] They asserted that the ethnocentric embrace of Hebrew culture prevented Judaism from becoming a world religion.[30] Actually, as we have seen, Judaism was an expansionist faith in the Hellenistic and early Roman period. But, concern with humanity as a whole did not diminish Jewish eagerness for the preservation and cultivation of their own national culture—their language, their land, their historical memories and associations. In fact, rightly or wrongly, they imagined that for the sake of humanity and universal culture, they are obligated to preserve their own cultural distinctiveness. A particular religion may well be associated with a particular culture in an intimate, organic way, even while it cultivates an openness and empathy for the cultures of other people and the vision of a universal culture.[31]

To be sure, there were times when the yearning for Zion reached fantastic proportions, as in the philosophy of Judah Halevi, who maintained that the Holy Land possessed a theurgic potency, which would be revealed in a revival of prophecy if a faithful Israel were once again settled in it (*Kuzari* II, 8). But, even Halevi remained true to the vision of a united mankind. He compared Israel among the nations to the heart in a living person; through the revitalization of the heart, all other organs will regain their vigor.[32]

Two questions arise in relation to the interaction of religion and culture. Should religions combat the rise of diverse ethnic cultures for the sake of a universal society, and if ethnic cultures are inescapable, should religions stand apart from them and subject them to criticism, or should they enter the secular world with a holy enthusiasm so as to sacralize the secular?

The first question was fiercely debated in western Europe in the nineteenth century. The founders of Reform Judaism insisted on eliminating the nationalistic residues in the Jewish religion, in order to render it worthy of serving in the vanguard of the world-religions of the future. So, they reduced the role of Hebrew in the liturgy, eliminated references to Zion, declared the dietary laws to be obsolete, and generally represented Judaism as the religion of reason and humanity. From Abraham Geiger to Leo Baeck, the Reform movement claimed that Jewry must preserve its faith as the nuclear religion of the future society of mankind.[33]

But history has a way of betraying those who cling tightly to its skirts. Today, classical Reform has lost its appeal to the Jewish mind. Modern Zionism affirms the worth of Hebrew culture, as well as of the Jewish religion. Yet, Zionism does not call for a return to the ghetto, or to a retreat from the humanist ideal. On the contrary, it is imbued with the faith that the revival of Hebrew life and culture in the land of Israel will contribute to the reinvigoration of western culture, which draws its inspiration from the Holy Scriptures. The universal ideal of a global society must be conceived in pluralistic terms, as an association of many and diverse ethnic cultures, all sharing in an emergent universal culture. The universal and the particular are not opposites but the two poles of one dynamic reality. In every generation, it is necessary to counter the absolutist claims of the proponents of each pole and to find the right balance between them.

As to the second question, concerning the interaction of religion and culture, we have seen in recent years the pendulum swing from Barth's "wholly Other" to Cox's "Secular City." Extremists draw attention, since they fall in with the alternation of popular sentiment. But, actually, it is obvious that to be effective religion must be intimately involved with the living culture of the moment and, at the same time, transcend it and subject its trends to relentless criticism. Religion performs the double function of celebrating the *status quo* and fueling the drive to transform it. It sanctifies the great ideals of society, yet if it has not lost its own vision of human destiny, it cannot but uphold standards and project social visions which loom far beyond the grasp of men at any one time.

The intimate association of Judaism with the empirical Jewish people provides a unique opportunity for the study of the interaction of a universal religion with a specific nationality. An ambivalent mood is generated, as dangerous as it is creative. The danger consists firstly in the temptation for outsiders to discount its message and to treat it as a form of sanctified ethnicism. Secondly, let it be admitted that the ethnocentric bias may indeed distort the message of faith. If the ancient proverb is true, "no one sees his own failings", how much more is this the case when one's communal interests are engaged. When a particular faith is organically bound up with a particular ethnic group and a political state, it is just as likely that religious values will be strangled by political interests as it is that politics and culture will be ennobled by the momentum of faith. On the other hand, when a faith is totally dissociated from culture and politics, it is just as probable that the faith will be "unspotted of the world", as it is that it will be ethereal and irrelevant, totally incapable of directing national policy.

For this reason, the Jewish faith-culture relationship, which is intimate and organic, and the Christian faith-culture posture, which is loose and indirect, are polar opposites; they should be juxtaposed and kept in a state of mutual challenge and tension. As in the realm of revelation, so in that of creation, God works through us, yet not through us alone, but also through the challenge to us of our neighbor's faith and that of the emergent society of mankind.

The emergence of the State of Israel did not transform essentially the character of Judaism as a historical blend of a universal faith and a national culture. Israel is a secular and modern state; yet, it is also the homeland of a widely scattered people, that defines itself by its religious faith. For this reason, it is perennially troubled by the recurrent question, "Who is a Jew?" And the Jewish people of the Diaspora, who may be in all respects other than religion totally integrated in the life of the nation of which they are part, nevertheless retain a particular affection for the land and people of Israel. Here, then, is a people that has been in the vanguard of progress in the western world, and yet in its social structure has somehow remained an anomaly. In its case, a universal religion and a particularist ethnicism were not bifurcated by the cutting edge of modern secularism, but on the contrary, both nationalism and faith were in modern times reinvigorated and re-combined. Because of its world-wide impact, Israel cannot run its affairs like any other secular state that is concerned only with its own security. Inevitably, it will strive to become a great center of man's quest for ultimate meaning and transcendent values. The momentum of history will impel it to serve as a force for interfaith and intercultural activities. And the faith of the Jews in the Diaspora will be challenged peculiarly by the concrete issues deriving from the realities of the Jewish state.

While the diverse loyalties of the Jews to God, to country, to humanity and to Israel are theoretically compatible, situations are bound to arise when these sentiments will pull in different directions. Thus, the Jew cannot afford to be complacent. Out of his inner turbulence, he must become sensitive to the subtle nuances of the ideals and beliefs that bind men together and generate the forces of history. And the example of the Jew will serve as a call to all peoples to transmute their parochial loyalties by the universal ideals of religious faith, to become "chosen people" with all the ardor and all the anguish that this task entails.

## Redemption

It is frequently stated that while Jews think of redemption in terms of exterior, visible developments, Christians think of it in terms of interior spiritual transformations. The contrast is also viewed as one of national vindication versus the salvation of all mankind. In both cases, we deal actually with variations of intensity in one spectrum of hope, variations which however are exceedingly important in our day and age.

Let us begin with the common theme. Redemption involves a fresh ingression of Divine power. It is God that redeems. While man can help through his repentance and good deeds, he cannot redeem himself. The Sages declare that if all Israelites were to attain the perfection of repentance, the Messiah would instantly arrive (Sanhedrin 97b). But, such a consummation is quite improbable, and repentance itself involves the help of God (Yoma 38b). So, even before the emergence of the modern concept of progress and man-made social advancement, a spiritual version of hopeful progress was implicit in the Judeo-Christian view of history. Yet, the distinguishing mark of that idea, in contrast to the modern concept of progress, was the central role of the trans-natural act of God. He is the Savior, in Christianity; "the Redeemer of Israel", in Judaism.

What is the negative significance of this belief? Manifestly, it implies that we must not assume the finality of any of our human achievements. The *eschaton* involves both a physical and spiritual transformation. And there is an abundance of metaphors in Judaism for both aspects of redemption. But, in both domains, we are cautioned to remember that none of our physical achievements is more than a passing phase in the divine scheme of salvation. Our industry and technology may be essentially flawed, with a terrible, even if, invisible price being exacted for every inch of progress. We must be constantly on guard against the sanctification of techniques and the smug assumption that human progress can be quantified and calibrated. To be sure, we must strive for advancement along the plane of external, visible progress, overcoming the anguish of privation in food, shelter and amusement. But, such progress, we are cautioned, is ambiguous. We cannot redeem ourselves. Our collective achievements, for all their grandeur, cannot bring ultimate salvation.

In the interior domain, as in the realm of physical progress, we must acknowledge our insufficiency. Our values and ideals may have to be transcended in ways that we cannot foretell. In the impetuosity of his genius, Nietzsche spoke of rising "beyond good and evil"; Kierkegaard wrote of "the suspension of the ethical", and in the last decade we endured the follies of the so-called "death of God" theologians. The facet of truth in these extremist outbursts is the recognition of the non-ultimacy of even our highest ideals and noblest values. There is a dimension of depth in the life of the spirit, while our value-judgments tend to be flat and fragmentary. Our concepts of God, need to be perpetually refined. Old concepts, like old shells, should be thrown back into the ocean of past history, where the natural processes of "recycling," will one day work their magic of resuscitation. Our perceptions of good and evil need to become ever more penetrating and critical, as our society becomes more complex; we should not be satisfied with a black and white checkerboard of human affairs.

By the same token, even our values and ideals may and probably will be overriden and, in due course, be supplanted by other attainments and norms, which will also be non-ultimate. In this way, man is kept from worshipping his own image in the mirror of time, much less the work of his hands.

Coming down to the events of our day, we need to maintain an open, yet critical, mind regarding the efforts of some of our youth to push beyond the old norms of personal and communal life, though we must insist on the compatibility of any new insights with the proven wisdom of the past. Any new Covenant "fulfills" but does not destroy the Old Law. We must not maintain that our patterns of the good life are absolute; at the same time, there are no breaks in the life of the spirit. The new emerges out of the old, creating new norms and generating new visions, but there is a deep continuity and essential unity, underlying all differences. Here, again, the course of revelation is instructive. Say the Sages, "all the prophets have delivered the same message, though not two prophets have spoken in the same style" (Sanhedrin 89a).

The youth-movement of our day flowed along the boundary between prophetism and apocalypse. At one end, it was critical of specific evils, but devoted to the grand ideals of the past, bitter but not despairing, visionary in its view of the high potential of their people, but not escapist. At the other end, it rejected the totality of existing society as irredeemably evil, embraced a revolutionary policy without any program, indulged in irrational fantasies and escapist utopias that reflected its despair and dreamlike irresolution. It was articulated in symbols of defiance and paradoxicality, an unculture, aptly called "counter-culture."

Religious leaders in both Judaism and Christianity have always had to contend against such quixotic movements of pseudo-messianism or chiliasm, which arose in times of widespread frustration. If authentic leaders keep the prophetic mood alive, they can hope to divert the energies of the apocalyptics into constructive and realistic channels.

In Judaism, the vision of redemption centers around the vindication of the destiny of Israel; in Christianity, redemption is of the individual, and the goal is to preach the message of redemption to all men. Again, the differences are in emphasis and centrality. The Jewish vision of the salvation of the people of Israel is viewed within the perspective of universal redemption, and the universalist outreach of Christianity allows for the role that an invisible *ecclesia*, "the people of God, have to carry out on the stage of human history". Yet, the differences are of immense significance.

In the Jewish view, the goal of redemption is not only an all-embracing universal society, but also the consummation of the particular cultures and dreams of the diverse nations and peoples. The universal goal must not be so construed as to preclude the fulfillment of the special qualities of each historic community. And if every individual is obligated "to say that the world was created for his sake", every individual nation is similarly enjoined to regard its own fulfillment as a supreme value. And just as in the case of an individual, the supreme importance of his own life is not interpreted as a license for selfishness; on the contrary, the motif of personal appreciation is embraced in the larger vision of a society of infinitely important selves, governed in justice and in freedom, so the particularist ambition of each people must be fitted within the concept of a universal society of peoples, abiding by a law that safeguards the rights of all.

Law, like love, is an expression of the Divine Will. While the rule of law is associated with harshness and privation in some literatures, including Kabbalah, it is viewed in the Pharisaic tradition as a sublime art, in which the Lord himself participates. The chief quality of the Messiah will be his supreme capacity as a judge. Hence, in the vision of the future, it is assumed that all nations will then be governed by a universal law. And the pioneering souls of the Kingdom of God may well be those who are even now engaged in preparing the world for the rule of law.

The application of universal law to the governance of mankind presupposes the attainment of three goals—first, the creation of a sense of community among the various nations of the world, second, the establishment of agencies for the investigation and determination of the true facts in every dispute among nations, third, the establishment of enforcement agencies. These three steps are needed in addition to the formulation of norms and principles comprising international law.

The third step can only be taken by governments, and we are still far from that consummation. But, the first and second steps can be taken by individuals, those who feel "called" to "improve the world through the Kingdom of the Almighty". A sense of world-fellowship or world-citizenship, as Philo put it, can only be built up by deeds which demonstrate our responsibility for one another as members of the human race. An international "peace corps" aided by governmental contributions on a generous scale, could be expanded in a generation to involve millions of people. The myriad deeds of helpfulness would generate in the course of time the feeling of belonging to "one world", a feeling which is still pale and feeble in our day. The Jews of the Diaspora and the reborn Israeli nation will, by reason of the impetus of history, as well as the promptings of their faith, ever strive for this consummation.

For the vision of a world-community is for the Jew the substance of his millennial history. It is the one hope that lends meaning to a hundred generations of travail. He has experienced the hurt inflicted by the barriers that divide mankind as thrusts of cold steel into his own flesh. Combining uniquely the roles of prophet and pariah, he stood at the center of the great issues that stirred the passions of the western world. The hydra-headed monster of Antisemitism was involved in all the struggles for the liberation of the mind of modern man from the burdens of ancient hates. Inescapable then is the place of the Jew in the vanguard of those who dream of a world redeemed from hate.

It is in the realm of redemption, that the recognition of mutual need is greatest in both Judaism and Christianity. So, Maimonides allowed that both Judaism and Christianity were "preparing the way" for the coming of the Messiah. In the nineteenth century, Formstecher, Rosenzweig and Kohler declared that the global destiny of Judaism was being fulfilled through the efforts of the Christians. Their scheme was based on the analogy between the sun and its rays—the sun is Judaism, the all-permeating rays are Christianity. Geiger clung to Halevi's analogy of the heart in a living organism, since he believed that the Jews had a special genius for religion. Kohler spoke of the Jewish faith as providing the standards as well as the source of progress toward a universal faith and a redeemed society. Still the bitter polemical note of medievalism was rarely overcome before our own generation. We still have to transcend the residues of bitter rivalry and sheer narcissism in the philosophies of the nineteenth century and return to fundamentals.

In the first place, we recognize that we do not know and cannot presume to know the course of redemption. The Talmudic sages excoriated those who "calculate the end" and those who "press the end". Maimonides adds wisely that in these matters we shall know what the prophets meant only after the events of the eschaton shall have taken place (*Hilkhot Melakhim*, XII). And Jesus, too, affirmed that no one knows the time of the End of Days (Mark 13,32; Acts 1,7).

In the second place, we have to transcend the rhetoric which foisted upon us mountains of misunderstanding. It is said that for Christians, the world is already redeemed, while for Jews, it is unredeemed. This is a specious juxtaposition. We might say with equal justification that for Christians, the world is in a "fallen" and corrupt state, while for Jews, the world is "very good". Actually, the tension in Judaism between an unfinished universe and a radiant vision of redemption was retained in the Christian philosophy of history, as presented in Augustine's "City of God," though Augustine rejected the chiliastic belief. A similar philosophy of history was contained in both faiths. The tannaitic Sages speak of the ongoing struggle between "the righteous who establish the world" and "the wicked who destroy the world", while Augustine speaks of the contention between the two cities; to the Jewish Sages as to the Christian Saint, the outcome was clear and firm (Abot 1,5; The City of God XII, 28). To be sure, Judaism and Christianity project different categories for the judgment of the course of history, but the categories are mutually supplementary at times, mutually challenging at times, and the variations within both faiths are so vast as to render meaningless the ancient controversies about the "fulfillment" of Scriptural verses.

Every creative act of God and every theophany is also redemptive. So, in many rabbinic passages, the Messiah was seen as another Moses, or another Adam. To many Christians, "the second coming" of Jesus was anticipated with the same ardor that the Jews displayed in regard to the Messiah. And in the major trends of Judaism, "the hope of Israel" is inseparable from the redemption of mankind. To a rationalist, like Maimonides, this result will come about through the normal developments of history, without any break in the laws of nature (*Hilkhot Melakhim* XII, 1); to a mystic, like Nahmanides, the End will be achieved through a miraculous intervention in the course of history.[34] To the truly religious person, the boundary between the natural and the supernatural disappears. In any case, during the messianic age, all redeemed mankind will form one universal society and "the covenant-people" will merge within the all-embracing "people of God." But, before the final consummation is attained, the diverse covenanted bodies must advance under their separate banners (Mic 4,5). Yet, they move toward the same goal, "when the Lord will be One, and his Name One". And as they advance along their own diverse paths, they must keep their minds and hearts open, so they can learn from one another. For the course of human history is studded with theophanies that are creative, revelatory and redemptive. The Deuteronomist, in our Massoretic version, calls upon the Israelites to discover their own true being by studying the careers of all nations and all epochs.[35]

The action of God in redeeming mankind, transpires in three dimensions—in release from suffering, in the overcoming of sin, in the attainment of a new scale of values. The pictorial representation of the messianic age in Judaism appears to stress the first more than the second, and the third dimension is in some versions reserved for the World to Come. Actually, the messianic vision of Judaism is complex and many-splendored, and the conquest of sin is central in all versions. If the Israelites repent truly, the Messiah will come and a "renewal of Torah" will take place.[36] The doctrine of the Second Coming in Protestant thought also emphasizes repentance and "rebirth."

A century or so ago, Friedrich Nietzsche articulated the inchoate feelings of his day by his vision of a progressive overcoming of the values of man by those of superman. He envisioned a transvaluation of all values, and he appealed to restless youth to take up the work of God in creating a nobler humanity, since, as he put it, "God is dead". His call sounded plausible to a generation shocked by Darwinian theories. But it led to the "youth-movement" at the turn of the century and then to Nazism. Today, we hear similar calls for new values, also similar declarations of the irrelevance of so-called "God talk." But, values are intrinsically non-disposable. What we do need is a keener grasp of values and their application in our complex times. New values grow out of the inner impetus of old values, not by their dissolution. In the realm of nature, the plants of this season grow out of the organic matter that derives from the rotted bodies of previous years. But, in the realm of spirit, we can transcend the wisdom of the past only if we understand it from within first. Every new advance presupposes the assimilation of ancient insights; else, our progress is illusory, like walking up on a descending escalator.

In our contemporary setting, the three phases of redemption are still very current. For most people the three quests of redemption are secularized. Sin is simply failure and values are sought in a retreat to privatism, or in various forms of negativism. As to suffering, moderns pin their hopes on the progress of science. However, science cannot cure the discontent that derives from interpersonal relations. We may be able to still the pangs of physical hunger, but poverty as relative deprivation is becoming more and more unbearable. For many people, the term sin has lost its theological significance, but if they are at all aware of social problems, they cannot but acknowledge that the malaise of our times is moral-spiritual. The smoldering volcanoes of hate in our urban centers and the bitter disaffection of our youth are fueled by a general feeling of loss of direction as well as by specific causes like war, unemployment and racism. And this absence of a sense of purpose is most disconcerting to us, as religious teachers, since it indicates the measure of our failure. Yet, each religious denomination can easily exculpate itself on the ground that its impact on the education of our youth is extremely marginal. In a society where church and state are separated, and properly so, can the several agencies of faith work together in providing a national *ethos* that is adequate to our times? I disagree most sharply with those who claim that we need a "theology of revolution", but equally, we cannot be content with the traditional role of unyielding conservatism, saying with Alexander Pope, "whatever is, is right."

In the maintenance and creation of new values, the pluralism of the redemptive work of God must be our basic axiom. As in the spheres of revelation and creation, the divine impact hits us from diverse and opposite sides. The Chariot of Ezekiel was lifted up by a wind that came from four directions at once. So, we have to cherish the basic values in our heritage, even while we listen hard to the new and strange music that assaults our ears. And our own way of life, wonderful as it is, may well not be the only way in which divine values are brought into society. Can a pluralistic ecumenism keep us from the sin of self-righteousness? It was this besetting evil of piety that constituted the main theme of the critique that Jesus leveled at the religious establishment of his day. The Sages of the Talmud agreed that the Pharisaic order, with all its greatness, was frequently guilty of false piety. This does not mean that Pharisaism was itself evil. On the contrary, it represented the institutional framework which served as the chrysalis out of which three universal faiths arose. But, every concrete body casts a shadow, when it stands before one source of light. The shadows disappear, though not altogether, when several lamps are lit at different points in the room.

In the Judeo-Christian tradition, God is identified now with one ideal, now with another. He is immanent in the moral order of life.—"Can it be that the Judge of the whole earth will not do justice?"; or, He is love; or He is freedom; or, "The seal of the Holy One is truth"; or, "The beginning of the Torah and its end are lovingkindness"; or, "the Name of the Holy One, blessed be he, is peace". But, while all these ideals are divine, we find that we arrive at a different posture in our social ethic, according to the primacy we grant to one or another to these ideals. Shall we stress freedom at the expense of equality, or compassion at the expense of justice, or truth at the expense of loving-kindness, or peace above all other values? These questions must always be open options to us, for God is the Source of all these values, and we become guilty of idolatry, when we substitute any ideal, no matter how lofty, for the fullness of his Being as the end of our worship. Virtually all the massive evils of our day, from Communism to Fascism to the shortcomings in our own society, may be traced to the exaltation of any one ideal to the point where it excludes the other relevant ideals. This is why the emphasis on pluralism is so salutary. Particularly so, in an age which deems itself to be living on the threshold of the Apocalyptic Era. And is not the crux of our anguish today precisely this widespread mood of apocalyptic hysteria?

It has been noted that a healthy society is one in which the forces of conservation and utopianism are held in balance. Is it not reasonable to hope that in a pluralistic faith-society there is less likelihood of either danger materializing, either a rigid stand-patism or a runaway utopianism?

The challenge of our youth confronts us in three areas—in the ideals of personal life, in the moral temper of the community and in the vision of national purpose. With all the unlovely outbursts of radicalism in recent years, we have to recognize a desperate groping for national integrity, a hunger for the genuine values of love and communalism. Perhaps, the strongest conviction of our radical youth is negativistic—somehow, we, the elders, have not been true to our own ideals. And this feeling is likely to persist. Even if we should establish equity in race relations, feed the hungry and end unemployment, we shall still have a vast problem of rebuilding the sentiment of dedication, of family loyalty, of pride in work and a sense of sharing in the greatness of the nation. And these qualities our nation possessed in far greater measure in the days when a larger percentage of its people lived at the level now called poverty.

Personal values need to be sustained by the bonds of fellowship. What the so-called "secular city" needs most is that intricate network of voluntary organizations, which has enriched the lives of small-town America. And those intertwined institutions were generated by the several covenanted communities. If the unchurched and the unsynagogued constitute today in many cities a seething mass of faceless individuals, some new social structures need to be devised by those who are churched and synagogued to reawaken the sense of personal worth. When Harvey Cox rhapsodizes over the joys of anonymity in the big city, he writes as an intellectual surfeited with public acclaim. He forgets that the biblical Adam demonstrated his humanity when he was able to name all living things. The attraction of communal living for the young is in part at least a frantic escape from loneliness, alienation and anonymity. There is need of an interfaith effort along experimental lines to encourage healthy forms of cooperative communities.

Finally, in respect of the world-community as a whole, we need to think of our collective mission, as members of the greatest industrial nation in the world. The problems are immense, but so are the spiritual rewards. Our national purpose in this space-age can be nothing less than to encourage the emergence of a world-community, viable in its population, with help for the backward peoples, and with security dependent ever more preponderantly on international agencies.

To achieve these ends, all of us that call ourselves "the people of God" must learn to labor together, shoulder to shoulder.

The last *mishnah* of Eduyyoth deals with the function of Elijah the Prophet. In a general way, all the Sages agreed that it was his function "to prepare the way" for the coming of the Messiah. But, how does he go about his work? Said one rabbi, he separates the true from the false; said another, he rectifies the evils and injustices of the past. But, the majority of the Sages, after due deliberation, concluded that reconciliation is more important than either the quest of truth or the demands of an abstract justice. Said they, "it is not his function to make clean or unclean, to repel or to bring near those who were repelled, but to make peace in the world". This is our task.

## Notes to *A Jewish View of the World Community*

[1]Yehezkel Kaufmann, *Toledoth Haemunah Hayisrealit*, vol. VIII. p. 283-300.

[2]See R. H. Charles' *The Apocrypha and Pseudepigrapha of the Old Testament II*, Introduction p. 292-295; references on p 312 and 358.

[3]Emil Schürer, *A History of the Jewish People* (New York 1891) vol. V p 291-292.

[4]See A. Marmorstein's essay on *Poshey Yisrael*. H. J. Schoeps, *Jewish Christianity* (Philadelphia: Fortress Press 1969) concurs in the identification of this term as referring to the Ebionites.

[5]See H. Strack and P. Billerbeck, *Kommentar zum Neuen Testament* on Acts 13, 16 (vol II p 715-723).

[6]H. A. Wolfson, *Philo: Foundations of Religious Philosophy in Judaism, Christianity and Islam* (Cambridge, Harvard 1947) vol. II p 364.

[7]Salo W. Baron, *A Social and Religious History of the Jews*, Vol. I p 375 note 15.

[8]The underlying philosophy of Menahem Meiri and his indebtedness to Maimonides is discussed in Jacob Katz, *Exclusiveness and Tolerance* (New York: Schocken 1962) p. 114-128.

[9]Jehudah Halevi, *The Kuzari* II, 44.

[10]Kaufmann Kohler, *Jewish Theology* (New York: Ktav 1968 reprint) p 323-324.

[11]G. Scholem. *The Messianic Idea in Kabbalism* (New York: Schocken 1971) p 46.

[12]N. Krochmal, *Moreh Nebuchai Hazeman;* Nathan Rotenstreich, *Jewish Philosophy in Modern Times* (New York: Holt, Rinehart and Winston 1968) p 48.

[13]Franz Rosenzweig, *The Star of Redemption* (New York: Holt, Rinehart and Winston 1970) Part I. The original appeared in 1920.

[14]*De Praemiis et Poenis* XX, 123; *Legum Allegoria* II, 69 (Leob Classics edition).

[15]Saadia, *Book of Beliefs and Opinions* (translation by Rosenblatt), Introduction, 6; Maimonides, *Guide for the Perplexed* (translation by Pines) III, 31; Joseph Albo, *Book of Principles* (translation by Husik) (Philadelphia: J.P.S. 1946) III, 25.

[16]*Book of Beliefs and Opinions* Introduction and 1, 3.

[17]*Guide for the Perplexed* I, 36.

[18]*Guide for the Perplexed* III, 28. See the commentary of Shemtov.

[19]*Guide for the Perplexed* II, 23. His "will to believe" is really an appeal to join in the quest of God's nearness as in III, 51.

[20]*The Kuzari* (translated by Hirschfield IV, 16). He regarded Islam and Christianity, for all the persistence of a pagan underground in their ritual, as closer to Judaism than philosophy—ibid. IV, 11, 12, 13.

[21]Moses Cordovero, *Or Neerav*, an introduction to Kabbalah. Understanding is ranked as *The Third Sefirah* after Wisdom and Crown.

[22]Mendelssohn's letter to the Duke of Braunschweig in January 1770; it is discussed in Ravidowitz's article in *Hatekufah* vol. 25 and 26.

[23]Shabbat 23a, where two reasons are given: one legal, based on Deut 17; the other moralistic, based on Deut 32, 7.

[24]*Sifre*, ed. Ish Shalom, Voet-hanan, 32. The text adds, "like Abraham," suggesting the role of a missionary.

[25]Strack and Billerbeck, *Kommentar* vol. IV p. 490.

[26]Rabbi Jacob Emden, *Eṣ Abot*, published in 1756, a commentary on the Ethics of the Fathers.

[27]*Hilchot Melachim*, 10;14 (Constantinople edition).

[28]See I. Heinemann, *Taʿamai Hamiswot* (Hebrew) II p. 95.

[29]Charles Guignebert, *The Jewish World in the Time of Jesus*, (New York 1959) p. 157; G. F. Moore, *Judaism in the First Centuries of the Christian Era* I p. 233.

[30]Strack and Billerbeck, *Kommentar* I p. 925; James Parkes, *The Foundations of Judaism and Christianity*, London 1960, p. 279.

146                        JACOB B. AGUS

[31]Martin Buber, *Israel and the World*, New York 1963 p. 183-213.
[32]Judah Halevi, *Kuzari* II, 44; II, 36. The Torah is the beginning of the manifestation of his Kingdom, III, 17.
[33]Abraham Geiger's battle for Reform was conceived by him as a war of "liberation" from the fetters of nationalism. See *Abraham Geiger and Liberal Judaism* by Max Wiener, Philadelphia 1962, pp. 156, 60, 71. Leo Baeck's conception of Judaism as a ceaseless, dynamic revolution aiming at the unification of man and of thought is summed up in his essay, "The Character of Judaism" in *The Pharisees and other Essays* (New York: Schocken 1947).
[34]See *Sefer Hageulah*, printed in *Kithvei Haramban* Jerusalem 1963 vol. I.
[35]Deut. 32,8. In the Septuagint, each nation has its divine Prince, as in the Book of Daniel. And the Kabbalists assumed that the reason the Israelites were exiled was that they might gather the "holy sparks", wherever they are found.
[36]Lev. Rabba 13,3. Whether a "new Torah" or a "renewal of Torah" was to be given by the Messiah according to the Sages, is a moot point. See Strack and Billerbeck, *Kommentar* III p 577. Recent discussion is found in Urbach's *Hazal* (Jerusalem 1969) p 264-267.

# CONSERVATIVE
# JUDAISM

# CONTINUING CREATIVITY IN
# MAIMONIDES' PHILOSOPHY

MAIMONIDES' CONCEPTION of God appears to be austere, remote and forbidding. He elaborated the historical notion of Negative Attributes in a way which seemed to rob it of religious import.[1]

He stressed that of God we can know only what He is not. God is not a physical being, moving within space, neither is He subject to influences from others, for He transcends the flow of time. We can approach Him most nearly by intellectual reasoning, but then He eludes the grasp of our intellect as well. Even such basic attributes as "wise, powerful and volitional" can be ascribed to Him only in a negativistic way—He is not not-wise, not not-strong, not incapable of willing (*Guide of the Perplexed*, I, 59, 60).

Attributes of action, that is, qualities inferred from the operation of nature, may indeed be postulated of Him, but then, it would seem that no more could be said of Him than could be inferred from the ordinary operations of nature (I, 53). He is "good," because life is on the whole more pleasant than painful (III, 10); He is compassionate because all living things seem to be endowed with all that they need for survival (III, 12). But, He does not break the chains of causality in response to human pleas, or in order to save the righteous from destruction (III, 27).

In medieval as in modern times, Orthodox pietists condemned Maimonides' way of overcoming the crudities of anthropomorphism as a snare and a delusion. Is there any sense in praying to a God, who cannot be placated by supplications; who does not soften the cold and indifferent physical laws of the universe by His gracious intervention; who remains impassive in the face of "the righteous suffering and the wicked prospering?"[2]

To be sure, Maimonides introduces the "leap of faith" as a decisive factor in affirming the doctrine of *creatio ex nihilo* (II, 25). He demonstrates that the Aristotelian argument for the eternity of the cosmos is no more convincing

Originally published in *Dropsie University Anniversary Volume*, ed. by A. Katsh and L. Nemoy.

than the contrary argument proving the creation of the cosmos at some moment in the past. In view of the scales of reasoning being equally balanced, he opts for creation, "in order to make the Torah possible." But, he does not make use of this pragmatic "will to believe" in order to prove the reality of a personal God. On the contrary, he castigates the theologians who design the world to suit their preconceived notions, instead of deducing ideas from the harsh, unyielding data of reality (I, 71). Divine creation makes it possible for us to allow that some biblical miracles did indeed take place, in reality, not merely in a dream, having been built into the unvarying causal chain of the cosmos in the moment of creation (II, 19). But, as to the concept of God, we are left with the strict injunction not to attribute to Him either wrath or compassion, either resentment of the evil ways of men or forgiveness for their sins, should they repent.[3]

David Kaufmann suggests that the *via negativa* is calculated to deepen man's apprehension of the incomprehensibility of God's Will. Its religious import is to impress upon us our human littleness and God's remoteness.[4]

However, Maimonides insists on the *comprehensibility* in principle of all the *mizvot*. And his goal is not the fear of God, but the love of Him. He ranks the ritual commandments below the inner truths of Torah, which lead through the activity of man's intellect directly to the Active Reason, and beyond it to God.

The various *mizvot* of the Torah are indeed designed to instill "the fear of God" in the hearts of the Israelites, as well as to promote the ethical perfection of the individual and of the "divine society" (III, 27). But, the purpose of the inner secrets of the Torah is to teach the love of God.

"Consider how it is explicitly stated for your benefit that the intention of *all the words of this Law* is one end, namely, *that thou mayest fear the Name*, and so on . . . As for the opinions that the Torah teaches us—namely, the apprehension of His Being and His unity, may He be exalted—these opinions teach us love, as we have explained several times. For these two ends, namely, *love* and *fear*, are achieved through two things: love through the opinions taught by the Law, which include the apprehension of His Being as He, may He be exalted, is in truth; while *fear* is achieved by means of all actions prescribed by the Law, as we have explained. Understand this summary" (*Guide* III, 52, Pines' tr. p. 630).

The final exhortation of this section is manifestly a summons to understand the hidden meaning of the entire book, which cannot be disclosed to the general public. Only the saintly philosophers can learn to pierce through the literal teaching of Torah and to reach the heights of metaphysical speculation. It follows that they, and they alone, can learn to "love" God, in the double sense of intellectual contemplation and whole-souled devotion. For it is "the intellect that overflows toward us and is the bond between us and Him, may He be exalted. Just as we apprehend Him by means of that light which He caused to overflow toward us—as it says, 'in Thy light do we see light' " (Psalms 36, 1) (*Guide*, III, 52).

The overflow of the divine intellect comes only to those who attain the highest level of moral and intellectual perfection. As Afudi points out in his commentary on this chapter, the love of God is reached through "true wisdom."

Doubtless, Maimonides was aware of Halevi's contention that "the God of Abraham, Isaac and Jacob" elicits impassioned yearning and personal love from His worshippers, while "the God of Aristotle" leaves them cold ("Kuzari," IV, 16). Throughout the *Guide*, Maimonides polemizes against Halevi and against all the naively pious who imagine that they can approach God either through emotions or through ritual actions. He insists that "it is pure thought deriving from the perfection of the intellect that leads to that impassioned love (*hoshek*) of God, may He be exalted, and as the intellect increases in strength, its light and its joy in what it has conceived are increased" (III, 51). Does he then shut the door to the love of God, and hence to the goal of human life for the majority of the Jewish community?—We note, too, that the counterpart to man's love of God, namely, God's love for man, is inseparable from the same intellectual overflow, for in God, reason, will and power are one.[5] Does Maimonides then deny God's love for the people of Israel, reserving it solely for the saintly philosophers of all nations, and for them only in rare moments of sudden illumination? Such an inference would contradict all that we know of his life's work.

Maimonides set out to reconcile the teaching of Torah with the doctrines of the scientific philosophers, chiefly Aristotle. Did he then achieve his goal by a laborious process of "interpretation," whereby the Aristotelian philosophy was shown to be the true and inner intention of the Torah, while its explicit instructions were meant only for the untutored masses?—Such a solution is ruled out by our knowledge of Maimonides' boundless devotion to Torah, and to Jewish people, wherever they lived.

The difficulty is compounded when we reflect on the fact that, to Maimonides, divine Providence seems to be limited to the philosophers and prophets, whose mind is open to the overflow of Active Reason, and even in the case of these pious sages, the protective guidance of God is restricted to those moments when they are actually enraptured in meditation (III, 51). He allows that the Patriarchs and Moses managed to cling to God, even when they went about their daily tasks. It is this suggestion that Israel Baal Shem Tov turned into the cornerstone of his teaching—namely, to train the body to attend to normal activities, while the soul is totally embraced in the ecstasy of the impassioned love of God (*Tsavoat Horivosh*, ed. Talpiot, 1951, p. 227). However, Maimonides specifically ruled out this possibility for virtually all men, by stating that one like himself cannot aspire to reach that exalted state.[6]

Indeed, Maimonides consistently exempted Moses and the Patriarch Abraham from the generality of mankind. With these exemptions from the range of Providence, it follows that all events are governed by the nexus of cause and effect. Can we then conclude that the universe is a physical mechanism, indifferent to human weal and woe? Did Maimonides himself subscribe to the view that he himself condemns as the essence of heresy, *leth din veleth dayan?* (Vayikra Rabba, 28). If God is conceived only through the *via negativa*, it is hardly possible to dispute this conclusion.

I. Husik blandly assumed that by asserting the supremacy of divine freedom in the original creation, Maimonides had managed to justify not merely the miracles mentioned in Scriptures but also petitional prayer and divine responsiveness to human needs. Husik goes so far as to describe Maimonides' concept of God as "personal."[7]

So wide-ranging a deduction from the doctrine of creation is belied by Maimonides' explicit disavowal of the belief that God listens to prayer, listing it among the "necessary" in contrast to the "true" beliefs (*Guide*, III, 28).

Julius Guttmann is undecided concerning the range of Providence in the Maimonidean world. Commenting on the inferences to be drawn from the doctrine of *creatio ex nihilo*, he points out that Maimonides might have concluded that God interfered regularly in the course of events, breaking into the physical chain of cause and effect in accord with His higher purpose. If He created the cosmos at one time, why not assume a succession of creative acts, miracles and wonders, interrupting the course of nature? But, Guttmann insists, Maimonides stays far from such naive views of popular belief. In particular, he distances himself from this view in his commentary on the *Mishnah*, where he teaches that the miracles were imbedded in the natural course of events at creation, and that all extraordinary events flow out of the immanent forces which were imbedded in nature at the time it was created.[8] "It seems that in the *Guide of the Perplexed* he no longer adheres to this extremist view which disallows any intervention of God within the course of nature, maintaining that such interventions are not breaches of the causal nexus, but that they are embraced in the original plan of the Deity."

If Maimonides believed in a succession of acts of creation, he would not have restricted the range of Providence, as we have seen, and he would not have insisted that the messianic redeemer would come in the normal course of history (*Hilchot Melochim*, end). In his notes, Guttmann casts doubt upon his own interpretation in the text.

Since Maimonides assumed that the cosmos was created through the Perfect Wisdom of God, he was compelled to conclude that no tinkering with its basic mechanism was needed in order for it to function, excepting only those actions which were specifically foretold in the Torah. Maimonides goes to some pains to show that the miracles performed by Moses were in a class by themselves. Decisive for the final import of God's attributes is the nature of Providence, and direct Providence was conceivable to him only for those prophets and pious philosophers whose intellect received the divine over-flow. (*Guide*, III, 18).

Maimonides' contradictory views on the nature of Divine Providence were noticed already by his first translator, Samuel Ibn Tibbon.[9] In his letter to the author, Ibn Tibbon pointed out the difficulty of reconciling the views expressed in III, 17, where Providence is described in the spirit of tradition, as operating in accord with the moral law, with the opinions expressed in III, 23, where the problem of Job is answered by the assertion that true felicity, which is the knowledge of God, is always available to the pious, and with the thoughts presented in III, 51, where Providence is said to be related solely to intellection. Guttman maintains that, in view of these contradictions, the least innovative view should be followed.

But, it would seem that Maimonides would not have covered his traces by deliberate contradictions, if he had intended only to state the traditional view, that God governs the world according to the law of Justice.[10] Indeed, Maimonides boldly separates himself from the prevailing view among the rabbis (III, 17).

S. B. Urbach resorts to some forced interpretations in order to safeguard the orthodoxy of Maimonides. In a note he writes,

"Maimonides asserts the reality of Providence in maintaining that a pattern of reward and punishment for individuals was built into the normal course of human affairs, and the intellectual bond is only a technical instrument, which makes possible the manifestation of this Providence . . . And it is a grievous mistake when some scholars write that 'not ethical considerations but the range of the intellect of people alone determines the nature of Divine Providence' . . ."[11]

Samuel Atlas, argues against Guttmann's notion that Maimonides changed his view of Providence in the *Guide*. The fact is that Maimonides quotes the same midrashim in the *Guide* (II, 19) as in his commentary on the

Mishnah. "Perfection and divine intervention are incompatible; they constitute a contradiction in terms . . ." Miracles, therefore, are pre-ordained
deviations from natural law, which were built into the course of nature, at
creation, and it is only the time of their occurrence that was revealed to the
prophets.[12]

Leo Strauss has expressed the view that Maimonides belongs in the
company of those medieval philosophers whose primary interest was political. Their real philosophy was imparted only to a select few, while their
public writings were designed to foster a well-regulated, well-disciplined
society. Hence, we may assume that the real philosophy of Maimonides was
worlds apart from the plain meaning of the *Guide*.[13]
      Strauss did not undertake to spell out the real philosophy of Maimonides.
However, another scholar, Jacob Becker, did not hesitate to carry this insight
to its logical conclusion. In a brilliant, introductory study, he calls attention
to the distinction between "true beliefs" *(emunot amitiot)* and "necessary
beliefs" *(emunot hekhrohiot)*—the latter being dogmas "necessary for the
abolition of reciprocal wrongdoing or for the acquisition of a noble moral
quality, as for instance, the belief that He, may He be exalted, has a violent
anger against those who do injustice . . . or that He responds instantaneously
to the prayer of someone wronged or deceived . . ." *(Guide*, III, 28).
      Maimonides himself warns time and again that his true teaching is both
concealed and revealed in the *Guide*. He set out to instruct the would-be
philosophers, without hurting the naive piety of those who are not properly
prepared for the dangerous flights of metaphysical speculation *(Guide*, Introduction). He claimed to reveal the mysteries of which the Mishnah speaks—
*maaseh bereshit* and *maaseh merkavah*, the works of creation and of providence. Such mysteries could not be revealed to the general public, only to
one or two worthy scholars in a generation (Hagigah 12b).
      Becker concludes that the entire web of religious attitudes, beliefs and
practices in Judaism was, to Maimonides, merely the outer garment, while
his real thought formed a consistent, philosophical system, best expounded
by Aristotle, but which, he believed, was derived originally from Moses and
the prophets. In this view, all contradictions are resolved, easily; in our view,
this reconciliation is achieved all too easily.
      As we have pointed out, Maimonides' personal integrity hardly squares
with so jaundiced a view of the dichotomies in his thought. We cannot but
assume that he saw an inner coherence between the true ideas, the "golden
apple" in his metaphor, and the external pattern of deeds and opinions, the
filigreed silver that encased the true philosophy *(Guide*, Introduction).

In our view, the so called "necessary truths" were only popular versions of ethereal concepts; hence, they were true in intention, even if in content they were so only in a qualified way. The best example of this relationship is the relation of the dogma of bodily resurrection to the belief in immortality, as described in the Eight Chapters. If we view his works as a whole, we see that in his popular works, Maimonides describes a steady ascent to the truth of speculation. He does not speak of an abyss between two categories of Jews, but of a unitary Torah-community.

Nor does he propound the doctrine of "two truths" which the Parisian Averroists later espoused.[14]

In Becker's view, the cleavage in the *Guide* between the truths of philosophy and the popular religion is so wide and deep as to be totally unbridgeable. It is the "necessary truths" and the laws of the Talmud that Maimonides has in mind when he writes, "For only truth pleases, may He be exalted, and only that which is false angers Him. Your opinions and thoughts should not become confused so that you believe in incorrect opinions that are very remote from the truth and you regard them as Law. For the Laws are absolute truths if they are understood in the way they ought to be" (*Guide*, II, 47).[15]

Becker assumes that the Thirteen Principles of Faith sum up the beliefs of the popular religion, while the truths of philosophy are only three—God's unity, His incorporeality and His eternity.[16]

These three ideas can, of course, be reached only through the *via negativa*. However, they were revealed to Moses "in the cleft of the rock," and through his prophetic successors this teaching was conveyed to the Greek philosophers (I, 71). In Becker's interpretation of Maimonides, the personality of Moses is exalted to the point of attaining a "superhuman" status.

"The entire trend of Maimonides' philosophy flows out of his deep conviction that Moses attained a level that is superhuman, supernatural, divine—he became pure reason."

"The foundation of the *Guide*, which I revealed in this study, is based upon this basic thought—the deification of Moses."[17]

From our standpoint, the radical conclusions of Becker are totally unacceptable. The entire impetus of philosophic thought is against the radical exemption of any one person or any one experience from the laws of logic and structure of being. In our view, the dogma which Maimonides lays down concerning the unique character of Mosaic prophecy was itself rooted in the Torah and promulgated for the same reason, namely, the need of providing stability to the Jewish community. That dogma is therefore in itself a "necessary belief," rather than a "true belief." Yet, as will be shown later, in this dogma, as in all "necessary beliefs," there is an intimate correspondence between the assertion that Mosaic prophecy was unique and its actual functioning as such in the history of mankind.

We can treat as a merely "necessary truth" that which Maimonides himself so categorizes or so suggests—for example, the resurrection of the dead—but not immortality and not the advent of the Messiah.[18]

However, both Strauss and Becker were impelled to suggest radical solutions to the puzzles in the *Guide* by the apparent poverty of Maimonides' conception of the Deity, Who is reached only through the *via negativa*.

We propose herein that the key to the *Guide* was actually the intention of Maimonides to open an affirmative way to God, a *via eminentia*, that would result in a rebirth of Israel and the nations of the world. The *via negativa* was already an accepted doctrine in his day; his contribution was to stimulate interest in the affirmative aspects of Divine Providence.

Four scholars have pointed the way to this interpretation:

Harry A. Wolfson—"While excluding God from knowable universal qualities, the attributes affirm of Him some unknowable qualities, peculiar to Himself, and identical with His essence."[19] In a later article, Wolfson states that Maimonides employed the negative attributes as a way "of justifying the affirmative form in which certain terms must be predicated."[20]

Z. Diesendruck, in his *Die Teleologie bei Maimonides*, refers to "the neovital-istic trends in recent philosophy" for an understanding of Maimonides' attempt to relate the purpose of creation to the noblest goal of human life.[21]

Prof. Solomon Zeitlin, pointed out in his book on Maimonides that the massive labors of Maimonides were future-oriented, toward the establishment of a constitution for Israel reborn.

Prof. Israel Efros brought to the study of the *Guide* his own central insight that the affirmative and negative dimensions of the Jewish religious experience were basically inseparable—*kavod* and *kadosh*.

In his view, Maimonides saw God as an Artist who blended Wisdom and Will in a continuous series of creations.[22]

The abyss between Maimonides' two major works—his *Code* and his *Guide*—is a grand demonstration of the gap between the two philosophies of life that he aimed to overcome. The *Code* is a faithful transcription of the entire Oral Law, without any concession to the claims of reason. So, the sacrificial system is included as a pattern for the future, not merely as an expression of "Divine Cunning," in weaning the Israelites from the practices of ancient pagans.[23] By the same token, the *Guide* follows, on the whole, the logical direction of speculative philosophy, concluding in the famous parable (III, 51), where the philosophers of all nations are ranked far ahead of the Talmudists.

But, with consummate skill, Maimonides proceeds to close the manifest gap, by including in the *Guide*, the reasons for the Commandments, and inserting his philosophical principles into the Code not only at its beginning, where it is clearly stated, but also at its end, where its significance in projecting a new philosophy of history was not generally noticed.

Insofar as the reasons for the Commandments are concerned, the striking fact is that he did not resort to the usual device of justifying all the *mizvot* on the ground that they were given by God, Who Knows best. He insists that they represent God's "Wisdom," as well as His Will; therefore, they must be transparent to human reason. Furthermore, he introduced the concepts of Primary Intention, Secondary Intention and "divine cunning," *beormo beelohit* (III, 32), thereby establishing the historical context for the assaying of the import of the *mizvot*. For this latter emphasis, there was no precedent at all in Jewish philosophy, and he opened himself up to the bitter criticism of all traditionalists. Evidently, this "historical" approach was not a secondary afterthought in his mind, but a central implication of his conception of the course of Jewish and human history.

In fact, the *Code*, for all its detailed description of a static and unvarying law, also stresses both the dynamic and historical aspects of Judaism in projecting the messianic era as a necessary outgrowth of the regular forces operative in history.

The first book of the *Code*, *Sefer Hamada*, was always recognized as a summation of Maimonides' philosophy. Those who attacked the *Guide* generally included this book in their condemnation. But, the intimate connection between the first book of the *Code* and the last chapters, depicting the messianic future, was not previously recognized.

Let us first note the reinterpretation of the messianic hope that Maimonides offers in the last chapters of the *Code*. The messianic era, he claims, will eventuate out of the regular course of history, without any supernatural intervention.

"Do not imagine that in the days of the Messiah anything will be changed in the operation of the universe, or that there will be any innovation in the works of creation."[24] Maimonides cited the dictum of the Babylonian teacher, Samuel, that "in the days of the Messiah, all that will be changed is the suppression of governments." But, then, Samuel and other teachers deferred the domain of total redemption to the appearance of *Olam haba*, when this cosmos will come to an end, and a new form of human life will come into

being, along with the bodily resurrection of the dead. An apocalyptic
*eschaton* is assumed in Talmudic literature. In Maimonides' view, *olam haba* is
the post-mortem state of the souls of the philosophical saints ("Eight Chapters"). And the doctrine of the resurrection of the dead is altogether scorned
in the *Guide* (II, 27). At most, it might be regarded as a "necessary belief,"
calculated to please the vulgar, in accordance with his reasoning in the "Eight
Chapters." In sum, the Messianic Era will grow out of the horizontal course
of history, not through a sudden interruption, or a vertical entrance of the
Divine into the affairs of mankind.

      Still, Maimonides was neither a naturalistic philosopher nor a rationalis-
tic believer in progress a la the nineteenth century liberals. The source of
ethical progress was, in his view, the persistent thrust of the Divine Power
and Wisdom, which are manifested in the operation of the Holy Spirit and
prophecy. He was liberal enough to recognize that this Divine nisus operated
among the Christians and the Moslems, as well as within Jewry, since these
religions promulgated faith in God and devotion to the ethic of Holy
Scripture.[25] But, the Torah-society was for him the unique instrument of
Divine guidance for all men, since "all of existence is like one living
organism" (I, 71). Hence, the task of readying the Jewish community for its
central role in the course of redemption.

      To be sure, the Jewish people generally cannot possibly aspire to the rank
of prophecy, but they can provide the social matrix for the emergence of
prophets and men inspired by the Holy Spirit. Here is where his organismic
view of society became central. All the cosmos is as one organism (I, 72),
with the saints and the philosophers bringing down the renewing vitality of
Divine Power to the society of mankind. And within the body of mankind,
the Torah-society is a similarly constituted organism. Since the Holy Spirit
stimulates statesmanship and inventiveness as well as devotion to the common good, we can readily acknowledge its significance for the advance of all
the aspects of human culture. Indeed, the rebirth of the Jewish people and
the revitalization of the human order are interdependent. The Messiah
himself is both a universal prophet and the King of Israel reborn.[26] His
advent depends on the general progress of humanity and on the resurgence of
the prophetic genius, in all its manifestations.

      But is there any hope for the reemergence of prophecy, either in Israel or
among the nations? Maimonides, unlike Halevi, did not confine the gift of
prophecy either to the people of Israel or to the land of Israel (*Kusari*, I, 93–
103). All that the Israelites lacked basically was peace of mind (II, 36).
However, as he saw it, the Talmudists circle around the "palace of the King,"
without daring to enter through its portals, by way of philosophic meditation

(III, 51). It was necessary for him to compile the *Code*, which renders superfluous the study of other works, in order to channel the intellectual energy of Jewish people first toward secular disciplines, and second, to the unflagging ardor of philosophic meditation, culminating in the rhapsodic states of the Holy Spirit (*Code*, Introduction). The preoccupation of Jewish savants with the perplexing casuistry of the Talmud prevented them from devoting themselves completely to the contemplation of the great truths—the problems of creation and providence.

As to Jewish society generally, the first book of the *Code* is intended to acquaint them with the elementary principles of philosophical speculation. "What is the right way to the love of God and the fear of Him?" His answer is to contemplate the wondrous works of creation, recognizing His Infinite Wisdom, so that we be transported by the ecstasy of His Glory, and then be moved to reflect on our human frailty and finitude, and that we tremble in fear (*Sefer Hamada*, I, 2).

Here, then, there is no attempt to approach God by way of *mizvot*, but through intellectual meditation, as explained in the *Guide* (III, 52).

Intellectual contemplation must be based upon the attainment of perfection in one's moral qualities. These in turn are described in the terms of philosophy—the happy medium between two extremes and "the imitation of God" (Hilkhot Deot, I, 4, 6). The latter principle, mentioned by Plato in *Theaetetus*, is manifestly contrary to the entire trend of Maimonidean thought. If we cannot ascribe to God any anthropomorphic qualities, how can we emulate His ways? Maimonides replies that the prophets attributed such qualities to God, for tactical reasons, in order to recommend the corresponding human virtues for imitation.[27] This dialectical twist might appear to be a *tour de force*, but it is really central to the Maimonidean philosophy. The goal of life is to attain "the nearness of God," as much as possible—first through moral training, then through intellectual disciplines, and finally by means of philosophical meditation. The imitation of God, in this sense, implies these three aspects of the unending quest, which is inspirational and prophetic in character.[28]

Second, the essence of the Divine influence, consists in the bestowal of wisdom and redemptive power to ever greater circles of humanity. Just as God is outgoing, with His "Goodness renewing daily the works of creation," so the recipient of the Divine power is driven to share his bounty with others. He is charged with the task of bringing more and more people to the high levels of devotion and inspiration that he has attained. The recipient of God's "flow" must undertake to bring *hesed*, steadfast love, and *zedek*, charity, as well as *mishpat*, justice, into the affairs of society (III, 54).

It follows that the inspired statesman and philosopher becomes an instrument of divine redemption within the course of history, helping to perfect human society, step by step, toward the climax of the messianic era.

This redemptive power, deriving from God through the Active Reason, is manifested in many and diverse ways that all can see, though God in Himself transcends our grasp. Human culture, in its esthetic forms as well as in its industrial arts, is reinvigorated by the impact of Divine energy upon the imaginative faculties of poets, artists, inventors and statesmen (II, 45). So culture and religion go hand in hand. The dynamic guidance of prophets is the key factor in the organization of an ideal society, one that promotes the intellectual climate of the community as well as its moral and esthetic disciplines (II, 38 and 40). But the esthetic and industrial arts are also produced by the Divine redeeming power and they are essential for the building of the noble society of the future. In a very real sense, Maimonides propounded a philosophy of universal culture, as well as of universal history, under the guise of an interpretation of biblical symbolism. His theological terminology served to conceal his broad-gauged humanism; indeed, his plea is for a manysided renaissance of culture, with the revived genius of prophecy at its heart.

But the impassioned humanism of Maimonides was not obtained at the cost of interpreting away the landmarks of Torah. On the contrary, he believed that he uncovered the original dimensions and full meaning of Torah. His philosophy remained theocentric, with the doctrine of *creatio ex nihilo* at its heart. All creation continues to be directly dependent upon the Creator—this thesis was to him not an abstract proposition, but the living core of his ardent piety (I, 69). For the purpose of man's life is "the apprehension of true opinions and clinging to the divine reason that flows toward him" (III, 8). *hasogat daat amiti bekhol davar vehidovek hasechel hoelohi hashofea olov.* This "Divine Reason" is inseparable from His Power, in the operation of Providence, which directs the lives of great men as well as the entire human race. *aamin shehahashgaha nimshechet ahar hasechel umdubeket bo.* His philosophy remained Israel-centric, in that a society patterned after the Torah is alone calculated to serve as the nucleus of mankind redeemed.

To recognize the new horizons of the Maimonidean philosophy, we have to give full weight to the two degrees of inspiration that he considers to be pre-prophetic.

The first degree is that known in our literature as *ruah hakodesh*. But in the scheme of Maimonides, it is purged of theurgic or magical implications. Instead, the term is given a broad, secular denotation.

"The first of the degrees of prophecy consists in the fact that an individual receives divine help (*ezer elohi*) that moves and activates him to a great, righteous and important action—such as the deliverance of a community of virtuous people from a community of wicked people, or the deliverance of a virtuous and great man, or the conferring of benefits on numerous people *hashpia tov al anashim zabim* (literally, 'making good overflow')" (Pines' trans. *Guide*, II, 45, p. 196).[29]

If we bear this definition of *ruah hakodesh* in mind when we read of the Divine Overflow affecting only the imaginative faculty, we recognize its broad, secular implications.

"If again the overflow reaches only the imaginative faculty, the defect of the rational faculty deriving either from its original natural disposition or from insufficiency of training, this is characteristic of those who govern cities, while being the legislators, the soothsayers, the augurs and the dreamers of veridical dreams. All those who do extraordinary things by means of strange devices and secret arts, and withal are not men of science, belong likewise to this third class."

Here, then is a description of skill in statesmanship and industrial inventiveness, as inclusive as one could possibly express in the last decade of the twelfth century.

The second degree of pre-prophetic inspiration is attained when some orators or authors are moved to compose great literary works. They experience the feeling of being seized by a superior power—"That another force has come upon him and made him speak . . . concerning governmental or divine matters."[30]

Maimonides includes in this category the wisdom and poetic works in the Bible. Their authors did not attain the double perfection of both the imaginative and the rational faculties. The imaginative faculty includes an intuitive power, which predisposes its possessor to anticipate future events.[31]

It is important to note that the two pre-prophetic degrees of inspiration are of a general, human character. "It is a part of the wisdom of the deity with regard to the permanence of the species . . ." (II, 40)—that is, the human race—that statesmen, legislators and governors should arise to impose laws upon their respective communities. If those laws do not take account of the need to develop speculative perfection, they belong to the class of *nomoi*—that is, they were designed by the impact of the Active Reason upon men "who are perfect only in their imaginative faculty" (II, 40, Pines', p. 384).

We note that Maimonides distinguishes between the law of pagans and those of cultured people (II. 39)—only the latter were the product of pre-prophetic, divine inspiration. But, all of mankind is a species that Providence seeks to preserve, even as it preserves all biological species by means of instincts. While man is not the purpose of all creation, he is the most perfect of all creation, and his perfection is in the future (III, 13). Divine inspiration, in its pre-prophetic levels takes the place of instincts, pre-disposing some to be governed, others to govern (II, 37). The latter fall into various categories—poets, statesmen, inventors, artists, and at their best, prophets. So prophecy is not a unique quality, but a blending of all other qualities, in their right proportions (II, 36). It follows that religion is the perfect harmonization of all of man's capacities (II, 39). It generates the various facets of culture and imposes a celestial harmony upon the conflicting forces in society.

From all the above, there emerges the outline of a philosophy that strikes a responsive chord in the hearts of moderns. We might describe it as panentheistic, in contrast to the pantheism of Spinoza. Nature is in God, but God is beyond nature. God works through the laws of nature, but He also supplements them by fresh infusions of spiritual power. Yet reason and the quest of truth are the surest guides to His nearness. "For only truth pleases Him and only falsehood angers Him" (II, 47). He imparts of His creative power most fully to prophets and fragmentarily also to philosophers and statesmen, inventors and poets. In this manner, He impels human society to ever greater heights of moral and intellectual achievement. Ultimately, the messianic world of moral and physical perfection will come into being, as a result of these successive upward thrusts.

But while the dynamic, creative energy of Divine Providence cannot be forced, it can be tapped with great assurance that it will be forthcoming. When a morally disciplined person, with a refined imagination and a keen intellect, achieves the climax of philosophical intuition, then "almost surely" the good God will not withhold prophecy from him (II, 32). Maimonides differs from both the Orthodox, who describe prophecy as a divine fiat, and the philosophers who consider it a purely human achievement. Since God is freedom, the entrance of His Reason and Will into the mind of man cannot be subject to the mechanical laws of necessity. Since He is also good, eager to bestow goodness, He will surely bestow the prize of prophecy upon the deserving ones. As a result of this antinomy, we can only prepare ourselves for the occasional thrusts of divine power, especially insofar as they affect those of us who can only qualify for preprophetic bounties.[32]

In assimilating prophecy to speculative perfection, on the one hand, and to all phases of culture, on the other hand, Maimonides created a theory of secular culture and progress, that is reminiscent of such modern panentheists as Bergson, Alexander, Whitehead and Hartshorne. While "the origin of species" was outside his ken, he saw the continuous creativity of Divine Providence in the course of human history, for "the final intention is to bring about perfection" (III, 13). He did not merely combine religion and philosophy; he created a religious philosophy in which prayer and meditation were organically related to all the domains of secular culture. The revival of prophecy was essential to the progress of mankind as a whole, and he expanded the horizons of prophecy far beyond their biblical limitations.

Far from being a divided soul, or a manipulative philosopher, Maimonides was a thoroughly systematic thinker and pietist—at once the noblest exponent of Judaism and a prophet of humanity redeemed.

Maimonides' image of the cosmos was so vastly different than ours that we fail to note its similarity to what Hartshorne calls the "convergent classical philosophy." In his view, the earth was the center of all creation, with a series of "spheres," surrounding it. The "spheres" were composed out of a heavenly matter that was not subject to corruption, and they moved in a circular fashion in order to articulate their love and knowledge of God. Each sphere was endowed with its own Intelligence. God Himself transcended all spheres (I, 71); and by means of the sphere of Active Reason, He continued to bestow the thrusts of His creative energy upon those individuals whose personalities had become receptive to His power. Furthermore, all living things were marked by the quality of purposiveness, in so far as their matter was capable of receiving the imprint of His Being (III, 19). All birds and animals manifest an inherent wisdom and an intricate network of interdependence. Indeed, the purposiveness of life is the noblest proof of the existence of God, for all living beings are impelled by the longing to imitate Him (I, 69):  . . .

Here, then, is a cosmos, that is truly one organism, and the soul of its soul is God. From Him comes the power that sustains life in all the species of plant and animal life and, in the case of mankind, the preprophetic and prophetic forces that impel human society to the perfection of the messianic era. Even death is "very good" in this perspective of continuous spiritual growth (III, 10). In a world where God is the Goal as well as the Source of all existence, it is but natural that the purpose of man's life should be, "to reach for truth in all things and to cling to the reason of God that streams upon him" (III, 8).

We recall that Leibnitz was led to postulate that ours is "the best of all possible worlds," since it was designed by the Perfect Being. To Maimonides, "the best of all possible worlds" for man was still in the future, and God was steadily propelling mankind upward and toward that goal. Even while insisting on His negative attributes, Maimonides suggests this goal when he asserts that he can think of no better metaphor for God acting upon His world than that of "a captain in the ship" (I, 58). Rather than make use of the rabbinic image of the Master of the Palace (Baal Habirah) (Genesis Rabba 39, 1), he prefers the dynamic image of the Captain in a ship, leading His charges closer and closer to the haven of perfection.

It is through the proliferation of divine wisdom and creative energy that all rivalries and hatreds will be overcome and the messianic era will dawn (III, 11).

The perfection of humanity in the days of the Messiah will be entirely "natural," as Maimonides takes pains to clarify in his *Code*. But this "natural" consummation is assured, because of the several ways in which the Divine nisus penetrates this earthly world.[33]

Nature *(teva)*, on its lowest levels, is totally mechanical and invariant. On a higher cosmic level, we encounter the complexities of organic life, which derive intelligent guidance from God. The complexity of structure in the eye cannot be due to fortuitous mechanical configurations (III, 19). "Nature is not endowed with intellect and the capacity for goverance . . . according to us, it is the act of an intelligent being." Organic life is then more than "nature," though at times Maimonides continues to speak of living beings as instances of nature's wisdom—"If you consider the divine actions—I mean to say the natural actions—the deity's wily graciousness and wisdom, as shown in the creation of living beings . . ." (III, 32, Pines' translation, p. 525).

There is no clear dividing line between the "natural" and the divine, but a steady ascent from Matter to God, from the simplest events in inanimate nature to the highest reaches of the prophetic personalities.

Above the level of animal life, the human race is more open to the constant "flow" of Divine power. Mankind was denied the sure guidance of invariant instincts, and humans differ in abilities and opinions. To survive, the society of mankind had to be sustained even in pagan or primitive times by preprophetic and pseudo-prophetic leaders, who managed to impose an order of some sort upon the undisciplined multitude (II, 40). Even the "Sabeans," or pagans, were governed by rulers and "diviners," whose gifts were imaginative and non-rational. The divine "flow" in their case was minimally rational and largely intuitive (III, 38).

On a still higher level, Providence operated in human society through the agency of statesmen, who worked out systematic laws for the governance of men, the so called *nomoi* of the Greeks and Romans. Here, the effect of the pre-prophetic divine power was manifested not merely in the relative rationality of the *nomoi*, but also in the readiness of cultured peoples to abide by these laws. For, as we have noted, the submission of people to government is an effect of a Divine incursion into society. Other consequences of preprophetic inspiration are the various inventions and artifacts which serve to enhance the quality of human life (II, 45, first degree) (II, 37).

The emergence of prophets, like Abraham, impelled humanity to a still higher level, but then only individuals were directly affected by the Patriarchs. The critical moment in the advance of humanity toward perfection occurred at Sinai, when Moses concluded the covenant with the people of Israel.

The prophecy of Moses was devoid of any imaginative elements. It was therefore in a class by itself. Yet he, too, was only human and when he was deeply anguished by the disaster that followed the report of the spies, he declined in his imaginative perfection, and for many years in the wilderness he failed to attain the noblest heights of prophecy (II, 36). For prophecy is the reception of God's *nisus* toward perfection and completeness. Hence, one must be perfect in all respects—physically, intuitively or imaginatively, morally and rationally.

Maimonides had to rank the prophecy of Moses far beyond that of other prophets, in keeping with the teaching of the Torah itself, and in order to foreclose the possibility of the Mosaic law being superseded by the laws of Jesus or Mohammed. As we noted earlier, this is an instance of a "necessary belief" (III, 32). Still, he makes a special point of stressing the exceptional character of "the miracles" performed by Moses—they were done "before the eyes of all Israel" (II, 35). In view of Maimonides' insistence that all miracles were embedded into the invariant nexus of the laws of nature (II, 25), this reference to the testimony of all Israel appears strange at first glance. Halevi employed this argument to prove the truth of the Jewish faith as against the claims of other religions. But Maimonides is not interested in this argument in the *Guide*. In general, he plays down the range and the persuasive power of miracles.

Manifestly, the presence of all Israel at Sinai was all-important to him, as proof of the divine potency of Mosaic prophecy. The divine flow that comes to the prophet compels him to disseminate his message (II, 37); at the same time, the divine power predisposes the people to listen to the prophet and to obey his message (II, 40). The role of the prophet is, after all, to satisfy the human need for inner coherence in society. The readiness "to be governed" is as important as the courage and intuitive power that statesmen need in order to govern.

So, at Sinai, the Israelites attained only the rational understanding of the first two Commandments; they heard a mighty voice and saw impressive sights. But, they did not attain the rank of prophecy and did not hear "the voice of God," as it were. But they were filled with the passive consequence of prophecy—the readiness to obey and follow the teaching of God through Moses. So they assented in the famous words, *na'ase venishma*. There was only one Torah and that was the Torah of Moses (II, 39). For if a thing is the most perfect of its kind, other things must be less perfect, "either through excess or defect."

The prophets who came after Moses called upon the people to be faithful to the Torah of Moses. So it is the assembly of the Israelites at Sinai that conveys to us the meaning of history. The prophet and the people stand as one before God, with the prophet attaining the highest degree of human openness to the Thought and Will of God, and the people dedicating themselves to live in accord with the Torah revealed to the prophet.

The prophet's vision, at its highest potential, and the humble obedience of the people were jointly solemnized in the convenant. The messianic era will achieve the fulfillment of the Sinaitic covenant, involving the whole of mankind in a renewed bond between prophetic-philosophical vision and popular obedience. Until that day, the virtue of obedience will be fostered by the Israelites through the observance of the Oral Law, as formulated in the *Code*, and the embers of prophecy will be nurtured and protected by the saintly philosophers of all monotheistic faiths.

Here, then, the *Code (Yad Hahazakah)*, in all its many-faceted complexity, and the *Guide*, in all its abstract rationality, converge to reveal the two aspects of Judaism—the infinite quest of the philosophers and prophets, on the one hand, and on the other, the balanced, harmonious way of the Israelites, in the first place, and ultimately of mankind.

In all these levels of the entrance of Divine power into human life, we cannot draw a line between the "natural" and the "supernatural," since the Divine power is the source of all purposiveness in nature, and there is a gradual ascent of beings on the cosmic ladder extending from inanimate nature to the Torah-society. Indeed, Maimonides writes of Torah as being both natural and not natural (II, 40). "Therefore, I say that the Law, although it is not natural, enters into what is natural. It is a part of the wisdom of the deity with regard to the permanence of this species of which He has willed the existence, that He put it into its nature that individuals belonging to it should have the faculty of ruling" (Pines' translation, p. 382):

Maimonides' philosophy is dualistic, in the sense that all things are composed of Matter and Form, with Matter being the source of imperfection—hence, of evil (II, 14). A righteous person might encounter many troubles, on account of the matter in his body, which the Lord cannot change.[34]

Maimonides designates Matter as Satan, but Satan is not a selfexistent force, cunning and malicious.[35] There is no hell, much less an inferno of eternal fire for Satan to preside over. The wicked, whose potential higher soul was never actualized, simply disintegrate at death. But the philosophical saints can actualize their potential rational soul and thereby attain immortality.

In this world, Satan cannot long delay the ultimate attainment of human perfection.[36] For the divine *nisus* in its two preprophetic stages is at work among Christians and Moslems, as well as Jews, impelling mankind to the *Eschaton* through the processes of history.

## Notes to Continuing Creativity in Maimonides' Philosophy

[1]The critics stated "that a being who cannot be comprehended by their thoughts and of Whom they cannot form a rational image, so that He can only be described by negations, does not exist at all." Iggeret Hakenaot, printed in *Kovez Teshuvot Ha-Rambam*, Lipsia, 1859, cited in the introduction.

[2]For a review of the Maimonidean controversy, see N. Brüll, "Die Polemik für u. gegen Maimuni," *Jahrbücher für T. Geschichte u. Literatur*, vol. IV. Also J. Sarachek, *Faith and Reason, The Conflict over the Rationalism of Maimonides*, New York 1935.

[3]In his *Iggeret Tehiyat Hametim*, he distinguishes between the miracle which breaks with "customary nature" and the one which defies reason.

[4]David Kaufmann, *Geschichte der Attributenlehre in der Jüdischen Religionsphilosophie des Mittelalters*, Gotha, Friedrich Andreas Perthes, 1877, pp. 471–501.

[5]A'had Ha'am maintained in his justly famous essay on Maimonides, "Shilton Hasekhel," that the latter was a pure rationalist.

"Whoever knows in what esteem our ancestors of that period held the study of the Torah will not be surprised that many wise men and rabbis were driven to the conclusion that 'this Chapter was not written by the Master, or if it was, it should be suppressed, or best of all, burned.' "

"Poor, simple men! They did not see that this chapter (III, 51) could not be either suppressed or burned except in company with all the other chapters of Maimonides' system . . ." (See commentary of Narboni on III, 51).

A'had Ha'am maintained also that Maimonides was impelled to write the *Guide*, not out of religious feeling, since "religious emotion certainly gained nothing" from his efforts, but only by "the national sentiment."

An English translation by Leon Simon of A'had Ha'am's essay is included in the reprint by Arno Press of the *Maimonides Octocentennial Series*.

[6]Pines points out that the Arabic phrase can be construed to say—"someone like myself cannot aspire to guide others with a view to their achieving this rank" (Pines, *op. cit.*, p. 624).

[7]"Mechanical necessity as a universal explanation of phenomena would exclude free will and the efficacy of prayer as ordinarily understood . . . A miracle is a discontinuity in the laws of nature brought to pass on a special occasion by a personal being *in response to a prayer* or in order to realize a given purpose" (I. Husik, "Medieval Jewish Philosophy," Macmillan, 1930, p. 274. italics, mine).

[8]J. Guttmann, *Haphilosophia shel Hayahadut*, Jerusalem, 1951, p. 158.

[9]Z. Diesendruck, *Hebrew Union College Annual*, 11, pp. 341–366.

[10]J. Guttmann, *op. cit.*, p. 392, note 453.

[11]Simha Bunim Urbach, *Amudai Hamahshavah Hayisrealit*, Jerusalem, 1956, vol. 4, p. 401.

[12]S. Atlas, "Moses in the Philosophy of Maimonides, Spinoza, and Solomon Maimon, *Hebrew Union College Annual*, XXV, p. 374.

[13]Leo Strauss, "On Abravanel's Philosophy and Political Thinking," *Spinoza's Critique of Religion*. See also J. Guttmann, *op. cit.*, p. 394, note 476.

[14]In medieval Jewish philosophy, this doctrine was maintained by Isaac Albalag, in *De-ot Haphilosophim*.

[15]J. Becker, *Mishnato Hafilosofit shel Horambam*, Tel Aviv, 1957, p. 47.

[16]Becker, *op. cit.*, p. 48, *Guide*, III, 28.

[17]Becker, *op. cit.*, p. 129.

[18]Bodily resurrection is expressly reinterpreted in the Eight Chapters. In the *Guide*, II, 27, it is referred to as the belief of those who interpret the Midrashim literally.

[19]*JQR*, New Series, VII, 22.

[20]"Ginzberg Jubilee Volume," pp. 411–46.

[21]*Hebrew Union College Annual*, V (1928), pp. 415–534.

[22]I. Efros, *Haphilosophia Hayehudit Bimai Habenayim*, Devir, 5727, I, p. 204.

[23]It is interesting to note that Rabad, Maimonides' critic, a mystic in the Kabbalistic tradition, foresaw an ethereal transmutation of the sacrificial regimen. "This has been revealed to

me by God's mysterious instruction to those who fear Him." Salo W. Baron, *A Social and Religious History of the Jews*, VIII, p. 41 and note 45, p. 292.

[24]*Code*, Hilchot Melachim, XII, 1.

[25]Hilchot Melachim, X, 12, the uncensored Constantinople edition.

[26]*Iggeret Teman*, edition Goldman, p. 96.

[27]Hilchot Deot, I, 6.

[28]In *Guide*, I, 69, Maimonides speaks of the purpose of all existence as being the imitation of His Being. Z. Diesendruck sees in the concluding sentences of this chapter the final summation of Maimonides' teleology—the purpose of creation is to make possible man's free *imitatio Dei*. Man can rise "above nature." *Op. cit.*, pp. 530, 533.

[29]We note that the "Messiahs of Israel," impelled by the Holy Spirit, may not always succeed in their endeavors. Samson and Saul failed in the end, though they were successful initially. So, in the last chapter of his *Code*, Maimonides describes Bar Kochba as a paradigmatic messiah, though his enterprise ended in a terrible catastrophe. Similarly, in his *Iggeret Teman*, he speaks reverently of a pseudo-messianic prophet in the days of his father, concluding, "may his memory be blessed." Similarly in Bergson's *Creative Evolution*, the élan vital does not always succeed. *Iggeret Teman*, edition Solomon Goldman, 1950, p. 112. *Iggrot Harambam*, edition "Rishonim," Tel Aviv, 1951, p. 195. Maimonides mentions this enthusiast as a *hassid*, in his responsa (*Kovetz Teshuvot*, I, 26).

[30]Pines' interpretation of "another force" as being different from the one operative in the first degree is illogical. The Divine flow is always the same. The differences are due to the variations of the receptive faculties. "Another force" is simply the subjective feeling of the recipient, since on this level, he is fully awake and conscious. The imaginative faculty makes one attribute inner experiences to external stimuli (II, 36. Pines, p. 379). Al Harizi's translation agrees with this interpretation.

[31]Pines' translation of the Hebrew, *Koah homeshaer*, as "the faculty of divination" is rendered by Friedlander as "an intuitive faculty," which is the meaning that best fits the context.

[32]See Afudi, II, 32, who assumes dissimulation on the part of Maimonides.

[33]Alvin J. Reines, in his *Maimonides and Abrabanel on Prophecy* (Cincinnati, 1970), describes Maimonides' religion as "naturalistic." He claims that Maimonides regarded "prophecy as a natural event" (XXXI). He disputes the notion "that the special divine will plays a role in every occurrence of prophecy." He takes issue with Diesendruck, who maintained that prophecy is the direct creation of God. (S. Diesendruck, "Maimonides Lehre des Prophetie" in *Jewish Studies in Memory of Israel Abrahams*, Vienna, 1927).

From our analysis, it appears that the categories of "natural" and "supernatural" do not apply to the universe of Maimonides. God's role in prophecy is not a capricious act of will that is totally undetermined. It is not a new act of *creatio ex nihilo*, but a thrust toward greater perfection and rationality. The contrast between the terms, natural-supernatural and immanent-transcendent, is great indeed. In the latter case, there is a persistent, creative drive, rising by degrees from the lower pole of reality that is Matter to God, Who is the "Purpose of all purposes" (III, 13). As Diesendruck points out, Maimonides expanded the role of purpose in the cosmos far beyond its range in Aristotle. Z. Diesendruck, "Hatachlit Vehataarim Betorat Harambam," *Tarbitz*, I, p. 106.

In our view, the Jewish philosophy of history, which Maimonides reinterpreted in the sense of a continuous drive toward perfection in human history, transformed his understanding of the relation of God to mankind. The remote God of Aristotle became a dynamic Presence, ever ready to inspire those who open their hearts and minds to Him, prodding the human race with "wily graciousness" (*he^cormo be^elohit*) (III, 32) toward messianic fulfillment.

[34]Shem Tov's summation in III, 14.

[35]David Neumark in his *Toldot Hophilosophia Beyisroel* (Jerusalem, 1971, III, pp. 341–418), maintains that Maimonides eliminated matter altogether from his view of reality. Neumark describes Maimonides' philosophy as an anticipation of the neo-Kantian, "critical" philosophy. In our judgment, his interpretation is unconvincing.

[36]We have referred to the two last paragraphs of Maimonides' *Code* "Hilchot Melachim," Constantinople, uncensored edition. A translation of these paragraphs is printed in Twersky's "A Maimonides Reader," pp. 226, 227.

Maimonides' universalism is expressed also in his famous letter to R. Hisdai Halevi, *Kovetz Teshuvot Horambam*, Lipsia, 1859, II, no. 24.

"In regard to your inquiry concerning the nations, know that the Compassionate one seeks the heart. Everything depends on intention. Therefore, our Sages said that the pious among the nations . . . belong to the World to Come."

# NEO-MAIMONISM

THE TERM, "Neo-Maimonism" is coined in the same manner and for the same reason as the well-known designations—Neo-Aristotelianism, Neo-Platonism, Neo-Thomism, Neo-Kantism and Neo-Hegelianism. Strictly speaking, we should speak of Neo-Maimonideanism, but we prefer the shorter form, for the sake of convenience.

There are only so many basic positions that a thinker can assume vis a vis the riddle of existence. And all serious scholars are aware of the historical roots of their thoughts. So, the ends of logical clarity and historical perspective are both advanced when a contemporary movement is described as a version of a well-known historical position.

In the case of Neo-Maimonism, this policy is all the more to be commended because the "Guide of the Perplexed" served as a touchstone of philosophic speculation ever since it appeared. To the religious liberals, it was the pillar of light, blazing a bold pathway through the arid wilderness of contending passions and superstitions. To the naive and the literalists, the philosophy of Maimonides was a snare and a delusion, even when they admitted that his Code was a most precious part of the sacred tradition. In a sense, the Maimonidean controversy continued unabated unto our own time. While in the thirteenth century, the question for the literalists in regard to the "Guide" was "to burn, or not to burn," the subsequent centuries rephrased the alternatives, but they continued the debate. The rise of Kabbalah and its triumph, after the expulsion from Spain, did not succeed in suppressing completely the influence of Jewish rationalism. And every new wave of enlightenment was powerfully assisted by the momentum of the Maimonidean philosophy. If Hassidism generally scorned the "Guide," the *Maskilim* felt that it propelled them directly into the intellectual world of the end of the eighteenth century. Moses Mendelsohn found that Maimonides prepared him to understand Spinoza, Descartes and Leibnitz. Solomon Maimon went directly from Maimonides to Kant. Several decades later,

Originally written for *Conservative Thought Today* (New York: Rabbinical Assembly).

Naḥman Krochmal and Samuel David Luzzatto defended opposing positions in regard to the place of Maimonides within authentic Judaism. In the past century and a half, when Jewish intellectuals were beguiled by the spirit of the times to move in different directions, drawn now to the nationalist-romanticist pole, now to the humanist-rationalist pole, it was the adequacy of the Maimonidean synthesis that they debated.

Our generation is called upon to undertake a basic reexamination of our convictions and goals. We are no longer driven by desperation to fight for sheer survival. In Israel and in the free world, we are sufficiently secure to face the ultimate questions and to take seriously Maimonides' admonition to let our ideas grow out of the facts rather than to tailor our convictions to suit our peculiar situation.

On the other hand, we cannot gainsay the obsoleteness of Maimonides' picture of the cosmos, with its basic categories of Matter and Form, its four earthly elements and the ethereal substance of the heavenly bodies, its many "spheres" and "intelligences," and its deference to Aristotle's authority in regard to all matters "below the moon." Also his knowledge of comparative religion and of history was inevitably minute by our standards, though he pioneered the exploration of these themes for the understanding of the *mizvot*. Again, we cannot assent to his aristocratic disdain for the common people. Yet, if we transpose the living core of his thought into the structure of nature and history, as they appear to us, we arrive at a philosophy of life that is balanced and harmonious. Neo-Maimonism also harks back to Maimonides in terms of the approaches he rejected—the personalistic voluntarism of Ibn Gabirol, the ethnic romanticism of Judah Halevi, the "reductionism" of those who confined all thought within "the four ells of Halachah," the imaginative exuberance of proto-kabbalists and even the mild, superficial rationalism of Saadia. Each one of the rejected viewpoints has its counterpart in our time. Neo-Maimonism, therefore, is defineable negatively, as well as affirmatively.

## Tension at the Heart of Reality

We begin with the pathways that Maimonides disdained to follow. He conceived his task to be the resolution of the perplexities troubling the educated Jew. On the one hand, such a person could not conceive of life without the guidance of Torah and the assurance of redemption contained in it. On the other hand, he was made uneasy by the literal meaning of many verses in the Torah, which described the actions of God in crass anthropomorphic terms. M.* prefaces his mighty effort with the confession that the contradictions in Torah cannot be understood with full clarity. The wisest can only get occasional, lightning-like flashes of the truth. ("More Nebuhim," Petiha. Pines' translation p. 7) Only Moses can be said to have perceived the mysteries of creation and providence in the full light of day. But, Moses is more a dogmatic than a historical figure, with the beliefs concerning him falling into the category of "necessary truths," to be discussed presently.

At this point, we call attention to the modernity of M.'s position. The modern age in philosophy was opened by Descartes, who proceeded to subject all experiences to the acid-test of total doubt. When we face the ultimate mystery of existence, we sense the tension between the polar opposites of being within ourselves. The rational points beyond the rational; the immanent feelings of holiness intimate His transcendence; the traditional accounts of God speaking to His Chosen People are somehow right, yet also far too narrow, too particularistic; since God addresses Himself to all men. In rare moments of inspiration, God speaks to those who are properly qualified, but excepting Moses, His "speech" is filtered through the thick strands of imagination. We are torn between our awareness of creaturely dependence on Him, without whose "everlasting arms" we should instantly disappear, and our rational conviction that we cannot say of Him aught that is meaningful and affirmative. Nor can we ever outgrow this state of tension. All our attempts at a synthesis are but so many words strung together, waiting to be fused into fleeting lights of meaning by bolts of lightning from above.

Is not this recognition of our human condition essentially compatible with the vision of reality in our time?—We no longer think of the flux of existence in terms of tiny billiard-balls in motion. Atoms, we know now, consist of many tiny particles, which can be described both as electro-magnetic waves and as bits of matter. Modern physics operates in terms of fields of force, which are condensed into relatively stable structures of congealed energy. Every thing is in reality an event, a series of tremors, fixed in space, yet infinite in outreach. Should not, then, the human soul in its confrontation with the Infinite Whole of the cosmos be similarly caught in a ceaseless tension?

On a more popular plane, we recall Pascal's famous remark—"reason which is small enough for the mind is too small for the heart; if it is big enough for the heart, it is too big for the mind." Here, then, in simple language, is that cluster of contradictions, which we can resolve only in those

*In this essay, we shall refer to Maimonides as M.

moments when heart and mind join to lift us temporarily above ourselves. Yet, it is not knowledge that we glimpse in those moments, but the assurance that our inner quest for wholeness and consistency is right, in direction, if not in content. We must try again and again to understand in love and to love with understanding, for only the whole man can approach the Creator of the Whole. We are launched on an infinite road.

### *"Sovereignty of Reason"*

M. maintained that his "Guide" was the first effort to deal with the mysteries of Creation and Providence (*maasai bereshit* and *maasai merkava*). (Moreh, Petiha: Pines, p. 16) He scorned the works of Saadia and Halevi, as being either superficial or fallacious. To him, a "philosopher" was an Aristotelian who recognized the sway of the unvarying laws of nature. Saadia associated himself with the Moslem school of Mutazila, and Halevi reflected al Ghazzali's critique of "the philosophers." (Moreh, I, 71; Pines, p. 176)

In a larger sense, Saadia and Halevi represented the "short but long road" that popular theologians prefer in all generations. Saadia's way is that of superficial rationalism. He rejected the coarse anthropomorphism of literalists. In M.'s view, Mutazilites thought they removed materialization from their notion of God, but, they did not really, since they ascribed to Him, emotional and psychological factors. (Moreh, I, 53. Pines, p. 119.) All the references in the Torah and the Bible to physical appearances of God apply to His temporary theophanies, not to His own Being. So, there is a "created light" or divine effulgence, which the Lord employs as a manifestation of His Presence. This luminous body called *Kavod* or *Shechinah* was seen by Isaiah and Ezekiel, by "the elders of Israel," and by some of the Sages. Similarly, the Creator formed a "created voice," which spoke in so many words to the prophets and to Moses. In this way, Saadia managed to retain the literal significance of the anthropomorphic passages in Scripture and Talmud, without ascribing to God Himself any material qualities. But, this method is, after all, an invention of the imagination. If the "lights" and "voices" are not themselves divine, why should we assume that they attest to the truth of prophecy? What is to prevent us from rejecting them as merely visual and auditory hallucinations?—If they are not temporary and detached events but integral manifestations of the Supreme Being, His emanations or His "Garments," then we fall back into the trap of idolatry, where all kinds of images might be said to be His representations and "incarnations." Furthermore, truth can only be self-authenticating, an extrapolation of man's outreach, but not an alien intrusion from another realm—a communication which man can only accept in blind faith. As a matter of fact, the "created light" and the "created voice" of Saadia became the basis of the neo-anthropomorphic school of the Ashkenazi Hassidim. They conceived of the Divine manifestations as permanent "forms" of the Deity, allowing the fevered imagination of mystics to rhapsodize on their visions of the various parts of the Divine anatomy.

M. did not altogether reject the doctrine of "created lights." He granted that it was helpful to those whose minds were too unsophisticated to grasp the concept of an immaterial Deity. At least, this doctrine kept them from ascribing materiality to God Himself. Also, it is extremely difficult to interpret the Pentateuchal description of the gathering at Sinai, without those "lights" and "sounds."[1] Yet, M. aimed to raise his readers to a higher philosophical level, which demands inner coherence and rejects the possibility of self-contained islands of truth, breaking into man's consciousness.

In M.'s view, the sustained quest of man for truth, as seen for example in the works of Aristotle, is itself the product of revelation. When a person's rational faculties attain a pitch of perfection, while his intuitive and imaginative powers are not equally perfected, he becomes a speculative philosopher. The school of Saadia was, according to M., remiss in that they accepted uncritically the premises of the Moslem Mutazilites. As a child of his age, M. believed that classical Greek philosophy was an integral part of the esoteric tradition of the biblical prophets and sages of the Mishnah.[2] M.'s historical knowledge was faulty, but not his reverence for the sovereignty, indeed the holiness of reason. To him, systematic and objective reasoning is the highway to truth, and God disdains those who forsake the manifest principles of truth for the sake of pleasing Him.[3] The anti-intellectualist mentality of a St. Paul, a Tertullian, a Luther, a Kierkegaard, with their subjective, or "existential" "truths" was to him an abomination.

Neo-Maimonism, too, asserts that rationality is of the essence of humanity. There is more to humanity than reason can comprehend, but the irrational and the subjective cannot serve as clues to the Image of God in man. To love God is to seek to know Him, and the greater our knowledge of Him, the greater our love of Him and of all who are created in His image.[4] And God's love of us is manifested in our love of Him and His Kingdom on earth.

## Rejection of Ethnic Mysticism

M. scorned the Halevian axiom that Jews and Jews alone are endowed with a special capacity for the "divine manifestation." To Halevi, Jewish people occupy an exalted level in the hierarchy of being, somewhere between the angels and the rest of mankind. All Jews inherit this unique intuition, which was given to them for the sake of humanity as a whole. As God has chosen the biblical prophets for the purpose of bringing His admonitions to the Jewish people, so too He has chosen the Jews from among the nations and endowed them with a unique capacity for things divine, and assigned to them the task of functioning as "the heart" of mankind. This "heart" will regain its vigor in the land of Israel, and then all mankind will be "saved" through Israel. However, even in the messianic future, ethnic Jews alone will serve as the channels of communication between God and mankind, for only ethnic Jews can function as prophets.

The Halevian approach has not lost its popularity even in our own day. Its plausibility derives, not alone from its seductive appeal to the hurt pride of a persecuted people, but also from the uniqueness of Jewish history. Here is a people that has been reduced to "dry bones," yet all the nations of the western world were brought to the service of God through its prophets. And the western world appeared to Europeans until recently to be synonimous with civilized humanity. If, then, in the past, Israel served as "a prophet unto the nations," why not in the future?—The fact that this self-image entailed the anguish of martyrdom and the aura of dedication to the service of all men kept this doctrine from turning narrowly chauvinistic and narcissistic. Furthermore, with the rise of romantic nationalism in the modern world, the Halevian approach was rendered the flattery of imitation by such popular "prophets" as Fichte, Mazzini, Mickiewicz, Danilevski and Dostoevski. Ethnic mysticism proved to be fantastically contagious.

Even the builders of classical Reform and cultural Zionism succumbed to the seduction of Halevian racism. Geiger, with all his rationalism, based his Jewish theology, especially his concept of Israel's "mission," on the axiom of an innate Jewish "genius" for religion. A'had Ha'am believed that "the national ethic" and "the national soul" were all but atrophied when the people of Israel was uprooted and driven into exile and that with the return of Jews to their native land Israel's ancient genius would be revived and revitalized. Echoes of mystical racism abound in the works of Buber and Rosenzweig. As Christian theologians are perpetually tempted to transfer the mystery of the Divine Being to "the secular city," so Jewish theologians are equally prone to transfer the mystery of Divine oneness and uniqueness from God to the people of Israel, or to the land of Israel, or to both. "Sanctified egotism" is the demonic underside and shadow of traditional Judaism.

M. refused to indulge in collective self-sanctification. The quest of truth is not a national monopoly. It is man qua man that is the subject of all speculations about God. To limit "the divine manifestation" to Jews living in the land of Israel is as unworthy of Jews as it is destructive of the principle of human equality, which is affirmed in the *Mishna*. To be sure, in his letter to the Jews of Yemen, M. found it necessary to descend to the level of popular mythology and to argue that those who are descended from the men and women that stood at Sinai cannot possibly disbelieve in the promises of the Torah. However, in his "Guide," he does not restrict prophecy either to the land of Israel or to the people of Israel. The reason prophecy is not attained in the lands of exile is due to the wretchedness of life in those countries. (II, 36) And in a famous chapter (III, 51) he ranks the philosophical saints of all nations ahead of "Talmudists" and *mizvah*-observers. Also, in the well known letter to R. Hisdai concerning people of other faiths, he avers, "God seeks the heart. . . ."[5]

Neo-Maimonism, too disdains the mystique of racism and ethnic narcissism along with the assorted brands of anti-intellectualism. All who base their faith upon their existential identification with the historical career of the Jewish people, affirming that such existence is unique and *sui generis*, simply beg the question. The task of reflection is to analyze, to discover relationships, to demonstrate the universal components in all particular events. All individuals, all historic peoples, are unique. And the conviction of being chosen by a supreme deity for high ends is by no means unique, either in ancient or in modern times. To insist on the uniqueness of the Jewish people as an irreducible phenomenon, that can be understood only by reference to the meta-historical, the meta-philosophical and the metaphysical is as irrational in principle as it is vicious in actual, historical consequences. For a people that is lifted out of the common run of humanity and enveloped in the ghostly haze of mythology is far more likely to be demeaned by opponents as subhuman than to be exalted as superhuman. If the holocaust demonstrates anything at all, it is the vulnerability of Jewish people to the mystique of racism. Jews should be in the forefront of the fight against this social disease, much less promote it. Haven't we been decimated by its ravages?—Yet, so strangely seductive is the temptation to mythicize our own being that the Jewish "meta-myth" is still a potent force in our midst and, owing to the mirror-image effect, among Christians.

## The Quest of Self-Transcendence

M. was a rationalist, but not in the flat sense of this term. Speculative reason, directed toward the ultimate mysteries of life, is far more than the sheer process of intellection. In fact, one must guard against the temptation to plunge prematurely into reflection on God and creation, before one has properly prepared himself for this arduous and perilous task. The preparatory disciplines are not only logic and mathematics, but ethics and esthetics. Also, one must be endowed from birth with a balanced disposition, which shuns all tendencies to excess and exaggeration. The prophet must be gifted in all the disciplines that are needed for the perfection and balance of the human personality. His imaginative and intuitive talents must be as excellently attuned to the reception of the divine Influence as his intellectual faculties. The prophet shares in the talents of the statesman, whose spiritual antennae relate him to the needs of the community as a whole, so that he senses "the general will" of the nation, to use a Rousseauist phrase. The prophet is also a gifted poet, creating myths and metaphors that reverberate with powerful resonance all through the ages. So, while the man of intellect can only gain from the Divine Influence some philosophical reflections, and the man of intuition and imagination can only be inspired by the same divine source to devise some ordinances and works of literary art, the one who is gifted in all the faculties of outreach can hope to attain moments of prophetic inspiration, that lead him to channel divine energy into the community of Israel and the society of mankind.[6]

It follows that man's pathway to God consists in the attainment of balanced perfection, or to put it differently, the quest of God is dependent on the attainment of wholeness and harmony, since God is the builder of wholes. This emphasis might be termed classical. It resists any endeavor to fragmentize the human personality and to set the ideals of the spirit over against the hungers of the flesh. To be sure, M. tended to downgrade sex as a "shameful" activity. (II,36) He described the Hebrew language as "holy," because it contained no words for the genital organs and employed "pure" euphemisms for the sexual act. In this respect, he was probably influenced as much by the feverish over-indulgence of the Moslem princes as he was by the teaching of Aristotle. But, his essential teaching was in keeping with the aims of the classicist. He regarded the health of the soul as paralleling the health of the body, rejecting the Augustinian claim that the love of self opposes and contradicts the love of God.[7]

Neo-Maimonist ethics is also a blend of the quest for balance of the classicist and the lyrical temper of the religionist. Along with M., we affirm the ancient principle of the Golden Mean. All virtues are happy syntheses of opposing tendencies. But, man's perennial quest for wholeness leads him again and again toward the brink of self-transcendence. M. supplements the classical ideal by the principle of *imitatio dei*, though in his view this principle could be asserted only in a metaphorical sense. To us, the urge for self-transcendence is a fact of human nature, for we cannot attain self-fulfillment without surrendering to a high ideal. The consequences of this hunger to be part of a greater whole are not always salutary. People are driven on occasion to serve idols and to reject the tensions of freedom. Here, again is an illustration of the dangers inherent in the polar tension within the human soul. Self-surrender to a partial good may be socially destructive as much as the anarchical drive for self-assertion. In the childhood of the human race, the limited whole which becomes the surrogate of God, is the clan, the tribe or the city-state. It is rare individuals, philosophers, statesmen and above all prophets, who have opened up wider horizons for the psychic need of self-transcendence. Plato, Aristotle and Xenophon shattered the naive idolatry of the Greeks. Isocrates expanded the meaning of the term, Hellene, to embrace those who acquire the culture of the Greeks. And, it was the long line of Hebrew prophets that most effectively contrasted the adoration of the One God with the sterile folly of worshipping any and all idols. The pathos of the prophets set its seal upon the deepest layers of the Jewish heritage. "Leave the Israelites alone—if they are not prophets, they are surely the sons of prophets." (Pesahim 66a.)

The rejection of idolatry is an ethical as well as a theological principle. It means that no ideal is more than a fragment of our total goal, more than a way-station on the road to personal and universal perfection. In every generation, the classical procedure of harmonizing conflicting interests and ideals issues in a consensus of what is reasonable and morally obligatory—a Way, which is then structured into laws and ordinances *(halachah)*. But, along with this legal pattern, there is also the beckoning ideal of greater perfection—a Vision of the sublime, which is only dimly reflected in articulate ideals. Beyond these ideals is the Nameless One, to whom alone our worship is directed. The concrete ideals of the age are all too readily transformed into idols, and the resounding No of prophetic monotheism, impels humanity to go beyond the "idols of the market-place" in quest of the receding horizon of perfection. "Without vision, a people is undone."

The religious Liberal, by virtue of his dynamic Vision, will be keenly conscious of the failures of the age and the limits of the regnant ideals. To him, the worship of the One God will result in an awareness of our human sinfulness. We ask forgiveness, not alone for the sins we have committed, but even more so for permitting some ideals to preempt our total loyalty, shutting all else from our view. Sin is the failure to heed the call of the whole—the whole of our self, the whole of society, the whole of the spectrum of ideals, that is the light of God.

There is an old pietistic comment on the claim of the Sages that in time to

180 JACOB B. AGUS

180 JACOB B. AGUS

come, God will slaughter Satan. Why should Satan be punished? it is asked. Was it not his duty to mislead and seduce people?—The answer is—Satan will be punished for the *mizvot* he urged, not for the sins that he commended. How beautiful!—The perfect world will be attained only when the demonic is totally separated from the divine—a consummation which can hardly be reached in our mundane existence.

## The Meaning of God

M.'s conception of God is the most misunderstood part of his system. It is taken to be "The Unmoved Mover," Who can only be described in negations. He is not this and not that. While we may think of Him as being One, Living, Almighty, All-knowing, we have to bear in mind that His unity is unlike that of all other forms of unity, that His Life, His Power and His Wisdom are totally unique, in no way comparable to the meaning that those adjectives normally convey. We seem to be left with a vacuous Naught. Since M. takes pains to hammer home the principle that "the end of our knowledge of God is to know that we don't know," (I. 59) many scholars in medieval and modern times have concluded that his God-idea was really devoid of religious content. At least one contemporary scholar even went so far as to infer that logically M. was a naturalist.

Actually, when the "Guide" is seen as a whole, the positive aspects of M.'s conception become clear. Existentially, M. confronted the Divine Being in times of meditation as the Ground of all being, the Purpose of all existence, the ultimate object of man's total devotion and affection. Intellectually, M. identifies the Divine with the marvelous wisdom that is apparent in living things, reserving the term, nature, for the mechanical laws that prevail in the inanimate world. (I, 69; III, 19; III, 23) In the designs of plants and animals, the reality of purposiveness is apparent. The whole is far more than the sum of its parts—one spirit dominates and controls the functioning of a myriad components. Furthermore, certain species depend for their existence on other forms of living beings. A Wise, All-powerful Will is at work, over and above the unvarying mechanism of nature.[8]

This blend of Wisdom and Will is manifested on a still higher level in the creation of humanity. Even in its most primitive stages, mankind received inflows of Divine Power and Wisdom from God. (II,40) These upward thrusts led to the development of skills needed for survival and of social customs that provided a modicum of order and justice. Among the Greeks and other cultured peoples, there have arisen statesmen, scientists, inventors and poets, who have contributed mightily to the formation of a civilized society. Yet, the laws of the Greeks (*nomoi*) did not meet the spiritual needs of their people. The only perfect law is the Torah, which addresses itself to the ethical and religious concerns of the individual as well as the economic and political interests of society. "So, the Torah, which is not a natural product is led up to by natural developments." (Ibid) The Torah was given to the Israelites, but in the course of time the "Torah of Truth" will govern the lives of all men and women. (Code, "Hilchot Melochim," end) "For all of existence is like one living individual." (I, 72, Pines. p.117) The thrusts of God, manifested in the biblical prophets and less perfectly in statesmen, poets and philosophers will ultimately redeem all mankind.

Here, then, is a holistic and evolutionary conception of God's work in history. The vistas of the contemporary theory of evolution were of course not open to M.. But, he conceived of God as being actively at work, creating the ideal human society of the future. Having postulated the doctrine of *creatio ex nihilo*, M. insisted that the Divine Flow from the sphere of Active Reason amounted to a series of additional creative acts, which transpired in the domain of history. While the material laws of nature have been fixed at creation, the spiritual horizons of mankind remained open, and the help of God is extended to the diverse builders of the ideal society of the future—to scientists, inventors, statesmen, poets, but above all to those who prepare themselves in mind and heart for prophecy. The perfect God must have designed "the best of all possible worlds," but only as a potentiality, revealed to prophets. And He is working in the dimension of time along with the elite of Israel and the nations in order to achieve this goal.[9]

The revival of prophecy is an indispensable step on the road to messianic perfection. The Messiah of the House of David will inaugurate the glorious era, but it will continue to grow in perfection for a long time, as the Messiah and his successors proceed to convert all of mankind "to the religion of truth." The laws of physical nature will remain unchanged, but man's productivity and prosperity will increase marvelously, so that people will be able to devote most of their time to Torah and religious meditation. (M.'s Code, Hilchot Melochim, Ch. XII) In M.'s view, then, progress is many-sided, economic as well as spiritual, secular as well as religious. And the ultimate source of this ceaseless advance toward perfection in time is the Supreme Being, Who is also the Purpose of all purposiveness in nature and in history, and the Ground of all that exists.

The important thing to remember is that M. combined a rationalistic version of the biblical philosophy of history with his philosophic system. Thereby, he resolved the contradiction between the Perfect God, Who is the Cause of an imperfect but steadily improving world. To be sure, M.

considered that goodness far outweighed all forms of evil in human life. The residual evil is due to the resistance of matter, and in the course of time, this resistance will be gradually overcome.

What is the contemporary religious import of this concept of God?—It does not allow us to think of God either as a loving Father or as a stern King, Who is placated by sacrifices, rituals and prayers. (III, 28) It does not console us with the assurance that we can win His magical intervention, whereby the laws of nature will be changed in our behalf. Neither repentance, in the popular meaning of the word, nor the recitation of prescribed prayers, nor the distribution of our possessions for charity will change the course of events.[10] We can speak of God as Compassionate only in the sense that He ordered the world in such a way as to provide for the needs of every living species.[11] But the concerns of the majority of mankind are, after all, self-centered. The truly religious personality will love God, without presuming that God must love him in return, as Spinoza later put it. Furthermore, our awareness of the Divine Being generates supreme joy within our souls.[12] The more we learn of His majesty, the more we yearn in love for His Presence, and this love is itself joy unalloyed. Indeed, God's love and concern is directed toward us, to the extent to which we prepare ourselves to receive His overflowing, creative energy. Providence is proportional to the readiness of our personality to serve as His vessel in behalf of the uplift of mankind.[13]

In M.'s philosophy, the only true miracles are those of the human spirit, when it is touched by the Divine Power.[14] The miracles of Scripture were built into the structure of natural law at creation. (II,29) Thereafter, we can look forward to the inflow of fresh freedom-generating creative power into the minds and hearts of creative men and women. All inventions, all the mighty achievements of the human spirit in every field of endeavor are the products of divine inspiration. (II,45) Man is not a passive victim of blind fate. On the contrary, God permeates the world only through the cooperation of great men and cooperative societies. (II, 40) He achieves human progress not by suddenly interrupting the chains of causality but by inspiring men to utilize the opportunities available to them. And the goal of this divine-human cooperation is certain to be the ever more perfect society of the future.

This concept of God is thoroughly in harmony with the modern spirit. We know the tremendous potential of the human spirit for the improvement of the living condition of mankind, where M. could only hope and trust. The parallels between M's philosophy, stripped of its medieval picture of the cosmos, and the views of such modernists as Bergson, Alexander and Whitehead are obvious. God is the unifying, integrating, perfecting Pole of the di-polar universe, but matter, the source of perpetual resistance and negation, is also His creation. The ultimate triumph of Freedom and Purpose is asserted in the doctrine of *creatio ex nihilo*.

M.'s philosophy could be decribed as panentheistic, in that God includes the world, but the world does not include God. While He is eternal, He works within time. God is both personal and non-personal, for personality is a blend of freedom with purposiveness, and God is at once the Purpose of all purposes in the cosmos and the Free Creator, "who renews the world daily by His goodness." He is immanent in the noblest momentary outreaches of the human spirit, but also transcendent, for we can affirm of Him only by negative attributes.

In sum, God is not only static perfection, but also a dynamic force, acting within history. Charles Hartshorne wrote, "Modern philosophy differs from most previous philosophy by the strength of its conviction that becoming in the more inclusive category." [than, being] (Ch. Hartshorne in "Philosophers speak about God," U. of Chicago Press, 1953, p.9) Also, reflecting the Kabbalistic tradition, A. J. Kook wrote of the two forms of perfection, attributable to God, though he hesitated to apply any potentiality to God in Himself.

"We say that Absolute Perfection is necessarily existent and there is nothing potential in it. The Absolute is all actual. But there is a kind of perfection which consists in the process of being perfected; this type of perfection cannot be applied to the Deity, since Infinite, Absolute Perfection leaves no room for any additional increments of perfection. In order that Being shall not be devoid of growth in perfection, there must be a Becoming, a process beginning from the lowest depths, the levels of absolute privation, and rising therefrom steadily toward the Absolute Height. Thus existence was so constituted that it could never cease from progressing upward. This is its infinite dynamics." ("Orot Hakodesh," p. 549, "Banner of Jerusalem," by J. B. Agus, p. 172)

The Kabbalistic solution is to distinguish the Pure Being of God, as *En Sof*, from His Becoming in the Plaroma of Sefirot. Modern philosophers feel no such compulsion—"there is no law of logic against attributing contrasting predicates to the same individual, provided they apply to diverse aspects of this individual." (Hartshorne, op. cit. p. 15)

## Meaning of Faith

Can we prove the existence of God? M. demonstrates the existence of God by a variant of the cosmological proof—for every existent effect there is a cause; hence, an ultimate Cause, an Unmoved Mover. But when the issue of creation vs. eternity of the cosmos is raised, M. takes refuge in a theory of faith. The issue cannot be decided by the arguments of logic alone. An extra-logical factor must be brought into the equation. If the cosmos is created, "then the Torah is possible." Since the scales of logic are evenly balanced, we are free to put our weight on the scale of creation and Torah.

M.'s resort to the Jamesian "Will to believe" must not be understood in superficial, tactical terms. M. made clear that his choice was not dictated by the literal teaching of the first chapters of Genesis. "The gates of interpretation are not closed to us." (II, 25) Nor did he opt for creation simply because of the possibility of including the miracles of Scripture in the primary act of creation. His argument moves on a deeper plane, so that it remains convincing in our contemporary universe of discourse. God does act in the world by relating Himself now to one person, now to another and by choosing a whole people as his instrument. (Ibid)

Torah, in the sense of the harmonious unity of the supreme values of life, is itself a form of cognition. To love is to seek understanding, as M. put it.

Speculative reason is intimately one with the imperatives of ethics and the intuitive perceptions of "the imagination." It is our personality as a whole that confronts the mystery of the universe, and when the judgment of logic is neutralized, the associated forms of outreach within us impel us to choose that view of the world which is consonant with the ultimate reality of spiritual values. In a created world, where the free spirit of God is sovereign, the human spirit finds its validation.

It follows that faith is not an alien element to the quest of truth, or a separate faculty detached from or even opposed to reason. On the contrary, faith is an extension of the adventure of speculative reason. Faith is the total posture of man, as "in fear and love," he confronts the awesome majesty of the Supreme Being. God is "the soul of the soul" of the universe, the Ultimate Whole, Whose Wisdom proceeds from the whole to the parts, rather than the other way around. Hence, in our quest of His "nearness," we have to integrate the whole of our being—our imagination and intuition, our balanced ethical virtues and our quest of God, our hunger for aloneness with God in the ecstasy of meditation, (III, 51) and our eagerness to redeem the world by deeds of justice and compassion. (III, 52-54)

M.'s teaching in regard to the meaning of faith and its decisive role in the trans-logical realm is applied in Neo-Maimonism to the issue of God's existence, not merely the creation of the world. Defining God as the Perfect Personality, the ultimate Whole in an evolutionary holistic-mechanical cosmos, we cannot demonstrate with mathematical logic that God does indeed exist. We point to the marvelous ladders of evolution, in which wholes of ever greater complexity and range of freedom have come into being. The appearance of the human mind marked the emergence of a new phase of holism—conscious, deliberate, multi-dimensional, creative. In the genuises of art, ethics, science, statecraft and religion, new phases of spirit are briefly glimpsed. All great achievements well up into the conscious mind of their own accord, as it were, like invasions from a sea of Super-Spirit, when the dikes are lowered, or like bolts of lightning, illuminating the dark night. The mysteries of life, mind, and flashes of genius point toward the possibility of divine thrusts, impelling us toward perfection. Indeed, we perceive, however dimly, intimations of the supreme source of all values in our ethical deeds, esthetic apprehensions and experiences of holiness. But, we cannot prove that the theistic hypothesis is true.

Still, and here we touch bases with M., our inner aspirations for growth in the realms of the spirit impel us to choose that view of the cosmos, in which Spirit, Freedom and creative Growth triumph over the dead entropy of matter. Our faith in God is an extension of "the lines of growth" in our personality—our hunger for justice, our thirst for beauty, our longing for truth, our experience of holiness, when we sense the cosmic resonance of eternity. Faith is the fragmentary arc within our being, extrapolated into an invisible, eternal circle. It is the outward reach of our entire being; hence, it cannot be unreasoning, or immoral, or blind. It becomes demonic when it sets itself over against the moral, or the rational, pretending to go "beyond good and evil." It is the whole of our self orienting itself toward and seeking support from that all-embracing Self, of which our minds are but so many cells. And faith, as M. points out, is not a steady, static condition. It is rather a tremor of the soul, an assurance and an inquiry, at one and the same time.

## Revelation

While prophecy is the central theme of the "Guide," the novelty of M.'s contribution consists in his tri-partite division of revelation. He discusses first two pre-prophetic stages, along with other protoprophetic phenomena; second, various stages of prophecy, the highest being that of Abraham; third, the super-prophetic quality of Mosaic revelation. In this way, the Torah of Moses is placed within the generally human context of inspired achievements and noble visions. The act of revelation is a quantum-extension of human perception, not the incursion of a totally foreign element.

Proto-prophetic are the diviners and the inventors, who discover new inventions intuitively, without any understanding of scientific and mathematical principles. (II,38) Their imagination and dedication are stimulated by the flow from Active Reason, enabling them to create instruments of human progress. Philosophers and scientists are also proto-prophetic, with their fresh visions of reality arising out of an inflow of Active Reason. However, in their case, the imaginative and intuitive faculties are short of perfection. (II,37) And the logic of the mind, however great it be, cannot suffice to reflect faithfully the total import of the divine thrust, which affects ideally man's entire personality.

The prophet is one whose imaginative, intuitive and rational faculties are all fully developed. Yet, even in his case, moments of genuine revelation occur infrequently. True, the good God is ever ready to grant His impulsions of goodness and wisdom. Though He is free to withhold His gift, He, in His Goodness, is ever ready to uplift men. But, even the noblest prophet can rise to the requisite levels of perfection only on a few occasions. Moses was far superior to all other prophets; indeed, he was unique and incomparable. Still, Moses was incapable of reaching the heights of prophecy during 38 of the 40 years that the Israelites wandered in the wilderness. (II, 36)

M. lists two pre-prophetic stages that great men may reach. Both are characterized by the influx of the Holy Spirit (Ruah hakodesh). (II,45 & II,41) In the first case this influx is manifested in great deeds, accomplished by leaders who are fired with the determination to redeem an oppressed people or to advance the cause of mankind. In the second case, the Divine power is employed to compose great works of inspiration and wisdom—such as, the Writings *(kethubim)* of Holy Scriptures.

Taking the proto-prophetic and the pre-prophetic stages together, we have here a conception of revelation that embraces all that makes for the advancement of mankind, unifying religion with the several branches of culture. Revelation is a thrust toward higher levels of holiness, in the life of the individual and of society. And the culmination of this advance will be attained in the messianic era, when material prosperity will be conjoined with ethical maturity and religious truth.[15]

In these stages of *ruah hakodesh* we are given a theory of universal progress, since philosophers, poets and cultural heroes address themselves to all mankind. We recall that, in M.'s view, Aristotelian philosophy was itself an integral part of the esoteric wisdom of the prophets and sages. His interpretation of the Noachide principles, as a body of "general revelation" fits into his scheme of an all-embracing philosophy of culture, consisting of artistic achievements and ethical principles intended for all men along with the Torah designed for the Jewish people.

If we now skip across the nine specific stages of prophecy and examine M.'s concept of the prophecy of Moses, we find that he takes pains to stress its radically dogmatic character. Everything said about other prophets and prophecy in general, he tells us, does not apply to Mosaic revelation. (II,35; II,39) Since his original problem was to reconcile the Torah of Moses, not merely prophecy in general, with the dictates of philosophy, it is certainly parodoxical that he exempts Moses from the normal category of prophets. Evidently, another principle is here involved, and we shall discuss it presently.

At this point, we note that the biblical prophets occupied the middle ground between the "general revelation" of the pre- and proto-prophets and the post or super-prophetic status of Moses. (II,45) While the prophets admonished the people to be loyal to the Torah of Moses, they dared to be extremely selective in their emphasis, as if they were authorized to weigh and measure the various *mizvot*. In regard to the sacrifices and the choice of Israel, they distinguished between the Primary Intention of God and His Secondary Intention. (III, 32) Accordingly they chided the people for their ethnic zeal and their preoccupation with sacrifices, pointing out that the ultimate aims of God were the same as in "general revelations"—namely, the ethical virtues of personal life and the perfection of society. So, while the spectrum of revelation ranges from the general principles of faith to the specific ordinances of Torah, it is basically the same phenomenon.

Why, then, does M. put Mosaic prophecy in a category all its own? In the first place, he was compelled to follow the teaching of Bible and Talmud, on this point. In terms of his own philosophy of prophecy, Moses is unique because there was no admixture of imagination in his teaching. (II,36) But strangely enough, M. states it as a rule that the prophet is superior to the philosopher, precisely because the latter lacks the qualities of imagination and intuition. (II,37) Evidently, in terms of prophetic receptivity, the more the imagination is developed, the better, but in terms of the content of prophetic revelation, the less it is enveloped by the fancies of imagination, the better. The role of the prophet is to serve as the "channel," whereby the divine uplifting thrust is conveyed to mankind. To this end, imagination or intuition is essential, since the prophet in distinction from the philosopher, addresses himself to an entire community, which is more likely to be affected by rites and symbols than by ideals and ideas. However, the inner content of revelation can be discovered only by penetrating through the poetic imagery of prophecy and isolating its rational content. The Primary Intention, say, of the sacrificial ritual, described in the Torah, is the purpose of the Divine Will. The Secondary Intention was the "cunning" of Providence in leading

Israel and mankind by slow and devious steps from idolatry to true religion. (III, 32) And the prophets, from Amos and Hosea to Haggai and Malachi, taught the Israelites to distinguish between the Primary Intention of God, reflecting His Purpose for mankind, and His Secondary Intention in providing the social institutions and rituals needed for the ultimate triumph of the Divine Will.

At this point, we note a most important distinction which M. draws between "True Beliefs" and "Necessary Beliefs"—the former are true in themselves, the latter, while strictly untrue, serve the cause of truth. (III, 28 & III, 32) As an example of the latter, he cites the belief that God listens to the prayers of men, turning from the policy of Wrath to that of Compassion, and changing the course of events in response to the earnest petitions of people. (III,28) In the case of rituals, the elaborate ordinances regulating the sacrifices in the Temple were designed to wean the people away from dependence on animal offerings. Similarly, the laws regulating family life continued relics of barbarism which the contempories of Moses were not willing to abandon all at once. (III, 32 & III, 47) So, too, in the case of ideas, the "Necessary Beliefs" were designed to establish a community dedicated to "True Beliefs." Some popular beliefs are essential to the formation of a community that would become the bearer of great, liberating truths. That the Torah of Moses can never be replaced by other prophets is one of those "Necessary Beliefs," that insure the continuity of the Jewish faith as against the claims of Christianity and Islam. In a larger sense, the entire dogmatic structure of Judaism, insofar as it reaches beyond the truths of philosophy, the impetus of prophecy and the messianic vision, belongs in this category of "Necessary Beliefs," particularly the teachings about hell and the resurrection of the dead.

What is the content of revelation, in M.'s scheme?

If we ignore for a moment the Torah of Moses, revelation is an energetic thrust, rather than a rational proposition. It is so protean that it assumes in different minds, forms as diverse as the speculations of the philosopher, the insights of an inventor, the visions of a poet, the arts of the statesman. In every case, the intent of the divine inflow is directed not alone to the prophetic personality but to the society of which he is part. And the nobler the level of prophecy the more it is oriented toward the entire community and ultimately toward all of humanity. Revelation contains a rational core; indeed, the Divine inflow affects reason primarily and imagination secondarily; but it is more than sheer reason, since the ideal prophet's grasp exceeds the reach of the philosopher. What, then, is the plus of prophetic revelation?

To say, as does Franz Rosenzweig, that God reveals His own Being is beside the point. "The entire world reveals His Glory." And in a more direct sense, God does not reveal Himself. The prophet receives a call, a command together with an intimation of God's reality. To assert that God reveals His love is true in a general sense, but this answer does not capture the special nuance of the Maimonidean philosophy, or the genius of Hebraic prophecy. The prophet loves his people, but he is also their severest critic. It would be more correct to characterize revelation as a thrust toward messianic perfection of the individual and of society. The two goals are one in essence, for the closer one comes to God the more he is dedicated to the promotion within society of "steadfast love," *(hesed)* "righteousness" *(zedakah)* and "justice" *(mishpat)*. (III, 54) An anticipation of the building of God's Kingdom on earth is implicit in the "inflow" from Active Reason, whether it occurs on the lowest, pre-civilizational level, or on the highest prophetic level. In each case, the recipient is impelled to bring some gift for the Kingdom; he is filled with "divine discontent," he must destroy as well as build, he is charged with a mission. All things are judged by Him in the light of the future kingdom. So he is hopeful when others are despairing and embittered when others are celebrating. His sole standard is the "nearness of God" and His Word. So, Job, who was not a prophet, came to realize that the highest good, "the knowledge of God," is available to us, even when we are troubled in body and anguished in soul. (III,23)

In a word, revelation brings a dynamic unity of reassurance, discontent and the vision of the long road ahead; hence, it impels the prophets to bless even as they curse, to speak of the glories that are to come, even as they expose the moral failings of their contemporaries. Above all, revelation is a "quest," a demand for creative action of one kind or another.

In our day, this concept of revelation is completely tenable, though our view of the world does not consist of Spheres and Active Reason. If we accept the world-view of what Hartshorne calls the "convergent philosophy," we recognize that new creative energy may well enter into us. God is the Pole of whole-creation, but He also includes the Pole of resistance or raw matter, in His Being. He is eternal, but He also lives in time. He enters into human history, when hearts and minds are readied for Him. To paraphrase Matthew Arnold, "He is the Power, not ourselves, that makes for growth in Life, Mind and Spirit." Is not the course of evolution, as analyzed by Morgan, Bergson, Alexander and Teilhard de Chardin, a demonstration of the continuing creativity of the Divine Being? Can we not discern an advance toward the emergence of creatures with greater measures of freedom?—If God is the Pole of wholeness building in the cosmos, then a series of pulsations toward ever greater wholes is precisely what we should expect.

Neo-Maimonism, then accepts the principle of revelation as an incursion of supra-human energy into the souls of creative individuals and into society. Along with M., we recognize the many-sidedness of revelation. It is by no means confined to the sphere of religion. It reinvigorates "the lines of growth" in the spirit of man. It is reflected in the realms of art, science, philosophy and statecraft. It ranges in power from everyday premonitions, that occur to most of us, to the creative ecstasies of geniuses.

Neo-Maimonism differs from the "life-philosophies" of Germany and the philosophy of Bergson, in the recognition that the fresh incursions of spiritual energy center on the expansion of the range of intelligence. The heart of reality is not the sheer impetus of a cosmic will, as in Schopenhauer and Nietzsche, nor is it a blind life-force, the *elan vital*, but spirit in the sense of the total outreach of man, including the disciplines of reason, ethics and esthetics. At the same time, Neo-Maimonism rejects the separation of religion from the other domains of culture. There is a goal and purpose to human history, and all efforts "to improve the world by the Kingdom of the Almighty" subserve that goal.

The essential characteristic of revelation is not the transmission of static information, but the confirmation of a direction. The recipient is powerfully oriented toward the achievement of "the nearness of God." The content of revelation is a hunger and a thirst for more and more of the things of God. As a dynamic phenomenon, revelation consists of three elements—an affirmation, a negation, a drive toward action.

As an affirmation, revelation is basically the reorientation of man's spirit toward the infinite goal of building God's Kingdom on earth. One comes to feel part of that wondrous company of great men and women who dared dream of the ideal society of mankind. One is reassured that this infinite quest will come closer and closer to realization. None of us comes to the experience of revelation totally alone and naked. On the contrary, we are sustained in our quest for God's "nearness," by the "sacred tradition" of our community. And in the experience of revelation, we find the values of the past confirmed and reinvigorated, in so far as their intent is separable from the external forms which they assumed in the various contingencies of history. God's Word at any one time cannot be in contradiction with His Eternal Will, as revealed to all men and women of good-will.

Neo-Maimonism applauds the principle of M. that the main road to true revelation is that of critical, objective rationality. Moses is praised for not daring to engage in metaphysical speculation before he has prepared himself fully for that task by means of mathematical and logical studies. And when the influx of Divine energy comes, it inspires man's rational faculty primarily. We cannot attain the insights of revelation by means of emotional rhapsodies, or by withdrawing from the world. Kierkegaard's slogan, "subjectivity is truth" is only partially true, in the two senses—first that the final fulcrum of truth is the mind of the individual; second, that all truth is inescapably filtered through the forms and limitations of our minds. Our formulation would be, "in all truth there is subjectivity," since it is the individual's hunger for truth and meaning that opens his mind to the influx of revelation. For this very reason, we are called to prepare ourselves for revelation by a critical analysis of the several ways in which we are subjectively structured. We are subjective, as individuals, as Jews, as Americans, as professionals. These varied influences increase our receptivity only when we have subjected them to critical analysis. The would-be prophet, even to the smallest extent, must emulate the prophets in the ardor of self-criticism.

So, we come to the second component of revelation—its negation. The prophet, knowing himself to be in the vanguard of mankind, condemns not merely the vices of his contemporaries but their virtues as well. His lips have been touched by the embers of eternity; he is impelled to surge beyond the landmarks of the past; he rails at the limitations and shortcomings of his contemporaries.

Above all, the divine-human encounter in Judaism must be translated into one action or another. In the first paragraph of the *Shema*, the love of God is carried out by way of teaching one's children, building one's home and spelling out its meaning in the market-places of the city.

In Neo-Maimonism, we have to recognize the role of "Necessary Beliefs"—that is, of ideas which are essential to the maintenance of the community. Without rituals and a common texture of ideas and sentiments, no community can live and serve as a bearer of truth. However, the "Necessary Beliefs" must be constantly subject to review and reexamination. Do they really, in our time, serve to provide a vehicle of truth and kingdom-building energy? Or is the opposite the case, with the rituals and "Necessary Beliefs" tying our people in knots and preventing them from facing up to the challenges of our time?

In general, the "sacred tradition" in its totality is our starting point. And this tradition is far from being monolithic. It is neither *Halachah* alone nor "ethical monotheism" alone, but the living texture of ideas and sentiments, ranging from the darkest hues of folk-mythology to the brightest ideals of humanity. We accept it with the greatest reverence as the deposit of revelations in the past, which is essential to the continuity of the Torah-community. But in the spirit of classical prophecy and philosophy, we accept it critically, distinguishing between the essence of faith and its external manifestations, at any one time or place. We recognize that what may have been a "necessary" belief at one time, may no longer be so today. We also affirm that a rite, devised by the "cunning of God" for a particular time might well become counter-productive in our day. So, we of the Conservative movement no longer pray for the reestablishment of the sacrificial system in the Temple, drawing the consequences of M.'s reasoning, though in his own time he could not do so, without tearing the Jewish community apart.

# Notes to Neo-Maimonism

[1]In his "Guide," M. makes use of "created lights" and "created voices," but only grudgingly, as a concession to the unsophisticated. See I, 5, where M. concludes, "If an individual of insufficient capacity should not wish to reach the rank to which we desire him to ascend and should he consider that all the words [figuring in the Bible] [for seeing] concerning this subject are indicative of sensual perception of created lights—be they angels or something else—why, there is no harm in his thinking this." (Pines, p. 31) Still, in I, 10, M. writes as if the "created light" was indeed there—that is, on Mount Sinai. Shem Tov on I,19 writes that "created lights" were indeed externally visible to the common people, but only the prophets apprehended the inner light. Generally, M. confines the hearing of God's voice to the dreams of prophets, save in the case of Moses, who heard Him in a vision. Afudi on *I,37*. In I,25, M. offers both interpretations of *Shechinah*—in the sense of "created light" and in the sense of Providence. We may assume confidently that the latter sense corresponds to his own belief. See also II, 44

[2]Guide, I,71

[3]"For the Lord, blessed be He, loves only truth and hates only falsehood" (II,47)

[4]Second paragraph of first chapter of Sefer Hamada.

[5]Whether M. believed that he had indeed attained the rank of prophecy is a question of semantics, for he refers more than once to quasi-prophetic insights that came to him. So, in the introduction to third part of the "Guide," he remarks, "no divine revelation (nevua elohit) has come to me to teach me . . . Now rightly guided reflection and divine aid in this matter have moved me." (vehine orarani bo hamahshavah hameyusheret vehoezer hoelohi) (Pines, p. 416) In Guide III, 22, M. exclaims, "see how I succeeded as if by prophecy" (kidemut nevuah) Pines translates—"see how these notions came to me through something similar to prophetic revelation." (p. 488)

In our view, M. assimilates prophetic revelation to the many kinds and variations of inspiration that come to the great benefactors of mankind.

[6]The role of courage and intuition (Koah Hameshaer) in prophecy is mentioned in II,38. The orientation of prophecy toward the greater society is stressed in II,39. See also II,37, "the nature of the intellect is such that it always overflows."

[7]This thought is more clearly presented in M.'s "Eight Chapters."

[8]The teleology of M. is discussed in detail in Z. Diesendruck's article, "Hatachlit Vehataarim betorat Horambam" in Tarbitz, II, pp. 106-134 & pp. 27-73. Also in his "Die Teleogie bei Maimonides," H.U.C.A. vol. V.

[9]M.'s conception of the positive functions carried out by Christianity and Islam in preparing the way for the Messiah is stated explicitly in his Code, "Hilchot Melachim," Chapter XI, uncensored version.

"But it is beyond the human mind to fathom the designs of the Creator; for our ways are not His ways, neither are our thoughts His thoughts. All these matters relating to Jesus of Nazareth and the Ishmaelite (Mohammed) who came after him, only served to clear the way for King Messiah, to prepare the whole world to worship God with one accord, as it is written, 'For then I will turn to the peoples a pure language, that they may all call upon the name of the Lord to serve Him with one consent' (Zephaniah 3,9). Thus, the Messianic hope, the Torah and the commandments have become familiar topics—topics of conversation (among the inhabitants) of the far isles and many peoples, uncircumcised of heart and flesh . . ." (transl. by I. Twersky, "Maimonides," p. 226).

M. makes use here of the conception of "Divine Cunning," (Guide III, 32) whereby God achieves His purpose indirectly.

[10]M. defines repentance as the actual transformation of the sinner's disposition, so that "He who knows all secrets can testify that were the sinner to be presented with similar temptations he would not ever commit that sin" (Hilchot Teshuvah, II,2)

[11](III,12) "His compassion in His creation of guiding forces [i.e. instincts] for animals."

[12](II, 29) "for faith in God and the joy inherent in that faith are two matters which cannot change . . ."

[13](III,17) "But I believe that providence is consequent upon the intellect and attached to it." (Pines' p. 474)

[14]In chapters III, 17 & 18, M. expatiates on the principle that divine providence is extended in proportion to a person's closeness to God. In opposition to the argument that a whole ship, containing hundreds of people might sink through the action of wind and water, he responds that the decision to enter the ship was in every case, a personal one. Presumably, the saint who is close to God would have been warned by some intimation (hearah) not to enter that ship.

[15]"Therefore I say that the Law, although it is not natural, enters into what is natural. It is a part of the wisdom of the Deity with regard to the permanence of this species . . . [i.e. humanity] . . ." (II,40)

# A THEOLOGICAL FOUNDATION FOR THE HALACHAH

MY CONTRIBUTION to this symposium on Halachah is a brief summation of views and ideas expressed in detail in other books and articles.[1] A philosophy of Halachah is an integral portion of one's world-view in general. At least, it is so in my case. I beg the reader's indulgence for the outline form of exposition, which necessarily raises more questions than it answers.

## God

I believe in God as the Ultimate Reality of the Cosmos, the unifying and harmonizing Principle of existence. The philosophic school which most nearly reflects my views is that of *panentheism*, where the cosmos is viewed as being *in* God. I consider that this school represents the "perennial philosophy" at which Aristotle and Maimonides aimed; Bergson reconciled it with the data of evolution; Alexander and Whitehead described it as "organismic" and Hartshorne defended it in contemporary thought. The cosmos contains a crescendo of "wholes," structured clusters of energy which function as if they were unitary beings. In the course of evolution, ever more elaborate organisms have evolved, with mankind representing the emergence of free personalities, capable of sensing the divine principle of organismic unity and harmony. The "image of God" in man is the fleeting, finite and fragmentary realization of the Divine creative thrust. For all its transitoriness, man's awareness of God is certain, intuitive and a source of self-renewal.

We may speak of God as Person, in both affirmative and negative senses. In its affirmative meaning, personhood means unity in space and time, imposing one Law upon the whole of creation, embracing the past in memory and the future in intention and in affirmation. In its negative sense, personality is self-defined by that which it excludes. So, in the case of God,

Originally published in *Judaism*, Winter 1980.

while all events are His work, through the operation of the laws of nature, not all events, taken in isolation, reveal His will. In a work of art there is a framework, material content which may be infinitely varied, and the intention of the artist that may be clearly manifested or only dimly apprehended by unconscious intuition.

Personality is the highest exemplar of holistic unity that we encounter in our human experience. Personality points to God, without delimiting Him. He is "the Soul of souls" (*neshamah lineshamah*). We dare not attribute the merely human qualities of speech and temperament to Him, except in a metaphoric sense. Rabbi Simlai's restriction of divine revelation at Sinai to the first two of the Ten Commandments is an apt description of divine-human encounters.[2] God opens ever new horizons by His self-revelation in our hearts and minds. He is revealed in man's ascent from slavery to freedom and in the progressive rejection of idolatry, be it gross or subtle.[3] Every revelation of God's Will in the human soul can turn idolatrous when it is taken to be the last word of the living God. Every step toward freedom that mankind takes is divine in inspiration and orientation, but it is just a finite step, no more, on an infinite road.

## Revelation

God reveals Himself to us in many different ways. His Will is manifested at the several cutting edges of the human spirit—in the infinite outreach of man's quest for understanding, in the imperative call to overcome the ills of society, in the inspiring moments of holiness. Plato's triad, the True, the Good and the Beautiful, was an inspired but time-conditioned formulation. Truth is an elusive goal and the awareness of limitation accompanies man's intellectual quest. Ethical imperatives are divine, but every step of social progress uncovers new tasks. The glory of beauty is most liable to perversion through the seduction of pleasure. True beauty includes the dimension of the sublime or the holy—hence, an intimation of infinity.

In each aspect, the awareness of negation, knowing that we do not know, is integral to the experience of revelation. As in the nineteenth Psalm, day speaks unto day and night unto night but "there is no speech, there are no words." Indeed, viewed in the perspective of the history of religions, the faith of the biblical authors stresses the negational dimension of the faith-event more than the affirmative one. The Hebrew Scriptures "de-sacralized" not only nature, but also history, setting strict categories for the manifestations of the divine will.

Several modern Jewish thinkers, succumbing to the influence of German philosophy, contrasted the pagan sanctification of nature with the Jewish sacralization of history. It is true that God is revealed most clearly in the expanding domains of the human spirit, but the course of human events is not identical with the advance of ethical sensitivity and moral vision. God is revealed *in* history, not *through* it. Judaism rejects the arrogant triumphalism of the historicists, whose slogan is "world history is the world court." The God of Israel appears in history as the champion of slaves, intent on reversing the course of history. And for two millennia, and against all odds, the Jewish people cherished the hope of rebirth. Only certain events in history manifest the divine will; others are consequences of the darker side of human freedom. As the *Mekhilta* on the crossing of the Red Sea points out, God appears at times as a leader on the battlefield, at other times as a sage teaching in a *yeshiva*.[4] As to which is which, in every instance the conscience of great and holy men must judge.

In addition to this general revelation, which is fleeting and unstructured, Judaism affirms the special revelation, which is embodied in its literature and its patterns of living. In the Hebrew Scriptures, the sacred tradition is mediated through the minds of three kinds of holy men—the priests, the sages and the prophets. "For Torah shall not perish from the priest, nor counsel from the wise, nor the word from the prophet" (Jer.18,18). (This is why we use the acrostic *Tanakh*—Torah, prophets, writings.) Different aspects of wisdom and piety are likely to be conveyed by each category of teacher. Because of the tensions resulting from these different approaches, the biblical faith was dynamic and many-sided. While archaic elements remained, countervailing influences were set in motion.

To consider matters of Halachah apart from their historic settings and deeper meanings is to follow in the wake of the ancient priests exclusively. The Talmud recognized that sheer legalism was a disease of religion. "Whoever says, 'I care only for Torah' will lack even Torah" (*Yebamot* 109b).

The "Sages of Israel," as the Pharisaic scholars called themselves, tried to preserve the ethical thrust of the prophets and the wisdom of the sages as well as the ritual of the priests. In the opening Mishnah of *Avot*, they even excluded the priests from the chain of transmission. The Aggadah contains, in gnomic form, maxims reflecting the philosophies of the ancient world, along with the impassioned ethical fervor of the prophets. Philo, the first philosophical exponent of Judaism, was a Greek-speaking Aggadist, incorporating into the tradition the so-called "beauty of Japheth."

Scholars have discerned two diverse approaches in the Palestinian schools of Rabbis Akiva and Ishmael—the former inclining toward literalism, the latter toward a reasoned interpretation. The literalist school produced also the *Shiur Komah* (descriptions of the Divine Glory) type of mystical literature which formed the foundation of Kabbalah, while the rationalistic school kept the gates open to the contemporary winds of philosophic speculation. Medieval Jewish philosophy, climaxed in Maimonides' *Guide*, was the most massive attempt to synthesize the three currents of tradition—that of priest, sage and prophet.

Maimonides effected this synthesis in three crucial ways—by viewing the tradition in the light of the history of religions and describing rituals as protests against ancient idolatries; by postulating Secondary Intention on the part of God as the source of the entire sacrificial system in the Holy Temple, and by introducing the distinction between "true doctrines" and "necessary doctrines". The former are true in themselves, the latter are affirmed by the sages in order to retain the cohesion of the community.

While lesser philosophers, both before him and after him, were content to separate and insulate the two domains of reason and religion, Maimonides insisted that worship must be whole-souled. Only if Judaism promotes philosophical piety does it have the right to demand self-sacrifice and even martyrdom. We learn from Maimonides that not all *halachot* are born equal. We have to study their origin in history, their justification in philosophy, their pragmatic consequences, their merit in terms of the primary intention of faith.

To be a Jew is to share in the priestly, prophetic and philosophical tradition of the living community of Israel (*K'lal Yisroel*), with the inevitable development of diverse schools of interpretation.


## Halachah

Conservative Judaism is one such school. It seeks to be true to the *whole* of our sacred tradition, to its inner philosophy as well as to its outer expression. As Conservative Jews we accept the Halachah as a starting point, not as a blueprint. It is one of the given components of our tradition, not all of it. Torn from its context in life and thought, Halachah is meaningless.[5] Every particular command should be open for evaluation in terms of the totality of the evolving sacred tradition.

For the purpose of clarification, some negations are in order:

We are not literalists—that is, we do not assert that the Torah was dictated to Moses, word for word, and that the Oral Law was transmitted verbally to him and to his successors. Therefore, the inner logic of a great deal of Halachah is, for us, not in itself persuasive. Nor is a custom in itself hallowed in our eyes solely because it has been practiced by many or even most of our people. For example, *shlogen kapores*. We have outgrown folkist romanticism. Nor do I and many of my colleagues follow the German super-conservative school of Savigny which idolized the institutions created by history as sacred, "positive-historical." We know all too well how many anti-Jewish horrors were sanctioned by that attitude.

We see the Jewish global community as centered in its religious life around sages—more exactly, priests, prophets and teachers of wisdom. In contemporary life, those categories do not coincide with any particular organized group. The rabbinate, in its totality, does not today exhaust the category of the ancient *hakhamim*. There are academic philosophers, individual scholars, educators and social workers, journalists and authors, who, in diverse ways, contribute to the making of the Jewish mentality. Associations of synagogues come closet, perhaps, to the representation of *Kenesset Yisroel*, the religious fellowship of Israel. With the progressive contraction of the domain of religious life to the precincts of the Synagogue, the norms and standards adopted by congregations will be decisive in molding the *Halachah* of the future.

## Takkanot

The Talmud speaks of those who violate an ordinance of the sacred tradition as rebellious children, disobeying their Father, who is God, and their Mother, the Congregation of Israel. Every ordinance is a product of both parents. We recognize the work of God in the living people, molded as it is by its historical institutions and guided by its spiritual leaders.

Therefore, in our view, the tradition develops by way of new *takkanot*, new *aggadot* and new *minhagim*. *Takkanot* are ordinances of conduct initiated by the spiritual elite; *aggadot* are new ideas that arise either out of Judaism or out of universal culture; *minhagim* are customs initiated by the people and concurred in by the *elite*. No strict lines of demarcation can be drawn between these several instruments of halachic development. Scholars used to draw absolute distinctions between the imposition of dogmas upon the free mind, which is intolerable, and the imposition of ordinances of conduct upon a free people, which is acceptable. The distinction is only partially valid, for there is no conduct that causes mighty changes in society, which does not imply certain ideas, and there are no ideas of consequence which do not affect the lives of people.

*Takkanot*, *aggadot* and *minhagim* aim to affect all concerned Jews, but they are usually initiated by individual congregations (*takkanot hakehillot*).


### K<sup>2</sup>lal Yisroel

The Conservative movement focused attention on the concept of *K<sup>2</sup>lal Yisroel*. I accept Dr. Gordis' interpretation of the term as the consensus of the concerned. In a free society, agreement will be gradational. In regard to essentials there will be a consensus, while there will be ample room for variations in ideology and practice.

A new factor of uncertain character is likely to modify the impact of *K<sup>2</sup>lal Yisroel*—namely, the government of Israel. Its relation to matters of personal status is well-known. Orthodox pressure in regard to Sabbath observance is also a factor. But, social issues are even more significant, if we think of Halachah in its ethical dimensions. We have to take account of questions in the realm of political science that our predecessors could comfortably ignore. What is the ideal relation of the Jewish religion, its Aggadah and its Halachah, to the Jewish state? Is the citizen of such a state ipso facto a member of the Jewish people? Should such a state be structured in keeping with the laws of Torah, or the principles of Torah, or the concepts of liberal democracy, the *hokhmah* of our time? Will the equality of the *ger*, affirmed thirty-six times in the Torah, apply to all the non-Jews in a Jewish state? Is a Jewish state conceivable that is not democratic? Shall Israel follow the model of western democracies, separating religion from government, or the model of an "Islamic state," à la Ayatollah Khomeini?

Manifestly, the character of Halachah in Judaism will be powerfully affected by the extent of its involvement with the government of Israel. Laws of religion and of government are different in essence. To make governmental privileges dependent on the practice of religious rituals and on the *kashrut* of those who administer them is a horrendous requirement in a western society. We cannot tell how Israel will develop in the future. So much depends upon whether a large Arab minority, consisting of the residents of the West Bank and Gaza as well as Israel proper, is embraced within the boundaries of the state. With a non-Jewish minority of nearly 40%, a new constitution may evolve, definitely separating religion from government. Also, spiritual forces emerging from grass-roots Israeli life may well lead to an acceptance of religious pluralism.

Halachah as religious law can be perverted into secular law, but, ideally, the two domains must be kept apart. For secular law takes no account of intention or relegates it to the background, while, in religion, the demands of spirit and piety are all important. In any case, the import and orientation of the *K'lal Yisroel* ideal is certain to be affected by developments in Israel, which cannot now be foreseen.

The negative implication of *K'lal Yisroel* is the refusal to read out of Jewish life those who differ from the majority in their interpretation of Judaism. A blurring of the lines of ideology within the Jewish community is the inevitable consequence of such a policy. There may not even be complete consistency within the Conservative movement, because of the need to reconcile the imperatives of progress with reverence for unity.

A case in point is the enfranchisement of women within congregational life. The first step was to institute *Bat Mizvah* observances as part of the Sabbath services. The next step was to grant *aliyot* and other honors to women, and to count them as part of a *minyan*. Once these steps have been accepted by the overwhelming majority of Conservative congregations, others, such as the ordination of women, might well be in order.

The gradational pace of change is itself part of the Conservative approach. In our endeavor to be faithful to the whole of our tradition, we need to shun the broad decisiveness of the ideologues.

## Ecumenism

If the rise of Israel is bound to affect the course of Halachah by changing the objective circumstances of Jewish life in Israel and by adding a fresh and triumphant note to our *aggadot*, the ecumenical movement is also likely to introduce new patterns of Jewish-Christian-Moslem relations. Like the State of Israel, the interfaith movement, involving Judaism, was a delayed reaction to the Holocaust.

It is important to recognize that the Halachah in regard to non-Jews was frozen in the form that it assumed at Yavneh at the end of the first century. Some general principles were enunciated—such as the Noachide laws, in all their ambiguities, the recognition that not all Gentiles are worshippers of "strange gods," etc. But, the relevance and application of these laws to Christians and, later, to Moslems, was left undetermined and was vitiated by the demands of apologetics. The times were not suitable for a positive evaluation.

In our day, the interfaith movement has already resulted in the breaking down of barriers in the field of learning and teaching. The old prohibition of "teaching Torah to Gentiles" is no longer taken seriously. In the field of *gemilut ḥasadim* there is bound to be increasing cooperation. Joint religious

services to celebrate great national events are becoming the norm, rather than
the exception, in American public life. What shall be the governing principles of such interfaith activities?

Other issues in this field have already moved to the forefront of our
agenda. Can we continue to close our eyes to intermarriages and refuse to
participate in their sacralization? Can we refuse to acknowledge the Jewishness *in potentia* of the child of a Jewish father and a Christian mother?

Must we regard intermarriage always as a loss, instead of as a potential
gain? If the living faith of liberal Christians is close to our "sacred tradition,"
where is the line to be drawn? Has the time come to revive the category of
*yirai hashem*, the Fearers of the Lord, insofar as Christian spouses of Jews are
concerned? What are the parameters of the obligation to welcome strangers
into our religious fellowship in our day?

These and similar questions are bound to open up new areas for the
different philosophies of Jewish law.


## Summation

In sum, Halachah is intimately related to the contemporary forms of
wisdom and the unfolding vistas of personal and social ethics. Hence, our
critical understanding of Bible and Talmud enters into our interpretation of
the dynamics of Jewish law, as well as our philosophical conception of the
nature of the divine thrust in history. Halachah must be responsive to the
best ideals of every age. To be sure, "whatever *needs* not to be changed, needs
*not* to be changed." Advances should be made with due regard to contemporary sensibilities, to the lessons of history and to the visions of the future. In
our age, the emergence of the State of Israel and of the inter-faith movement
present fresh challenges to the making of Jewish law.


## Notes to A Theological Foundation for the Halakhah

[1]Following is a selected bibliography on the themes of revelation and halachah: *Guideposts in
Modern Judaism*, chapters four to nine; *Dialogue and Tradition*, pp. 427-501 and 523-553;
Proceedings of the R. A., especially '76; the chapters on revelation, the covenant and
Maimonides in this volume.
[2]B.T. *Makkot* 23b. In the name of R. Yishmoel, *Horayot* 8a.
[3]Philo interprets "the image of God" in man to be the capacity for freedom.
[4]Additional references in A. Urbach's *Hazal*, p. 29, note 1.
[5]In this sense, the Midrash speaks of Torah as "the decayed fruit of the wisdom that is above"
(Genesis *Rabbah* 17,5; 44,17).

# JEWISH—CHRISTIAN DIALOGUE

# JUDAISM AND THE NEW TESTAMENT

Father Florovsky summed up the challenge of an interfaith dialogue in these well-chosen words—"It is delicate and painful, but not hopeless." The subject of this paper illustrates the aptness of his judgment. The long centuries of historic hostility demonstrate the anguish, yet the essence of both testaments, as Paul understood it, was precisely hope (Acts 28:20; Eph. 2:12).

Judaism and Christianity meet theologically on the following common ground: The Hebrew Bible, reverence for Wisdom, and the genius of prophetic inspiration. Beginning with the last element, we note that rabbinic Judaism maintained that biblical prophecy had come to an end. Yet, it also asserted that the Holy Spirit guided the deliberations of the sages. Hillel attributed this blessing to all pious Israelites—"You may rely upon the Israelites, the Holy Spirit is upon them. If they are not prophets, they are sons of prophets."[1] The deliberations of the sages were aided by a divine echo.[2] The medieval philosopher, Judah Halevi, expressed the general belief when he asserted that the Mishnah and Talmud were composed with divine assistance (*The Kuzari* 3:73).

The concept of prophetic inspiration consisted in attempting to penetrate the deeper meaning of Torah and the concomitant belief that God works through history, generating ever greater understanding of God's revelation. So, in the rabbinic tradition a prophet could not set aside a *halachah*, or establish a new *halachah*, but could decide which *halachot* were to be applied in his day.[3] Divine inspiration in the interpretation of a biblical book was claimed by the writers of the Dead Sea Scrolls.[4]

A parallel development of the operation of the Holy Spirit lies at the very heart of Christianity. Whether the view prevailed that the Holy Spirit worked through the community as a whole or through the bishops or through the papacy or through the mystics, the obligation of penetrating to the deeper meaning of the Bible was incumbent upon every generation. And Jesus illustrated this obligation by the comment on divorce, sifting the divine intent from "the hardness of the heart," which conditioned an earlier saying.[5] We dare say that in every faith deriving from the Bible a renaissance took place whenever theologians returned to a fresh study of Holy Writ. The reinterpretation of Scripture, in the light of the prophetic emphasis on justice, compassion, and love, is the common task of Jews and Christians.

In our day, we bring to the study of the Scriptures in particular, and the

Originally published in *Journal of Ecumenical Studies*, 1976.

past generally, certain tools and insights that were scarcely available in previous generations—which brings us to the second component of theological common ground, the element of wisdom. The obligation to pursue the quest of wisdom in order to understand the implications of faith is of the essence of biblical religion, since the books of wisdom formed part of Holy Writ. The sages formulated the matter succinctly—"If there is no wisdom, there is no piety; if there is no piety, there is no wisdom" (Abot 3:14). Similarly in Christianity wisdom was extolled, and Greek philosophy preoccupied the attention of the Fathers of the Church beginning with Clement of Alexandria.

Wisdom today has the added dimension of history-mindedness in all its facets—a recognition of the context in which every event must be viewed, a critical and comparative approach to all documents, an understanding of the fluidity of meaning, and its determination by psychological and sociological factors.

The duty to study history in order to understand the meaning of providence is already stated in Deut. 32:7. But while history was in the past the handmaiden of theology, it now asserts its own independent validity, compelling theology to take account of its data. History-mindedness need not degenerate into an all-questioning historicism; on the contrary, by deepening our awareness of our human limitations, as individuals and as heirs of a specific tradition, it heightens our appreciation of the third part of the prophet Micah's admonition, "to do justice, to love mercy, and to walk humbly with the Lord, thy God" (6:8).

When we speak of Judaism in relation to the New Testament, we have to make clear that we view Judaism as a river which contains many trends and flows on several levels. Modern Judaism contains a broad range of views, from a tenuous attachment of those who are primarily ethnicists to a whole-souled, mystical absorption in Torah as the embodiment of the divine will. We speak of three main branches of the Jewish faith—Orthodox, Conservative, and Reform. But, in actuality, each of these divisions is a loose grouping of diverse views. On the whole, there is greater emphasis today on the historical-cultural matrix of faith, hence a willingness to include within the tradition sects, trends, and opinions that were previously excluded. We include the Karaites, for instance, and appreciate the boldness of their founder's slogan—"Search well in the Torah, and do not rely on my opinions." These audacious rebels against the rule of the Talmud articulated a Jewish ideal, although their maxim proved to be impractical. By the same token, we look upon the spectrum of Jewish groups in New Testament times without identifying ourselves completely with any one of them.

The discovery of the Dead Sea Scrolls expanded further our awareness of the immense fermentation in the spiritual life of ancient Israel. The Qumran sectarians drew a sharp line between "the children of light and the children of darkness," but in modern Israel their writings are ensconced in a special building, *Bet Hasefer*, as a great national treasure. Each sectarian group considered itself to be "the true Israel," as did the Pharisees, who spoke of their teachers as *hachmai Yisroel*, the sages of Israel; the Sadducees who stigmatized their opponents as Pharisees, or separatists; the Zealots; the Essenes; the Samaritans; and the Apostolic Jewish-Christian community in Jerusalem.[6] The Pharisees captured the loyalty of the masses of the people even before the Great Revolt and, following that disaster, the Hillelite school of Pharisaic thought came to predominate. Because of a series of catastrophes, the treasures of Hellenistic Judaism were neglected. The sages of Yavneh were compelled to limit the range of Scripture, eliminating the apocryphal and pseudo-epigraphic works.[7] They acted in order to lower the fever of messianic speculation and provide a protective shield against the inroads of Gnostic sectarians.

Ever since the opening of the modern era, Jewish scholars endeavored to reclaim the works of Philo, the books of the Maccabees, and the entire library of inter-testamentary literature. Judah Maccabee, unmentioned in rabbinic literature, was reclaimed as an exemplary hero. It is now evident that the apocalyptic writers formed circles or schools within either the Pharisaic or the Essenic movements. And Philo's thought is now regarded as essentially and authentically Jewish.[8] As we see it, the tannaitic sages of the Hillelite school did not approve all that the Pharisaic order represented, either in fact or in popular fancy.[9] As to the high priestly hierarchy, it consisted largely of Sadducees, and the Talmud contains ample evidence of the resentment they aroused among the people (Pesahim 57a, Yoma 18b, Kiddushin 66a.). Considerable latitude was allowed for differences of opinion among the tannaitic rabbis, heirs of the Pharisees. It was considered a blessing that "disputes for the sake of heaven" would endure (Abot 5:20).

In the historical interpretation of Judaism, which was begun in the nineteenth century, we take it as our task to acknowledge the dark shadows as well as the bright glories of the Pharisaic movement. We are also aware of the distortions and perversions that crept into the two Talmuds by reason of the fact that they were not edited, with the result that unworthy and unhistorical references to Jesus and Christianity found their way into the Talmud and Midrashim. We regard such passages as the debris of folk-myths, rather than as teachings of the faith. Modern Jewish scholars can find ample justification for this attitude in the authoritative works of the rabbinic tradition.[10]

From all the above, it is clear that the theological spectrum of historic

Judaism is far bigger and more diverse than either Bousset's concentration on the Apocrypha or Moore's concept of "normative Judaism" would suggest. Schechter's stress on rabbinic Judaism and Moore's classic description of the ideas implied in rabbinic literature were needed correctives of the previously prevailing views, especially among German scholars, which described first-century Judaism largely in terms of the Apocrypha. On the other hand, it is equally one-sided to ignore Philonic and intertestamentary literature.

The great historian, F. Baer, has proposed the thesis that a synthesis of Judaism and classical Hellenism was effected by the sages of the fourth and third pre-Christian centuries, when the ideal of a *Hassid* emerged as a blend of the Greek philosopher and the prophetic disciple. There was born the concept of an earthly society of ascetics, striving heroically for spiritual perfection and for the establishment of a perfect society here on earth, mirroring the harmony prevailing in the cosmos. Even if Baer's theory is not accepted in its totality, we cannot doubt that for generations Greek philosophers and Jewish sages recognized one another as kindred in spirit.[11]

Philo, then, was not an exceptional figure who undertook an impossible task, but the heir of a long tradition to which, as a matter of fact, he refers from time to time. The Alexandrian school of Jewish thought helps us to see the roots of the New Testament in the teachings of diaspora synagogues. There is, for instance, the distinction in Philo between God who is unknowable, and God's manifest powers, chief of which was the Logos.[12] Whether the origin of the "heavenly man" be sought in Persia or in Greece, this concept was employed by Philo in his description of the creation of Adam and Eve (Philo, *Legum Allegoria*, I, XII, 31, Ed. Loeb Classics).

The Alexandrian Jews and Christian historians were convinced that Plato and Aristotle were disciples of the biblical prophets.[13] A bold, universalistic outreach to all people informs the entire range of Hellenistic-Jewish literature—from Philo to the author of the Testaments of the Twelve Patriarchs.[14] Philo interprets "the reasons of the commandments" in purely human terms, as sign-posts for the human soul in its struggle to attain perfection. Even the name "Israel" is for him a title, rather than an ethnic designation—the mark of one who has attained the vision of God.[15] Philo's use of the allegorical method to discover the inner meaning of Torah is today no longer regarded as an alien importation into Judaism. The authors of the Dead Sea Scrolls employed a similar method. Furthermore, Hillel or his teachers did not scruple to adopt the methods of Alexandrian grammarians in the interpretation of the written law.[16]

Philo's description of the Theraputae, Josephus' description of the Essenes, and the Dead Sea Scrolls allow us glimpses of the variety of schools within first-century Judaism. We now recognize the tremendous polarity between a gentle, all-embracing humanism and a fanatical dogmatism seeking to limit the circles of the "elect." In the Babylonian Talmud itself we encounter the two contrasting attitudes—the constricting one, limiting the rewards of heaven to the few pietists, and the outreaching one, opening its blessings to all "who direct their hearts to heaven."[17]

From the standpoint of historical Judaism, the documents of the New Testament acquire a special importance. They reflect the process whereby the central concepts of the Jewish religion were transferred to the great non-Jewish world. Yet this transfer was carried out in a way which cast the Jewish people in the role of the dark, satanic force. This double effect—an acceptance of the Jewish message in essence, and a rejection of the Jewish messenger in fact—has determined the character and destiny of Jewish history. Hence, there is a renewed interest in the study of the New Testament and its ancillary literature on the part of Jewish scholars.

For a long time, Jewish scholars studied the New Testament only for the purpose of holding their own in debates with Christian counterparts. Such disputations centered on the meaning of certain proof-tests or, as Nahmanides and Albo pointed out, on the logical tenability of certain Christian dogmas.[18] By far, the vast majority of medieval rabbis ignored the New Testament and shunned interfaith discussions for fear of being accused of blasphemy. Even in our day, some rabbis maintain that, while Christianity must take account of Judaism, the latter does not have to evaluate the import and truth of the former. While for Christianity Judaism is the foundation, they say, for Judaism, Christianity is simply a development outside its own walls.

Indeed, the Orthodox, who are comfortable with dogmatic walls, frequently take this view. But, if our self-awareness as Jews is determined by our overview of Jewish history, we cannot but regard the emergence of the Christian branch out of the Jewish stem as the most momentous event in our millennial experience. The Jewish self-image is largely affected by this development, as well as the image of the Jew among the nations. The "big idea" of our heritage was demonstrated in this phenomenon, in that "the God of Israel" triumphed over the pagan deities and all their works. But also the "big burden" of Jewish life was here heaped upon our shoulders, since the Jew was in effect compelled to wear the sign of Cain. While in actuality the Jewish spirit achieved a magnificent triumph, this process was associated with a systematic denigration, even the demonization, of the Jew.

Hence, the thoughtful Jew who desires to follow the ancient counsel, "know thyself," must grapple with the many riddles posed by a study of the

New Testament. To begin with, the Jew knows that the entire New Testament was composed by Jews. Luke was probably a convert to Judaism before he joined the Christian community. Yet, the Jew also knows that the various documents constituting the New Testament were edited by Christians at a time when the church consisted largely of Gentiles and was engaged in bitter fights against Jews. The two communities broke apart in the generation following the destruction of the Holy Temple (70 A.D.), amidst bitter curses and implacable hatred.[19] We cannot tell whether the *birchat Haminim* of the Jews preceded or followed the anathemas of the Christians. In any case, neutrality appeared impossible to both sides. The historical approach makes it possible for us to rediscover our kinship with one another, while repudiating the seeds of malice that the duststorms of history have scattered over the pages of sacred Scripture.

The central theses that emerge from the study of the New Testament in the context of Jewish rabbinic literature include:

*First*, that the teaching of Jesus did not imply the repudiation either of Judaism or of the Jewish people.

*Second*, that the closer we come to the Apostolic community centered in Jerusalem, the less we encounter any suggestion of the "rejection" of Israel.

*Third*, That the New Testament passages implying the "rejection" of the Jewish people, as a reversal of their having previously been chosen, were superimposed upon the earlier traditions of the church after the fall of Jerusalem; that the essence of Christian teaching, according to medieval interpreters, consisted in the repudiation of Judaism.

*Fourth*, that all such anti-Judaism and anti-Jewish passages resulted in part from the gradual transference of the Gospel tradition from the Jewish to the Hellenistic culture sphere, during the seventy-year period, 65-135 A.D., and in part from the impassioned bitterness of the second and third centuries when the New Testament canon attained its present form.

*Fifth*, that it is incumbent upon Christian scholars, as seekers of truth in love and love in truth, to eliminate anti-Jewish and anti-Judaism inferences from their interpretation of the New Testament.

*Sixth*, that it is incumbent upon Jewish scholars to reclaim the New Testament as an integral part of their domain of study and to develop the implications of the teaching that Christianity is an "ecclesia for the sake of heaven," employed by God as an instrument whereby humanity is being prepared for "the kingdom of heaven," *malchut shomayim*.

1. The first thesis has been established for several generations among Jewish scholars. Jesus was a supremely original personality, and his views

did not coincide completely with those of any of the movements that existed in his day, but the building blocks of his spiritual edifice were taken from the Jewish world of that day. Jesus stood closest to the Pharisees, in that he believed in the resurrection, in angels, in the worship of the synagogue, and in the role of providence within the life of the individual and within Israel; but he was also close to the Essenes, as is evident in his ethics, in his relation to John the Baptist, in his closeness to the apocalyptic circles, and in the life of the Apostolic community of Jerusalem.

But Jesus differed with *some* of the Pharisaic leaders. After all, James the Elder testifies that many Pharisees had joined the early Christian community without giving up their zeal for the Law (Acts 21:20). Jesus' arguments with the Pharisees referred to specific issues of the oral law, which were probably topics of disputation in the schools. His critique of the high priests reflected popular sentiments that are also echoed in the Talmud (Pesahim 57a.). Jesus' chief complaint was the non-recognition on the part of most Pharisaic leaders of his claim to be the apocalyptic Messiah.[20] As we learn from occasional references in the Talmud, some apocalyptic circles taught that the Messiah would bring down the Holy Temple from heaven and put it in the place of the earthly one.[21]

2. The second thesis is proved by scholars through the comparative textual analysis of the Gospels. Paul Winter, in his book *On the Trial of Jesus*, puts side by side the various references to the enemies of Jesus. He takes the passion chapters of Mark to be the most ancient portion, and he concludes his analysis as follows (p. 124):

> *The oldest synoptic tradition* (however restyled it may have *become in the process of literary formulation) does not include the Pharisees among the enemies of Jesus at all;* there is not a single instance in which Pharisaic hostility towards Jesus finds mention.

A similar view was already put forward by the famous scholar, Daniel Chwolson, who suggested that the second-century editors changed in many places the word "scribes" for the word "Pharisees," since in their day there were no longer Sadducee scribes.[22] Joseph Klausner pointed out that Jesus debated as a member of the Pharisaic movement. Paul Winter argues similarly: "Yet in historical reality, Jesus was a Pharisee . . . when an eschatological emphasis may have pervaded Pharisaic thought more strongly than in the tannaitic age" (p. 133).

The viewpoint of Jewish scholars was summarized in the old *Jewish Encyclopedia*, published in the first decade of the twentieth century (article on the New Testament):

. . . that the old and the more genuine the records, written or unwritten, of the doings and teachings of Jesus, the more they betray close kinship with and friendly relations to Jews and Judaism; but that the more remote they are from the time and activity of Jesus, the more they show of hostility to the Jewish people and of antagonism to the Mosaic Law.

The gulf between the Jews and Christians was deepened by the lynching of Stephen, and the persecutions directed by the Sadducee high priest were opposed by Rabban Gamaliel the Elder. Agrippa probably followed the counsel of the Sadducees. The Pharisees still resented the execution of James the Elder, but with the approach of the Great Revolt (65-70 A.D.) tempers were inflamed throughout the Jewish world. In some places, Jewish leaders sought to remove the protective mantle of Judaism, as a *religio licita*, from the proliferating Christian churches. Thus, the soil was prepared for Nero's persecutions. With the outbreak of the Revolt, which was spurred by intense messianic expectations, and punctuated by outbreaks of pogroms throughout Syria, the Christians left Jerusalem, according to a tradition recorded by Eusebius.

With the disappearance of the mother church in Jerusalem, leadership fell into the hands of Gentile Christians. The remnant of Jewish Christians were beset by pressures from both Jews and Christians. The Jewish curse formulated by Rabban Gamaliel the Second and the Christian anathema combined to crush the middle position. In addition, when the Roman Empire imposed a special tax upon Jews, the Christians were exempt; and when Marcus Aurelius Antonius was friendly to Jews, he was implacably hostile to Christians. The course of history raised a high barrier of hostility between the two communities just at the time when their respective traditions were taking firm shape. But it was the rise of Gnosticism that contributed most effectively to the introduction of mythological Antisemitism in Christianity

3. The third thesis points to the most persistent anti-Jewish animus that is inculcated almost unconsciously by the New Testament. To illustrate its dark impetus, I will cite a recent popular scientific commentary on Matthew, edited by the late Professor Albright, who yielded to no one in his stout defense of Judaism and the Jewish people. Yet, in commenting on Matt. 9:17, he wrote (p. 108):

Romans IX-XI is evidence of the great concern felt about the precise relationship of the Messianic Community to Judaism. On the view that vss. 16-17 are to be regarded as Jesus' teaching on the relationship of his Community to Judaism, then the final clause "*and both are preserved*" is either editorial comment, or a misplaced saying from another context in an attempt to deal with the question.

But this must be regarded as unsatisfactory. The whole tenor of Jesus' teaching, in all four gospels, makes it hardly possible to suppose that he looked to a continuance of his Messianic Community and Judaism side by side.

So, even Albright assumes that the establishment of the Messianic community implied the rejection of those who did not join it. But, is not this attitude a retrojection of later attitudes? If Paul could not reconcile himself to such a rejection, could Jesus, whose Jewish roots were far deeper, adopt such a judgement? Whether or not we adopt Schweitzer's interpretation of Jesus' eschatological attitude, we cannot deny that Jesus' central concern was to preach "the good news" to his own people. And his few acts of benevolence toward Gentiles were entirely in keeping with the teaching of Jewish ethics, certainly not a repudiation of his people. But the pervasive feeling to which Albright calls attention embodies an impetus, deep and strong. What is its source? The answer uncovers a fundamental struggle which continues to the present.

The canonization of the New Testament was brought about through the partial rejection and the partial acceptance of two contending philosophies—Judaism and Gnosticism. Marcion formed the first canon, and he excluded the Old Testament altogether, consigning the God of Israel and God's Law to the sinister role of demiurge, the creator of this world and its numberless evils. Jesus was the Son and Messenger of the good, transworldly realm, whose followers, by repudiating this world and all its works, would inherit that glorious realm. Marcion was repudiated by the emergent Catholic Church, but Gnosticism was too insidious and too deep-rooted to be altogether eliminated. The Church looked for the middle way between Judaism and Gnosticism.

What were the essential differences between these two poles of the spirit? We take Gnosticism to be the opposite of classical Hellenism as well as of prophetic Judaism. While the stars were "gods" to the Hellenes and noble creations of God, or angels, to Jews, they were part of the evil order of reality to the Gnostics.[23] The essence of Gnosticism is the myth of catastrophe, describing how Sophia, or the heavenly one, or supernal light was imprisoned by Satanic forces, and the belief that the way of redemption depends on a special knowledge deriving from beyond this world, whereby the soul reverses its path and ascends to heaven. Hence, the polarity is threefold—whether or not truth is co-extensive with natural human powers of reason;

whether or not goodness is that of human effort and conscience; and whether or not certain people are provided from birth with a pneumatic soul, rendering them capable of redemption. Gnosticism asserts the *discontinuity* of human wisdom and redemptive knowledge, of sanctification through deeds and intentions, or through an inner spirit and Divine Grace. Similarly it asserts the dichotomy of the human race between ordinary people and pneumatics.[24]

Paul wavered between Judaism and Gnosticism, inclining sufficiently to the latter pole to provide a handle to Marcion. Some portions of John contain the reverberations of Gnostic rhetoric. Generally, the Gnostics were bitterly anti-Judaistic and anti-Jewish. Within Christianity the Gnostic orientation, identifying the divine with the discontinuous, the transcendental, and the ascetic, triumphed especially in heretical movements. But, it frequently generated a powerful undertow, even within the official forms of the faith. And whenever Gnostic anti-Judaism prevailed, anti-Jewishness was always the result.

The Gnostic theory of pneumatics is easily translatable into mystical racism. Fichte, prophet of modern German nationalism, demonstrated the perennial appeal of Gnosticism in his philosophy of history, stigmatizing the Jews as the children of worldly cleverness, *Verstand*, and elevating the Teutons to the rank of people of *Vernunft*.[25] A great deal of modern biblical study expatiated on the contrasts between Jewish "good deeds" and Christian grace; between Jewish intellectualism, which is presumably barren, and the noble intuition of Teutons, or Nordics, or Aryans; between the Jewish ideal of equality before the Law and the arbitrary "election" of the Gentiles.[26] Naturally, in German Gnosticism, the Slavs and the Greeks are condemned equally with the Jews, though a special hell on earth was reserved for those who were "chosen" by the evil Creator. Ideas are "carried over" from religion to politics and back again. Gnostic, that is non-Hellenic and non-Jewish, was the asserted discontinuity between the Old Testament and the New Testament, between the Old Covenant and the New, between the old Israel and the New, between the Old Morality and the New, between Jew and Gentile. It is time to allay this metaphysical mythology, wherever it appears—in Christian as in Jewish thought.

4. The fourth thesis purports to explain how what was originally a fervently Jewish faith became so bitterly anti-Jewish. In part, the answer is simply the transference of the same rhetoric from a Jewish to a Gentile popular base. When an Isaiah or a Jeremiah castigates his people, he does not infer that they are indeed degenerate and God-forsaken. The prophet demands so much because he trusts the essential nobility of his people, and

his words are preserved by the people as expressions of their own conscience. But, when the same words are taken out of context by external enemies, they add up to a verdict of condemnation.

A contemporary Jesuit scholar summarizes the import of the biblical prophets as follows:

> Ancient Israel was played out and had to go. . . . This new Israel could, however, only be born of the downfall of the old. . . . The salvation of the new people of God was the reverse of the divine judgment passed on the ancient people of God.[27]

Yet, note that the same words which convey this meaning to the Catholic scholar were cherished by Jews as "the hope of Israel."

So, the occasional bitter outcries of Jesus or Paul or Matthew or John were spoken in the revered vein of prophetic admonition, but their Gentile editors, living in a different milieu, edited them in keeping with their own lights. Following the fall of Jerusalem, the mother church fell apart, and the branches in the Gentile world had to establish their legitimacy on their own grounds, despite the fact that they were worshipping one who was condemned and executed by Rome. Modifications and qualifications that existed in the original document, describing various personalities within the Jewish community, were all generalized into the term which made sense only in the new social environment—i.e., the term "Jews" was substituted for "witnesses" or "crowds" or "opponents" or "skeptics."[28]

In part, this editorial policy was a reflection of the bitter animosity between Jews and Gentiles during the Civil Wars of 65 to 135 A.D. By the middle of the second century the Jewish Christians were reduced to a marginal minority. How could the hatred of Jews coexist with the love of so much of the Jewish literary and spiritual heritage? The sad truths of human nature provide the answer, and history corroborates the insights of psychology. Josephus tells us that in Damascus the Syrian women were "God-fearers," attending the synagogues on the Sabbath, while many of their husbands were Jew-haters, planning physical massacres of their Jewish neighbors.[29]

5. The fifth thesis is an appeal to Christian conscience and truthfulness. There is absolutely no reason to interpret the documents of the New Testament in such a way as to teach that the Jews are condemned or accursed or rejected, much less that they are eternally guilty of deicide. The Catholic Church is to be heartily commended for its decisiveness in confronting this issue. I can say without fear of contradiction that no passage in the New

Testament gives aid or comfort to Antisemitism, if it is seen in the light of the social-cultural context of contemporary Jewish life.

The disputations with Pharisaic leaders are instructive examples of the arguments that went on in the schools. Their general import is an emphasis on inwardness and principle that is indeed laudable and by no means rare in Jewish tradition. The numerous parables, so rich in meaning, are all-human, not Jewish-Gentile in reference. Always the concept of Israel included an all-human dimension in hope and faith. And the narration of Jesus' life and death, read in context, is free of any anti-Jewish animus.

By way of example, the sentence of Matthew 27:25 which served as the foundation for the myth of deicide can be easily understood in its Jewish context. As it reads it is utterly incomprehensible. "All the people" could only refer to the crowd actually present. Why should people voluntarily take guilt upon their children as well as upon themselves? The medieval mind understood this action as the work of Satan, but medieval myths have a way of persisting beneath modern rationalizations.

If we see the crucifixion in the light of the practices then prevailing, then we know that witnesses were indeed warned, prior to the execution of the defendant, that the guilt for that death and the death of any potential descendants down to the end of time would rest upon them. In turn, the witnesses would reassert their testimony and say they are so sure that they are willing to assume this blame.[30] Now, Jesus was condemned on the basis of the presumed testimony of witnesses, or of those present in the house of Caiaphas. The followers of the high priest, then, stated their willingness to be judged in heaven for the blood of Jesus and his potential descendants. When this incident was transferred to the milieu of a different culture, "his children" seemed blasphemous, if Jesus were God, and the term "witnesses" were simply generalized to the phrase "all the people"; as in most other cases, the specific term was generalized to the all-inclusive category, "Jews."

A similar example may be taken from John 8:44, wherein the devil is said to be the father of the Jews. We have here a sermon, given presumably in a synagogue, with Jesus addressing "those Jews who had believed him" (8:31). The author dramatized the tension between belief and unbelief within the soul of Jewish people. When this inner dialogue is transferred into a Gentile-Christian universe of discourse, the inner voice of admonition is transformed into an external verdict of condemnation.[31]

6. The first part of the sixth thesis deals with the reclamation of the New Testament. It is part of Jewish history as literature and life, but with respect to the sacred heritage it marks the boundary between Judaism and Christianity. Frequently, we can see how the same words acquired different meaning as they were transferred from the Jewish to the Hellenistic context.

So the name "son of God" was applied to Jewish people generally, to righteous men, to the kings of the house of David, and by implication, also to the Messiah.[32] But, within the ideological context of Judaism, the concept of divine unity precluded any notion of a "son of God" in any essential sense. Precisely because Jews lived in a society where Caesar was proclaimed son of God and *Kyrios*, Jewish opposition to this notion was firmly established. Philo could speak of God being three in appearance—i.e., God's sovereignty, benevolence, and unknowable being—but he added that, to the thoughtful, God is One.[33] So, the same series of titles of "Messiah," "son of Man," "Son of God," and "Kyrios" could by degrees acquire totally different meaning as the Jewish culture-context was replaced by the Hellenistic.[34]

Similarly, the concepts of redemption, faith, the Law and its inner meaning, the ideal congregation of Israel, the salvation of Gentiles, the replacement of the sacrificial ritual by deeds of "steadfast love"—all these and many more—are observed in the process of transformation.

In one century, the nascent Christian community underwent several transformations, brought about by a series of "scandals." The first "scandal" was felt within the Apostolic community, which was almost entirely Jewish—the Messiah came unto his own people, and "they" rejected him. "They," in this case, meant the leaders and teachers, the Pharisaic masters "who sit in Moses' seat." In the light of this "scandal," the differences between Jesus and the Pharisaic teachers were magnified, but the belief prevailed that this resistance of Jewish leaders and their followers was provisional and temporary. The second "scandal" was felt on the boundary between Jewry and the Hellenistic world as a result of the progressive transference of biblical and rabbinic ideas to the Hellenistic realm of thought. What was "unthinkable" in Judaism became the mark of a transcendent wisdom, the sign of a fresh upsurge of the Holy Spirit in the churches which continued to develop the ideas of Paul and John, particularly after the church became entirely Hellenistic. While Philo represented the synthesis of Judaism and Hellenic philosophy, the Pauline churches represented the blend of Judaism and Hellenistic religion. The third "scandal" was felt by the Gentile converts, following the fall of Jerusalem. How could they adore one who was convicted and executed by Roman authority? Gradually, the notion prevailed that Jesus was condemned by the Jews, while Pontius Pilate was the passive reluctant agent of Jewish, or demonic, fury.

In the modern world, all of us are bidden to live in two universes of discourse—within our traditions and in spirit, in an all-embracing universe of discourse. *On the Boundary* is the title of Paul Tillich's autobiography. And to live "on the boundary" is part of our universal experience.

The second portion of the sixth thesis might be called a Jewish theology of Christianity. This task will be carried out in diverse ways by the theologians of present and future generations if the contemporary irenic orientation within the Christian and Jewish worlds is maintained and deepened. It takes time for old ideas to fade away totally. Who can tell whether the old demons will arise from their graves and once again point to Jewry as anti-Christ, whose sin is the free intellect or a conscience geared into universal law or piety ossified in ritual? If the ecumenical movement endures, we can expect a deepening of the sentiment of community in the family of God's children. Let me outline some of the sign-posts of a Jewish theology of Christianity:

a. God judges individuals, one by one, as well as groups as a whole. A rabbi who lived through the siege of Jerusalem taught "that the pious among the nations share in the World to Come," even if they are not converted. According to their personal merit, the Holy Spirit rests upon them. Pious Gentiles are described in the Talmud as examples for Jews.[35]

b. Christianity, in all its variations, was declared by the Tossafists to be a monotheistic faith. Gentiles were allowed to associate other divine beings with God in their worship (*shittuf*), though this practice was not permitted to Jews. The "curse of heretics" (*birkhat haminim*) was not included in the prayers of European Jews, since the close of the Babylonian Talmud.[36]

c. Occasional hints of a still more affirmative relation to Christianity should now be developed systematically and in depth. Such an orientation is contained *in nuce* in the rabbinic characterization of the church as an "ecclesia for the sake of heaven" that God causes to endure and expand through the vicissitudes of history.[37] This estimation of the church as a divine instrument by no means implies the ending of Israel's role. The high purposes of God require many instruments for their "fulfillment." So, we return to the view of Rabban Gamaliel the Elder, as recorded in Acts 5:33, and to the opinion of James, "the brother of Jesus" (Acts 15:13-21). Highly significant is the imagery of the twelfth-century philosopher, Judah Halevi, who spoke of Israel as "the heart"; other faiths, like other internal organs, are equally necessary for life. He also employed the figure of a tree with three branches, growing out of the same seed (*The Kuzari* 4:23).

d. While Jews cannot accept the dogmatic framework of the New Testament, they can and do recognize its sublime teachings. Many scholars, including preeminently Martin Buber, saw in the revivals of Jewish pietism at various times, and particularly in Polish-Russian

Hassidism, a similar efflorescence of religious genius—an emphasis on inwardness, an aspiration for "the nearness of God," an anticipation in the present of the glories of the blessed future. Some modern Jewish philosophers regarded Christianity as the outstretched arm of the Jewish faith, seeking to redeem humankind.[38]

Above all, the historical approach with its strong dash of relativism orients our thinking along the lines of pragmatism. Truth *is* as truth *works*. Does any proposed idea really motivate people to sow the seeds of justice and truth, of faith, hope, and love? Indeed, Jesus anticipated this mode of thinking in the maxim. "By their fruits shall ye know them" (Mt. 7:16).

In the pragmatic orientation we focus our attention on the task that faces us, the task of regaining for the living Word of God a society which is so largely atheistic, materialistic, and bitterly cynical. It is an overwhelming task, far more "delicate and painful" than the interfaith dialogue, but by no means "hopeless."

All of us are called upon to share in the covenant of the spirit which transcends all ritualistic and historical differences. It is in this way that we see the contemporary meaning of Jeremiah's "*berit Hadashah*," which underlies the term "New Testament" (Jer. 31:30). Neither the old ritual nor the new is in itself decisive. What is decisive is the spirit in which rites are performed and the consequences that flow from them (Lk. 22:20; 1 Cor. 11:25). To the extent that any of us individually or collectively achieves the prophetic ideal, we share in an enterprise that is eternal. Whether we derive our inspiration through the rabbinic tradition, which in turn is linked to the Hebrew Bible, or through the Christian tradition and the New Testament, which are also linked to the same sacred Scriptures, our ultimate quest is the same—*malchut shomayim*, the Reign of heaven in our hearts and in society.

220                          JACOB B. AGUS

## Notes to Judaism and the New Testament

[1]Tosefta, Pesahim 4,13. Jer. Talmud 6,1. The version of the Babylonian Talmud, Pesahim 66b, does not mention the Holy Spirit.

[2]The reference to Hillel in Tosefta Sota 13,3. Pesikta Rabbati, Ch. 35. The relation of Halachah to prophecy is examined in detail by A. Urbach in *Tarbitz*, 1947.

[3]B. T. Shabbat 104a. He could revive a law that was forgotten. The term used here is "Tsofim," which means mystical visionaries. In this sense, the sages were considered to be the heirs of the prophets. [B. T. Baba Bathra 12a. where the strange comment is given—"A Sage is better than a prophet." A prophet's authority did not extend to concessions to idolatry, even as a temporary expedient (Sanhedrin 90a).]

[4]"The Habakkuk Commentary," *Pesher Habakkuk*, is a case in point. Note particularly this sentence, "And as for what it says, *that he may run who reads it*, this means the teacher of righteousness, to whom God made known all the mysteries of the words of his servants, the prophets" [Millar Burrows, ed., *The Dead Sea Scrolls* (New York, 1955), p. 368]. The ideal of the prophet has continued in Judaism, down to our own day. See my essay, "The Prophet in Modern Hebrew Literature" in *Dialogue and Tradition*, p. 385.

[5]Mt. 19:8. A similar view is stated in the Talmud, Kiddushim 21b, in reference to the law described in Deut. 21:10-14.

[6]The Pharisees, it had been noted long ago, do not refer to themselves under that title. On the time and the issues that brought about the split between the Pharisees and Sadducees, see S. Zeitlin, *The Rise and Fall of the Jewish State*, vol. I Prolegomena. L. Finkelstein, "Haperushim VeAnshai Keneset Hagedolah" (1950), p. 81, note 243.

[7]Rabbi Akiba favored proclaiming the exclusion from *Olam Haba* of those who read "external books" (Sanhedrin 100b), but there is considerable uncertainty as to the meaning of "external books." The only example offered in both the Palestinian and Babylonian Talmuds is the work of Sirach, or Ben Sira, yet Sirach was quoted in the Talmuds. It seems that Rabbi Akiba's maxim was his own private opinion. In the Midrashim, echoes of apocalyptic writings are heard. Even the books of Enoch, so close to New Testament thought, are praised in Zoharic writings, which contain echoes of the ideas of pharisaic circles in the first century. It is noteworthy that the Tossafot assert that in some areas we follow the teaching of "the external books," as against the Talmuds (Berochot 18a, Zohar, Bereshit 72b., 37b., Shemot 55a., Vayikra 10b. See also the Jerusalem Targum on Gen. 5:24.).

[8]See Harry A. Wolfson's *Philo*, in two volumes (Harvard University Press).

[9]The description of "Pharisaic Plagues" in the Babylonian Talmud is already undecipherable (Sota 22a). Clearly, the condemnation referred to external acts of piety which were contrasted with "the Pharisee out of love," who follows the example of Abraham.

[10]That some raw passages were inserted by "immature disciples" was already acknowledged by Judah Halevi (1085-1140) in *The Kuzari*, III, 73. Maimonides in the Introduction to the "Guide of the Perplexed," and in First Part, Chapter 59. Nahman Krochmal devoted chapter 14 of his classic work to this problem, *Moreh Nebuhai Hazeman*. In regard to the Pharisees, he stressed that they represented normative tradition only in a general way, not insofar as they defended their own sectarian interests (ibid., ch. 10, Edition Lemberg, 1863, p. 51).

[11]F. Baer's studies appeared in the Hebrew magazine, *Zion*, vol. 27-28 (1952-1953), and vol. 37 (1962); in *Molad* (1964); and in his small book, summarizing his position, *Yisroel Bo-amim* (Jerusalem, 1956).

[12]Harry A. Wolfson points out that God's "unknowability" was Philo's contribution to religious philosophy. While Plato considered that the human mind was closest to the Logos, Philo insisted that our mind is not self-activating, but that it reflects divine power and initiative. See *Legum Allegoria*, II, 69. Harry A. Wolfson, *Philo* (Harvard University Press), II, p. 110.

[13]Josephus, "Contra Apionen," I, 22. Eusebius, Praep. Evangelica XIII, 12.

[14]The universalist note in the Testaments of the Twelve Patriarchs is particularly striking. Test. of Benjamin, IX, 2; Test of Naphtali, II, 5; Test. of Levi XIV, 4.

[15]*De Spec. Leg.* I, 58. "Quod Deus sit Immort.," 30,144. Good and holy men of all nations are called by him, "Sons of God," *De Spec. Leg.* I, 318.

[16]Saul Lieberman, *Hellenism in Jewish Palestine* (New York, 1950), chapter on "Rabbinic Interpretation of Scripture." David Daube, "Rabbinic Methods of Interpretation and Hellenic Rhetoric," *Hebrew Union College Annual*, 22 (1949): 239ff.

[17]Berachot 18b. ". . . for I run, and they run. I run to the life of World to Come, and they run to the pit of destruction." Berachot 17a. ". . . The Sages of Yavne used to say, 'I am a creature and my colleagues (who do not study Torah) are creatures. . . . Lest you say, 'I do more and he does less,' we have learned. Alike are those who do more and those who do less, for all depends on the directing of one's heart to heaven. . . .'"

[18]Joseph Albo, "The Book of Principles" allows that two religions may coexist at one time and be equally divine. However, he disputes the validity of Catholic doctrine in his time, the beginning of the fifteenth century, on the ground of its logical impossibility. See I. Husik's edition, published by the J.P.S., volume III, chap. 25. Nahmanides argued at Barcelona, in 1263, as follows:

> The core of the true dispute among us is not the concept of the Messiah . . . but the crux of the issue and the reason for the argument between Jews and Christians is the fact that you impute to the Deity things which are exceedingly repugnant. . . . For what you state, and this is the essence of your faith, reason cannot accept, nature does not permit, and the prophets never implied . . . (*Sefer Havikuah Lehoramban*, 12).

[19]In a series of books, S. G. F. Brandon sought to uncover the implications of the catastrophic fall of Jerusalem on the formation and crystallization of the New Testament. His major works are *The Fall of Jerusalem and the Christian Church, Jesus and the Zealots,* and *The Trial of Jesus of Nazareth.* The disappearance of the mother church of Jerusalem is, in his judgment, the crucial fact.

[20]Ezekiel Kaufman elaborates this view in his monumental study, *Goleh Venaichar,* vol. 1, chap. 8.

[21]"Jerusalem that is above" in II Enoch 55, 2. The heavenly Temple in B. T. Hagigah 12b. Jer. T. Berochot 4,5. B. T. Sukkah 41a. Rashi's Commentary.

[22]*Das letzte Passamahl Christi u. der Tag seines Todes* (1892, 1908), p. 118. Jesus' condemnation of evil Pharisees (in Talmud, "Pharisaic plagues," Mishin Sota 3,4) was generalized by later copyists. This was also the view of M. Friedlander, *Die religiösen Bewegungen innerhalb des Judentums im Zeitalter Jesu* (1905).

[23]One blesses God, "The Creator of the beginnings," on seeing the stars (Berachot 59b). While the stars were occasionally made responsible for a person's fate (mazal), this dependence did not apply to Israel (Shabbat 156a).

[24]Jaroslav Pelican, *The Christian Tradition* (University of Chicago Press), vol. I, p. 85. The ascription of marriage to Satan by the Encratites was the clearest expression of their unworldliness. The supposition of a third mediating kind of human being was a compromise to give substance to conversion. Wilhelm Bousset, *Kyrios Christos* (New York, 1970), p. 266.

[25]F. G. Fichte, *Characteristics of the Present Age* (1849).

[26]It has long been noted that the prophets of Teutonism were also exponents of "cultural despair." Such men as Ludwig Jahn, Julius Langbehn, Paul de Lagarde, Richard Wagner, Eugen Dühring, and Oswald Spengler were agreed that the values of the democratic West were all degenerate. They looked for the awakening of a dark, slumbering soul, a peculiar racial psyche.

[27]Henry Renckens, *The Religion of Israel* (New York, 1966), p. 238-239.

[28]The Gospel of Mark was believed to have been written in Rome after 70 A.D. It includes older Aramaic logia and personal reminiscences, but it was composed with the aim of separating the Christian community from the odium that was then attached to Jewish people.

[29]Josephus, *Wars of the Jews,* II, 20,2.

[30]B. T. Sanhedrin 37a. and 44b. There was no independent rabbinic tradition regarding the crucifixion, else there would have been some consistency at least in regard to the time or the place of execution. But the time is supposed to be roughly a hundred years before, and the place Lydda, instead of Jerusalem (Sanhedrin 43a; 107b).

# 222                                    Jacob B. Agus

[31]Raymond E. Brown, in his introduction to his commentary on the Gospel of John, *Anchor Bible*, vol. 29, p. LXXI, writes as follows:

> . . . there is one stratum of Johanine material, particularly evident in XI-XII, where the term, Jews, simply refers to Judeans . . . the Fourth Gospel uses "the Jews" as almost a technical title *for the religious authorities, particularly those in Jerusalem, who are hostile to Jesus*.

[32]The messianic interpretations of Psalms 2 and 110 occur in the late Midrash Tehillim, ed. Bober, but with the qualification that "sonship" is metaphorical, "as when a Master says to his slave, 'you are my son' " (Ps. 2:54). Midrash Tehillim, ed. Bober, 110,14. The Yalkut on Tehillim, 110,869, speaks of the Messiah sitting to the right of God, with Abraham sitting at God's left.

[33]Referring to Abraham's vision of the three angels, Philo writes:

> Rather, as anyone who has approached nearest to the truth would say, the central place is held by the Father of the Universe, Who in the sacred scriptures is called 'He that is,' as His proper name, while on either side of Him are the senior potencies, the nearest to Him, the creative and the kingly. . . .
>
> . . . presents to the mind which has vision the appearance sometime of one, sometimes of three (Philo, *De Abrahamo*, XXIV, 121, 122).

[34]W. D. Davies, in *Christian Origins and Judaism* and *Paul and Rabbinic Judaism*, demonstrates that Paul's ideas were rooted in Judaism, though they were transformed in later years into concepts that could no longer be fitted within a Jewish ideological context.

[35]Tosefta, Sanhedrin, 13. Rabbi Joshua ben Hanania's opinion. The twelfth-century authors of *Tossafot* on the B. T. Avoda Zara, 2a, declare that Christianity does not fall under the category of idolatry. The contrary opinion of Maimonides in his Code is mitigated by his letter to R. Hisdai Halevi, in which he points out that "God seeks the heart." Of Gentiles as examples, Jerusalem, Peah I,1. B. T. Kiddushin 31a.

[36]Avodo Zara 2a. The Palestinian version of *"birchat haminim,"* which specifically includes Christians, was unknown to the Jews of Europe prior to its discovery by S. Schechter in the Cairo *Genizah*.

[37]This application of a maxim in the *Ethics of the Fathers* (IV,14) is offered by the eighteenth-century sage. Rabbi Jacob Emden, in his commentary, "Aitz Avot."

[38]See the original edition of Martin Buber's *Reden*. Solomon Formstecher in the nineteenth century and Franz Rosenzweig in the twentieth century used the image of the sun and its rays as symbolizing the respective roles of Judaism and Christianity.

# ISRAEL AND THE JEWISH-CHRISTIAN DIALOGUE

The six-day war between Israel and the Arab states came perilously close to precipitating a breakdown of the dialogue movement between Jews and Christians. To Jews the world over, Israel was the brand plucked from the fires of Auschwitz and Treblinka. Therefore, the essence of the six-day war was for them the threat of the Arab propagandists to complete the process of annihilation begun by Hitler. On the other hand, many Christian church-men tended to disregard the Arab threats as idle rhetoric. While Jews cannot help but see the lurid events of our day against the background of the smoking chimneys of Auschwitz, Christian observers are likely to be more general in their identification of evil. The six million Jews who died in camps were for them only part of the forty million or so victims of the Second World War—thirty million on the Russian front alone. And the ultimate causes of the conflagration were the pagan idols of nationalism and the modern myths of communism and anticommunism.

Yet the different conditioning of Jews and Christians by the atrocities of the Nazi era is not sufficient in itself to account for the feeling that a wide gulf in sentiment and thought had opened up between the two communities. It became clear that the theological dimensions of the state of Israel had not been explored in the Jewish-Christian dialogue. In fact, neither Jewish nor Christian theologians had come to terms as yet with the reality of the state of Israel and the mystical aura that clings to it. Does it represent the "fulfill-ment" of biblical prophecies? Does Israel usher in the *eschaton*, the days of the Messiah, so that it must be viewed in the many-splendored light of a new dawn of hope? Or is it simply another nation-state, hence a regressive step in the evolution of a world order, the more so, when it bears the incubus of theocratic entanglements? More specifically and to the point, since it was the dispute concerning the nature and destiny of the people of Israel that bifurcated the Jewish and Christian communities, does the emergence of the state constitute a "refutation" of the Christian thesis—hence, a "stumbling block" for Christians—or have we now through God's grace and human

Originally published in *Journal of Ecumenical Studies*, 1969.

travail risen to the point where the ancient stumbling block might well be transformed into a cornerstone of the new era of interreligious cooperation?

## God of Israel—God of All

Every attempt to explore the theological dimension of Israel must begin with an examination of the so-called "scandal" of particularity that marks the world view of the biblical authors and underlies the thinking of both Judaism and Christianity. The universal God of the philosophers is at the same time the personal God of the prophets and the psalmists. He who is far, transcending all experience, is also near, as near as our awareness of selfhood, underlying all our experience. The God who is unknowable and transcendental is also the God of revelation, and in Christianity, of the incarnation.

We have here a way of thinking that is intrinsic to the religious situation, where man, in all his littleness and because of his being "brokenhearted," encounters the Supreme Being and Creator of the universe.[1] The dialectic of this encounter consists of the awareness of polarity, followed by the act of commitment and the feelings of self-scrutiny.

In Judaism the polarity was not resolved in favor of one or the other side. There was no controversy corresponding to that between Pelagius and Augustine, except if we go back far enough and accept Josephus' version of the division between the Sadducees and the Essenes, the former removing God from the direction of human affairs and insisting that man was free to make his own destiny, the latter asserting that all was previsioned, determined and fixed in advance by God. The Pharisees whose teaching became the basis of Mishnah and Talmud retained the dynamic equilibrium of the religious encounter. In the words of R. Akiba, "all is foreseen, but choice is given,"[2] or in the later formulation of this thesis, "all is in the power of heaven save the fear of heaven."[3]

The paradox of polarity lies at the heart of the (nuclear) religious experience. God is at the opposite polar end of one's own being; yet, He deigns to look upon "the poor and the lowly of spirit, who trembles at my word."[4] An affirmation as well as a negation is contained in this awareness— man feels he has been accepted in all the uniqueness of his individual being; he is embraced in "great love," elevated into His companionship, made part of His household, a "son"—no less. He responds with love and the pledge of loyalty, he accepts the command and submits to a covenant. At the same time, he feels the severity of the divine negation. God is "other" than man. All that we can do falls short of His mark. We are sinful, weak, unclean.

The affirmation of the divine encounter issues in a determination to become a "partner of the Lord in the work of creation."[5] His command is translated into a regimen of conduct, a pattern of good deeds and sacred rites, or into the readiness to sacrifice all in His name. In either case, the deed and the feeling of being covenanted are followed by the feelings of self-criticism and penitence. If the "yes" of the divine encounter issues in positive acts and redemptive feelings, its "no" instills the awareness of inadequacy and insufficiency.

"Do not believe in yourself till the day of your death,"[6] counseled Hillel the Elder. Certainly, Paul, the disciple of Rabban Gamaliel, Hillel's grandson, was aware during the days of his Jewishness of a ceaseless inner tension. The struggle is never finally won. Rabban Yohanan ben Zakkai taught this lesson to his pupils with his dying breath:

"When he lay on his sick bed, his pupils came to visit him. When he saw them, he began to cry. Said his pupils to him, 'The lamp of Israel, the right pillar, the mighty hammer, why do you cry?' Said he to them, 'If they were bringing me before a king of flesh and blood, who is here today and in the grave tomorrow, whose anger is not eternal, . . . I would have cried. Now they will bring me before the King of Kings who is eternal and whose wrath is eternal, should I not cry?' "[7]

Similarly we learn that Israel Baal Shem Tov dreamed persistently of two thrones in heaven and two holes in hell being reserved for him. He would not know his place till his life was ended.[8]

The infinite demand cannot be fulfilled by finite beings. Hence, the feelings of humility and lowliness, sinfulness and self-scrutiny. "The soul of man is a candle of the Lord, searching his inmost parts."[9]

In the last stage, man returns to the state of anxiety and eager waiting for the word that characterized his initial quest. But, following the first nuclear experience, there is a deepened awareness of the polarity: the infinity of His demand, the limitations of man's weakness and sin. Another encounter may well advance the course of one's spiritual growth. In the absence of self-scrutiny, the finite reactions are absolutized. An idol of deed or of dogma takes the place of the living God. The initial experience turns into a blind wall, instead of serving as a telescope. "Pride," says the rabbis, "locks God out."[10] In authentic religion there can be no finality of attainment. The quest is ever renewed—"Seek me and live, said the Lord."[11]

## The Mission of Israel

In Judaism, the concept of the Covenant is the nuclear experience of religion writ large. The spiritual life of prophets and saints is projected upon the people as a whole. The covenants with Adam, Noah, and Abraham foreshadow the Covenant at Sinai with the children of Israel. Thereafter it is the people who take the place of the individual. The people endure the pangs of desire, of yearning for God. They follow after Him, forsaking the amenities of civilization, the so-called "fleshpots of Egypt." In later years the wilderness of Sinai symbolized the arduous seeking of the Lord. "I remembered unto thee the kindness of your youth, your going after me in the wilderness, in the land that was not sown."[12]

Then came the dramatic climax of the revelation at Sinai. The people, all of them, accepted the Covenant, asserting, "We shall do and we shall listen." They were now a covenanted people, determined to become "a people of priests and a holy nation." Soon enough they discovered that with the best of intentions they had committed a "great sin." Moses assured them that other prophets would continue his work. They would stray in diverse paths, but the call to repentance would be sounded in their midst again and again. They would "return" and start afresh. The Covenant itself is unbreakable. Israel is the instrument of salvation of all mankind. It is the "chosen people," or the "treasure people."

Both Jews and Christians are apt to forget the stage of self-scrutiny in the covenantal situation. Christian scholars at times describe Judaism as a religion of laws or deeds, or as a "self-redeeming" faith, forgetting that penitence was ordained for all, for every day of one's existence, and in particular during the High Holiday season. Through one moment of true penitence, one may start life afresh, and on the highest level of saintliness.

Jewish scholars are likely to err in considering the chosen people as an end in itself rather than as the vanguard of humanity. Is the people Israel set apart from humanity, "a people that dwells alone," or is it "the first born" of the Lord, part of the family of mankind, from which more is demanded because more has been given to it? Was Israel chosen as an example or as an exception?

As we examine the contemporary mentality of Jewish people as well as the sacred tradition, we find that the answer oscillates between the two positions. At times it is the exceptionalist interpretation that predominates; at other times it is the awareness of Israel's role within the human family that surges to the forefront of consciousness.

There can be no sense of a universal mission or a redeeming vocation without the conviction of chosenness. But if this feeling is confined within the boundaries of the people itself, the concept of chosenness ceases to be self-critical, progressive, and relevant to the times. It then becomes self-sanctifying and self-glorifying, enacting the Narcissus tragedy on an ethnic scale. Whether exceptionalism or universalism prevails in the interpretation of "chosenness" depends on the strength of the experience of self-scrutiny that follows after the nuclear religious encounter.

So long as Israel's feeling of vocation was part of a powerful pattern of intense religious life, the feelings of sin and failure were certain to maintain the universalist, messianic aspect of Jewish piety. The messianic vision projected the hope of Israel's redemption within the context of the conversion and the salvation of all mankind. The plea for the return of dignity to Israel follows after the petition for the banding together of all men in one fellowship to serve the Lord with a perfect heart. This unity of national and universal redemption was characteristic of the ethnic-romanticist current of Jewish thought as well as of the mystical and rationalistic trends.

No one stressed the exceptionalist character of the people of Israel more than Judah Halevi. He regarded the Jewish people as being a higher species than the rest of humanity.[13] For Israelites alone were endowed with the genius for "the divine phenomenon"; they alone were capable of prophecy.[14] Yet it was Halevi who also projected two wonderful images of the place of Israel within mankind—"Israel among the nations was like the heart among the limbs, possessing more vitality than the other organs, but also more liable to illness than they."[15] Second, Israel is like seed planted in the soil, with Islam and Christianity being two branches of the tree sprung from that seed. In the fullness of time, the same seed will be found in the ripe fruit of all the branches. "These faiths are introduction to and preparation for the awaited Messiah. . . ."[16]

Both images of the seed and the heart presuppose an organic relationship of Israel to humanity as a whole so long as awareness of sin and failure is strong.

The universal role of Israel was consigned to the messianic era. While in the Greco-Roman period Judaism obtained many "spiritual converts," those who rejected idolatry and accepted the ethical-religious principles of Judaism, and many full converts, its sages regarded the conversion of mankind as a goal that would be attained only in the messianic era.[17] So, the early Christians, looking forward to the speedy return of Jesus, were eager to convert and save as many persons as possible. They exalted the *mizvah* to bring Gentiles "under the wings of the *Shechinah*," into the supreme command of the hour. The sages of the Mishnah urged every Jew to do his part, but they cautioned, "It is not for you to finish the work."[18] The early Christians, expecting the *eschaton* almost daily, were fired with zeal to complete the work in their own lifetime.[19] If the Messiah had already come, then the conversion of mankind or of a goodly portion of it must be accomplished in the shortest time.

The famous commentator Rashi interprets the meaning of the Shema to

228 JACOB B. AGUS

be as follows: "Hear, O Israel, the Lord is our God now, not the God of other nations; but in time to come He will be the God of all," as Zephaniah put it, 'Yea, at that time I will change the speech of the peoples to a pure speech, that all of them may call on the Name of the Lord and serve Him with one accord.' (III, 19) Also, Zechariah said (XIV, 9) 'on that day, the Lord will be One, and His Name One.' "[20]

Both Philo and the rabbis of the Talmud hoped for the total conversion of mankind in the fulness of the messianic era.[21] Philo and the rabbis looked forward to a peaceful society of nations, not to a homogeneous humanity as did the Stoics.[22] No Messiah was conceivable who would not redeem the nations as well as Israel. Indeed, some of the rabbis identified the image of the "Suffering Servant" of Isaiah with the ideal community of Israel, while others saw in him the Messiah. In the minds of the Jewish teachers, the visions of the Messiah and of the ideal community coalesced. The Messiah would redeem Israel, and redeemed Israel would then redeem the nations. Those who portrayed the Messiah as suffering voluntarily in order to atone for the sins of Israel also thought of Israel as suffering for the sake of the ultimate redemption of mankind. Commenting on the verse (Ex. 19:6), "Ye shall be unto me a kingdom of priests and a holy nation," a medieval commentator notes, "In this shall ye My treasure, in comparison with the others, that you will be a kingdom of priests, to teach and to guide the entire human race that all of them may call on the Name of God, serving Him with one accord, as the role of Israel will be in time to come."[23]

Contrary to the opinion of some scholars, there was no such thing in Judaism as a purely national Messiah, one who would redeem only Israel.[24] However, Jews believed that the Messiah would begin his work of redemption with them; then, constituting Israel redeemed under the leadership of the Messiah, they would proceed to redeem mankind. Akiba could proclaim the military hero, Shimeon bar Kosiba (Bar Kochba) as the Messiah, but only in the sense of inaugurating the messianic era. For he looked forward to the time when the Messiah will sit on a throne, at the right side of God, to judge all men.[25]

So Maimonides describes the messianic hope in his code:

"Do not imagine that the regular course of the world will be altered in the days of the Messiah, or that the work of creation will be changed. . . ." He describes the era in wholly natural terms; yet, it is a rule of nature that borders on the supernatural.

"A prophet will arise in Israel before the wars of Gog and Magog. . . . All the nations will accept the true faith. . . . The Messiah will gather the scattered ones of Israel, build the Temple in its place and lead all men to serve God together. . . .

"At that time there will be neither famine, nor war, nor jealousy, nor competition, for good things and pleasant foods will abound, and all men will have but one occupation—only to know the Lord."[26]

In his essay on the resurrection, Maimonides dissociates that event from the initial efforts of the Messiah, but he affirms the belief in the resurrection, as an article of faith.[27] Nahmanides adds that in the time of the Messiah, the evil desire will be removed.[28]

## Israel as Instrument of Fulfillment

The priority of Israel in the scheme of redemption is of the greatest importance in understanding the Jewish hope and its relationship to modern Israel. If in the Jewish view we now enter the category of fulfillment of the work of God in history, then we have to bear in mind all that the messianic vision implies. It is easy to concentrate on the immediate goal and to forget the spiritual context of the vision as a whole. Maimonides, who was in so many ways ahead of his time, could recognize the steps of messianic redemption within the Christian and Muslim worlds, though in his day the two monotheistic faiths were locked in a deadly struggle. The two daughter faiths of Judaism were helping to prepare the way for the advent of the Messiah.[29] There is much more to the "kingdom of heaven" than the restoration of Jewish sovereignty—namely, the elimination of injustice, of wars, of slavery, of greed. A revived Jewish state would contribute to the winning of these goals in behalf of all mankind, but it is only one component of the messianic process which is all-pervasive and inseparable from the entire course of human evolution.

In modern rhetoric, "the light of the Messiah" means the triumph of divine values in human society as a whole and within Israel. It also means the emergence of opportunities and instruments for the realization of these values within Israel, as an example, and within the universal society that is struggling to be born. There can be no assurance that opportunities and social instruments possessing messianic potentialities will in fact be so used. A cosmic question mark hovers over all that is human, especially in its encounter with the divine. This is why the classical prophets, in contrast to the apocalyptic visionaries of later centuries, offered their predictions invariably in conditional terms. And the Talmud, when it speaks of the advent of the Messiah, declares, "if they merit it, 'like the son of man in the clouds,' if they don't, 'like a poor man riding on a donkey.' "[30] The Talmud also speaks of King Hezekiah as having had the opportunity to become Messiah, but he muffed it.[31]

To speak of the "theological dimension" of the state of Israel is to project a vocation, not to stake out a claim of achievement. In keeping with the progressive current of Jewish thought, we are challenged to recognize the human-divine values and the opportunities for such values that the state opened up for its citizens, for the Jewish Diaspora and for humanity. At the same time, we must recognize the entanglement of the demonic with the messianic components. The state, reflecting the ethnic base of Jewish consciousness, may become a surrogate for the superstructure of the faith. The beginning may be viewed as an end, the opportunity as a fulfillment.

## Secular Interpretations

The secularization of Jewish messianism did not begin with the Zionist movement. In the first decades of the nineteenth century, the rising tide of European liberalism was hailed by Jewish intellectuals as the dawn of "the light of the Messiah." The apostles of the reign of reason shared with Kant the belief that war and slavery, together with all their attendant evils, would be eliminated through the spread of education. Hegel's rejection of this belief was regarded by the liberals of the mid-century as the personal aberration of a typical Prussian.

The Jews of the West generally transferred the messianic fervor of their heritage into the channels of liberal causes for the uplift of mankind. Moses Mendelssohn and his followers put Palestine and the messianic era into the metaphysical-mystical limbo of the hopes for immortality and resurrection. In this mundane world, Jews ought to labor for the ideals of humanity, leaving the *eschaton* to God.[32] Typical of the mood among enlightened Jewish laymen was the declaration of the Frankfurt Society of the Friends of Reform:

"A Messiah who is to lead the Israelites back to the land of Palestine is neither expected, nor desired by us; we know no fatherland except that to which we belong by birth or citizenship."[33]

While this radical formulation was too extreme for the majority of devout Jews, even in the West, the conservative philosophy of Frankel in Germany and Marks in England reflected the prevailing attitude. It asserted, first, that the traditional Israel-centered eschatology depended altogether upon a divine initiative, and second, that a resurgent Jewish state would be but another step in the fulfillment of the messianic hope for all mankind.

So the Rev. D. W. Marks, of the West London Synagogue, wrote as follows:

"When God shall be pleased by means of a moral revolution to bring back the seed of Abraham to Judea, we shall then rejoice in our title of a 'Kingdom of priests and a holy nation' and in that title . . . bringing all mankind to acknowledge the unity of His name, and in making blessed all the families of the earth."[34]

More forthright and entirely in line with the triumphant faith of the latter decades of the nineteenth century was the declaration of the American Reform rabbis in 1885:

"We recognize, in the modern era of universal culture of heart and intellect, the approaching of the realization of Israel's great Messianic hope for the establishment of the kingdom of truth, justice, and peace among all men. We consider ourselves no longer a nation, but a religious community, and therefore expect neither a return to Palestine, nor a sacrificial worship under the sons of Aaron, nor the restoration of any of the laws concerning the Jewish state."[35]

The Columbus Platform modified this purely universal version of the messianic hope, declaring that it was an obligation "of all Jewry to aid in its upbuilding of a Jewish homeland by endeavoring to make it not only a haven of refuge for the oppressed but also a center of Jewish culture and spiritual life."[36] The homeland would be a social instrument of national as well as human values and provide the opportunity for the realization of these high ideals.

The emergence of the modern Zionist movement in the *fin de siècle* atmosphere of neutral Switzerland represented a synthesis of the secularized messianism of the West, which was universalist in character, with the secularized messianism of the East, which was nationalistic in character. The Zionist movement did not, as is widely believed, amount to a repudiation of liberal hopes and ideals. On the contrary, the liberal intellectuals and statesmen were the only friends the Jews had. But it represented the melancholy realization that the path of human progress would have to go through the stage of nationalism, and European nationalism as a mass movement would have to embrace the follies and fantasies of racism. The upsurge of antisemitic fantasy and fervor at the height of the Dreyfus controversy indicated to Herzl that feverish chauvinism was quite capable of generating new myths. But, in his wildest nightmares he could not imagine the horrors of the Nazi holocaust. The universalist vision was not abandoned by the Zionist ideologists, but they assumed that the unity of mankind would take the form of a friendly association of nations rather than of individuals. In 1934 Buber wrote, "There is no re-establishing of Israel, there is no security for it save one: It must assume the burden of its own uniqueness; it must assume the yoke of the Kingdom of God."[37]

In the course of its development, Zionism absorbed the mystique of ancient messianism, in which the very soil was endowed with unique metaphysical qualities. The land itself was held to be holy, not merely certain places in it, although the holiness of Jerusalem is in a higher category and that of the Temple Mount still higher.[38] Certain rituals can be observed only in that land.[39]

While the moral laws of God apply everywhere, the soil of the Holy Land would "spew out" transgressors, lest it be "defiled."[40] Halevi maintained that the phenomenon of prophecy was possible only in the land of Israel, "or for its sake."[41] Nahmanides asserted that all the *mizvot* were designed for life in the Holy Land,[42] which was governed by the Lord himself, not by angels, and the earthly, rock-bound Jerusalem corresponded to "Jerusalem that is above." Even the rationalistic Maimonides wrote, "The greatest sages used to kiss the borders of the land of Israel, embracing its rocks and rolling in its dust. . . ."[43] Every upsurge of piety would lead to a migration to Palestine.

Even a modern American rabbi could speak of the land of Israel as "standing under a more watchful Providence" than the rest of the world. The momentum of sentiment and mystery is likely to continue even when its intellectual substratum is cut off.

Is not this transference of myth and mystery from one ideological context to another simply the application of the Newtonian law of momentum to the realm of social mythology? Anyone who wishes to see a recent illustration of this law should stand at the Western Wall and note the great variety of people visiting that shrine. He will see dyed-in-the-wool secularists pushing through the crowd of zealous pietists in order to put a hand against the Wall.

The mystique of Israel derives not only from the impetus of tradition but also from the peculiar tragedies of Jewish history, which were brought to a head in the fires of Auschwitz. The Jewish feelings of "exceptionalism" were confirmed in a macabre way by the Nazi policy of separating the Jews from the rest of mankind and consigning them to extermination camps. The very massiveness of the Hitlerian challenge required a powerful, concrete, historical reply. The state of Israel is the one positive answer to the antisemitic myth that Jews cannot build a state and lead a "normal" life. It is proof to Jews the world over that their survival as a people is worthwhile.

Yet this mystique is not necessarily anti-universalist. It retains as a matter of fact the universalist elements of the messianic vision that are comprised in the secularized forms of Jewish messianism. We recall the philosophy of A'had Ha'am, who reaffirmed the worth of Jewish nationalism, assigning to it the task of serving mankind by evolving a nontheological universalist ethic, a modern version of the good life. He transferred the Jewish vocation from the realm of metaphysics to that of ethics. Martin Buber similarly stressed the ethical implications of the Jewish faith. He regarded the Hebrew Scriptures as being by far the most authentic revelation of true faith. Within Judaism, this faith was concretized in deeds; within Christianity, in dogmas; but essentially, the vital kernel of religion is nonmetaphysical and purely ethical in character. According to Buber, the spirit of scriptural faith did not disappear from Jewish life; in the last two centuries, the awareness of the "Eternal Thou" came to life in the Hassidic movement. Buber was certain that in Israel the "I-Thou" relation will create new patterns of living that will redeem mankind from the emptiness of its "I-it" distractions.[44] In America, the Reconstructionist philosophy of Mordecai M. Kaplan synthesizes the feelings of Jewish ethnicism with a humanist interpretation of the faith.

## The Universal Vision in Modern Israel

The universal aspects of the secular messianic impetus are basic to the self-image of the contemporary Israeli intellectuals. They cannot help but think of themselves as an integral part of world Jewry, especially western Jewry. And in the West, the messianic vision of Jews has long been secularized into the ideology of liberalism. In fact, following the six-day war, the Israeli and the Jews of the world discovered that their "family feeling" was intensified. More than ever before all Jews realized that they constituted a family of communities, a family of adult brothers and sisters who normally lead their own lives, rallying together in times of crisis to aid the one who happens to be in trouble. Furthermore, the very existence of Israel is dependent upon the sympathy and aid of the liberals of the West, and to some extent also upon the nascent liberalism in the Soviet world. The amazing achievement of Israel in the domain of foreign aid to under-developed countries is at least in part an expression of the messianic impulse in its liberal, secularized version.

In modern Israel the afterglow of the messianic mystique is a potent reality, and Jews the world over respond to its perennial allure. But this mystique continues to be bipolar, embracing the entire spectrum between the supernatural redemption of the people Israel and the secular redemption of the whole of mankind. The drive to build the Kingdom of God on earth is surprisingly strong, although the tension persists between the exceptionalist, restrictive expressions of this ideal and its exemplary, universal versions.

It is at this point that the importance of the Jewish-Christian dialogue becomes apparent. It can only be meaningful if both the Jewish and Christian interlocutors have moved away from their respective medieval conceptions. The Jews have to see Israel as a *part* of the universal messianic vision; the Christians have to acknowledge the indispensable role of the Jewish homeland in the solution of a historic problem and in the building of the Kingdom of God. They have to accept the necessary *existence* of the state as a realm of opportunity for the realization of Jewish and universal values. This very acceptance, we need hardly add, is an invitation to Christians to join in its evaluation, not a call for the silencing of their criticism. Both groups have to recognize that to disentangle the divine from the demonic in all historic developments is a never-ending task. God works in history through all of us, and we need one another's helpful criticism, lest we forget.

## Christian Concepts of the Kingdom

In Christianity the concept of the Kingdom of God ranged all the way from the original Jewish ideal to the subtle version which interpreted the Kingdom as a present, metaphysical reality. Jesus felt that in his person the Kingdom was already present in nuclear form, like a mustard seed.[45] One version of the Kingdom continued to view it as a dimension of reality, or as the tangential point where the linear flow of time and the circular, self-contained silence of eternity coincided. Interpretations of the Second Coming oscillated between versions which regarded it as being at least initially historical and human and doctrines which removed it altogether from the realm of history. Augustine's "City of God" may be seen as a philosophy of history, in which the invisible "congregation of the saints" progressively gathered strength, culminating in an eventual triumph. In that case it would coincide with the Jewish hope of the messianic kingdom growing out of the earthy impulses of this world. But Augustine's heavenly city could also be identified with the hierarchy of the church, in which case his concept was metaphysical and also metahistorical. Needless to say, both versions proved to be extremely influential in the history of Western thought.

In the context of anti-Jewish polemics, Christian theologians tend to stress the non-national and the nonhistorical character of the Christian concept of the Kingdom. These emphases belong to the perpetual dialogue between Judaism and Christianity, where they are embraced within the one field of tension between two polar positions that were rejected in both traditions. In Judaism, the Kingdom centered around the physical nucleus of the empirical community, the people of Israel. Yet the valid role of the individual's choice was not denied. The "ten tribes," said Rabbi Akiba, will never return, a judgment which the popular imagination refused to accept.[46] Individuals could certainly remove themselves from "the congregation of Israel," and they could join it of their own accord, either as full converts, or as "spiritual converts." In a sense, the Talmud asserts, "any one who denies idolatry is called a Jew."[47] Yet the ideal community is the repository of the Promise and the instrument of redemption in history.

Similarly in Christianity, the invisible congregation of saints was constantly in tension with the visible one. Calvin asserted that the children of those who are "saved" are also among the "elect," tempering Protestant individualism with the consciousness of communal life. In history, Christianity allied itself more than once with ethnic sentiments. During the nineteenth century, the so-called "national" parties fostered loyalty to the national church—the Anglican in England, the Catholic in Ireland, the Pravoslavna in Russia, the Armenian in the Turkish diaspora.[48] Bergson recognized the consciousness of nationality as one of the two sources of religion.[49]

Today we are more aware than ever before of both the destructive and the constructive potentialities of the national ideal. If Judaism contains the component of "sanctified ethnicism" and Christianity a persistent emphasis on the inner life of the individual, the Jewish-Christian dialogue faces the task of evolving a dynamic equilibrium, clarifying the roles of the national and the humanist ideals in every age.

From the Jewish standpoint, liberalism is a secularized version of the messianic ideal. By the same token, Toynbee has correctly described European liberalism as a secularized version of Christianity and communism as a Christian "heresy." To be sure, the neoorthodox movement of the twentieth century presented itself as a critique of liberalism. However, its major impact was to correct excesses of the liberal mood, not to deny it totally. It is the perpetual task of the Christian to stand apart from "the world," to say "no" to it and to remind it of the "sinfulness" of all that is human and historical. But the Christian is far from being a cynical philosopher of classical times. His "no" is meaningful because, standing on a Jewish base, he already has said "yes" to the world as the creation of God and to history as the locus for the operation of divine providence. Reinhold Niebuhr's category of "irony" is that of a devout liberal, one who works within history for the amelioration of its evil, yet is perpetually ready to question the worth and the efficacy of his own efforts.[50] In the dialogue, the Christian "no" and the Jewish "yes," insofar as history, nationally, and the Kingdom are concerned, are brought into dynamic tension for their mutual enrichment.

## *The Modern Question of the State of Israel*

With the emergence of Israel as an indubitable reality on the international scene, the old polemic and debate concerning the identity of Israel and the meaning of the Kingdom were revived and placed in a fresh context. Some Jews believe that Christians cannot reconcile themselves to the thought of an Israel reborn—it is too blatant a contradiction of their ingrained belief that Israel belongs to the past; resurrections, however they be interpreted, are somehow "out of this world." Some Christians believe that the state necessarily represents a retreat of the Jew into his past, a repudiation of Jewish-Christian coexistence in the West under the auspices of liberalism, and an insensitivity to the plight of the Arab refugees. There is little justification for either opinion.

Actually, the state of Israel is the product of Jewish-Christian symbiosis, such as it was, with all its ambiguities. Christian prejudice generated the harsh social pressures for the upbuilding of the homeland, and Christian sympathy generated that atmosphere of international acceptance which made the homeland possible. Moshe Sharett, the one-time Foreign Secretary of Israel, noted after a journey through Asia and Africa that wherever the Bible was unknown, the Zionist movement was totally incomprehensible. Sympathy for the idea of a Jewish homeland in Palestine could only have emerged in cultures that were rooted in the Scriptures.

The state of Israel is inescapably shadowed as well as illumined by the uncertain, flickering "light of the Messiah." Israelis may be tempted to see this light only in the triumph of their arms and their enterprise. It is up to the Jews of the Diaspora and the Christian world to keep alive the universalist colors in the messianic spectrum. For messianism, bringing the Absolute into the course of history can turn narrow and fanatical. Is not the danger of pseudomessianism the perpetual shadow of every messianic appearance?

Christians have to accept the existence of the state of Israel and its security as an obligation of all who undertake to speak for the evolving conscience of humanity. That state was founded on the basis of two worldwide commitments by agencies which came closest to the vision of a parliament of mankind: the League of Nations, and the United Nations. At the same time, Christians should bring to the dialogue a candid criticism of the state of Israel in terms of the insights cultivated in their tradition.

Christians cannot in conscience turn their back upon the state of Israel; they participated in its creation. But the state cannot be dissociated from the vision of the Kingdom, emerging in history. It is an instrument hopefully of "the light of the Messiah," which dawns whenever human freedom and dignity reach new horizons. It is inevitably part of the rhetoric and symbolism of the Promise in the Judeo-Christian tradition. In turn, it is subject to evaluation and criticism in the light of these religious ideals. If we entertain the hope that the monotheistic religions can contribute to the making of One

World, founded on justice and equity, we must acknowledge that this hope is now being tested in the fires of the Israel-Arab crisis.

Far from serving as a stumbling block to the Jewish-Christian dialogue, the state of Israel with all its manifold domestic and foreign problems should become a major focus of the ecumenical discussions. The ecumenical movement, I feel, is also laboring within the Christian world under the category of Fulfillment: that is, in the recognition that the insights and circumstances of today provide opportunities for the realization of the vital core of faith.

A visitor to Israel is struck by the close proximity of the places that are most holy to the three monotheistic faiths: the Western Wall, the Dome of the Rock, the Church of the Sepulchre. Is not this juxtaposition itself a perpetual reminder of our need for one another's insights in love and in truth?

An international presence of some sort may eventually be needed if Jerusalem is to be truly a city of peace. An ongoing interreligious dialogue, moderating the conflicting mystiques, may in the long run become a powerful force for peace. If the participation of Muslims is initially impossible, the Jewish-Christian dialogue should be regarded as a preliminary step, "preparing the way" for the future conclaves. Ultimately, all religions should be represented. More than ever before, the words of Isaiah ring out with contemporary resonance: "Out of Zion shall Torah go forth and the word of the Lord from Jerusalem" (Isa. 2:3).

In sum, the aura of the messianic vision, the category of Fulfillment in the nuclear covenantal experience, looms large on the religious horizon of our day. It hovers over the state of Israel, the ecumenical movement, and the humanist hopes of secular liberals. It is particularly in this category that the theological "no" is likely to be silenced by the ecstasy of attainment. In the past such silencing has led to the sterility of the Covenant experience, to its becoming a blind alley of exceptionalism instead of the open highway of progressive religion. In our day the danger of a narrow interpretation of Fulfillment lies in the international and sociological, rather than in the theological, domain. Still, Christian as well as Jewish theologians face the task of maintaining the dynamic equilibrium between the political-nationalist and the religious-universalist components of the messianic category of Fulfillment.

Notes to "Israel and the Jewish-Christian Dialogue"

[1]Isaiah 60:1.
[2]Abot 3, 16.
[3]Berochot 13a.
[4]Isaiah 66:2.
[5]Sanhedrin 38a.
[6]Abot 2, 4.
[7]Berochot 28b.
[8]Shivhai HaBesht.
[9]Proverbs 20:27.
[10]Mechilta, Yithro, 9. Sotah 4b.
[11]Amos 5:4.
[12]Jeremiah 2:2.
[13]"The Kuzari," Hirschfield translation, N.Y., 1964. II, 8; II, 36.
[14]Ibid. IV, 5, 17.
[15]Ibid. II, 36.
[16]Ibid. IV, 23.
[17]Aboda Zara 3b.
[18]Abot, 2, 21.
[19]I Thessalonians 4:12.
[20]Commentary on Deuteronomy 6:4.
[21]"De Praemiis et Poenis," XVI, 93-95.
[22]H. A. Wolfson, "Philo," II; pp. 417-419.
[23]Commentary of R. Obadiah Seforno, ad loc.
[24]Strack-Billerbeck, "Kommentar," II vol., p. 242, on Luke 24:26.
[25]Jerusalem, Taanit 4, 3. Hagigah 14a. Sanhedrin 93b, 97b.
[26]Hilchot Melochim, XI & XII, 1-5.
[27]Iggeret Tehiyat Hametim, VI.
[28]Commentary on Deuteronomy 30:6. Also, Sefer HaGeulah II, printed in "Kithvai Ramban," I, p. 280, Jerusalem, 1963.
[29]Hilchot Melochim, X, 14, in uncensored editions.
[30]Sanhedrin 98a.
[31]Ibid. 94a.
[32]For a bitter critique of Mendelssohn's teaching and influence, see A. Cohen's "The Jew, Natural and Supernatural."
[33]Jewish Encyclopedia, Vol. X, p. 356.
[34]W. Gunther Plaut, "The Rise of Reform Judaism," N.Y. 1963, p. 137.
[35]Point 5 of the so-called Pittsburgh Platform, printed in Phillipson's "The Reform Movement."
[36]Yearbook of Central Conference of American Rabbis, Vol. XLVII.
[37]A. Hertzberg, "The Zionist Idea," N.Y., 1960, p. 457.
[38]Encyclopedia Talmudit, II Vol. p. 211.
[39]Ibid. mizvot hateluyot ba-arez.
[40]Nahmanides Sefer Hamizvot, Root 5. Sifre on Numbers 35:34.
[41]Kuzari II, 14.
[42]Commentary on Genesis 26:5.
[43]Hilchot Melochim, X.
[44]Martin Buber, "Israel and Palestine," London, 1952.
[45]Mark 4:31; Luke 10:23; 17:20.
[46]Sanhedrin 110b; Yebamot 16b; Megillah 14b.
[47]Megillah 13a.
[48]Salo W. Baron, "Modern Nationalism and Religion," N.Y., 1960.
[49]H. Bergson, "Two Sources of Religion and Ethics."
[50]Reinhold Niebuhr The Irony of American History, N.Y., 1952.

# PERSPECTIVES FOR THE STUDY OF THE
# BOOK OF ACTS

THE FAITH and career of Paul are generally regarded as marking the tragic break between Judaism and Christianity. While many Jewish scholars maintain that Jesus lived and taught within the ambience of Judaism, they argue that Paul was responsible for the separation of the two faiths and their mutual hostility. So, Joseph Klausner can find in the case of Jesus only the "seed" of denationalized piety. Kaufmann and Buber include Jesus completely within the sphere of Judaism.

But as to Paul, Klausner blames his alienation on the fact that he was a Jew from the Diaspora, hence inauthentic and anguished by contradictions. Montefiore similarly asserts that Paul could not help but experience the serene piety of the Pharisees, had he lived in the land of Israel. Raised in an alien environment, Paul was troubled by foreign influences and familiar only with the unlovely exterior of Jewish observances. Paul seems especially ignorant of the central ideas of Pharisaic Judaism—namely, repentance and forgiveness.

In sum, it is said by Jewish scholars that while the religion *of* Jesus was part of Judaism, the religion *about* Jesus, inaugurated by Paul, broke radically and completely with the Jewish faith.

Christian scholars find in the life of Paul additional confirmation of the thesis that the Jews, as a people, were "rejected," if not placed under a curse, and then replaced by the Gentiles.

Johannes Munck, in the *Anchor Bible* volume of Acts, commenting on Acts 28:17–28, says: "Israel's unbelief became the cause of his preaching the Gospel to the Gentiles." The same author comments on Acts 21:20, where James speaks of tens of thousands who joined the Christian community, while remaining "faithful to the law": "There could not be so many Jewish-Christians, since Jesus complained that his message was rejected."

Originally published in *Perspectives on Jews and Judaism* (New York: Rabbinical Assembly, 1978).

239

The axiom of a mutual rejection that was immediate and total distorts the teaching of the New Testament generally. Paul would have preached to Gentiles, whether or not all or most Jews had accepted his message. After all, Peter had also preached to Gentiles. Here, we are concerned with the Book of Acts.

May I suggest the following perspectives for the interpretation of this book:

First, the concept of monotheism, as it emerged in Judaism, *included a set of polarities that were reconciled only in the Will of God.* Judaism is what it is, and it is what it will be. Its being is also its vision of the future.

God was absolutely transcendent, beyond the grasp of man's senses or man's imagination or man's intelligence. Already, Philo speaks of God as being unknowable. At the same time, God was revealed at Sinai, to the prophets, dimly also to the Sages. Mediating divine entities were conceived, such as "The Word," the *Shekhinah*, Primal Man, Metatron, "whose name is the same as that of his Master." In the interpretation of biblical oracles, God's help was granted from time to time, through these entities.

The Torah, too, was bi-polar. Given at Sinai to Moses, it contained specific commands, whose purpose was "pedagogical," "to refine human nature," and inner principles, which corresponded to the structure of the cosmos.

The Temple in Jerusalem was believed to correspond to a heavenly Temple.[1] God dwells in heaven and in the human heart, as well as symbolically in His earthly Temple; the Archangel Michael or Metatron functioned as the heavenly high priest offering the souls of the righteous, or "lambs of fire," by way of atonement for the sins of Israel.

Israel, too, was bi-polar. It refers to the empirical Jewish people, but also to "the pious among the nations of the world." "Whoever denies idolatry is called a Jew," says the Talmud. The so-called God-fearers of the New Testament were in this category.

This bi-polarity was evident in all the relations between God, Torah, and Israel—God deals in terms of law, but He also extends His mercy freely; man is free, yet all is determined; God forgives, yet man must earn forgiveness by sacrifices as well as by repentance; Israel was chosen, by the fiat of divine love, yet only individuals are so chosen; Israel will be vindicated in time to come, yet all of redeemed mankind will constitute the Israel of the future, while not all Israelites will be redeemed. Characteristic is the language of the Mishnah: "All Israel have a share in the World to Come, but the following classes of people, do not . . ." (*Sanhedrin* 10:1).

This bi-polarity in every aspect of the Jewish faith is inescapable in a living faith, based on monotheism, that seeks to do justice to the fullness of human aspirations. It grows out of the realities of human existence, on the one hand, and the nobility of man's ideals, on the other hand.

Now, in the Jewish vision of the future, the Messianic Era shading off into the World to Come, the gentler, bolder, more dreamlike pole of hopes and ideals was expected to predominate—God will be more present to His worshippers, His Holy Spirit being "poured out" in abundance; the inner light of Torah will be revealed; Israel will become the redeemed nucleus of humanity; forgiveness will be offered freely, conditioned only on one's willingness to accept; Jerusalem and the Temple that is Above will take the place of the concrete Temple in the earthly Jerusalem; the policy of Compassion, or love, will prevail over that of Law: redeemed mankind will be liberated from the body of flesh and join the company of angels, in whose company they truly belong.

Now, "the Time to Come" *(leatid lavo)* will begin with the days of the Messiah, eventuate in a cosmic Day of Judgment, and culminate in the revelation of the "World to Come" *(olam haba)*, when the "Saints will sit with crowns on their heads delighting in the radiance of the Presence [*Shechinah*]."

Had the aeon of the Time to Come dawned already? At this point, the Christians diverged from the rest of the Jewish community.

Jesus and his disciples believed that the new aeon had begun. The religion *of* Jesus contained a firm belief *about* Jesus. Paul believed the culmination of the new aeon would come in his own generation. He was living in the Eschatological Age. It was incumbent upon him to be the instrument of saving those that were predestined for salvation. Otherwise, their "blood would be upon his head."

All of Paul's teaching is to be seen in the context of the appearance of the new aeon—hence, an Immanent Divine Presence, a Messianic Torah, a new Israel, the redeemed nucleus of humanity, the assurance of the Holy Spirit, and the belief of the speedy coming of the Parousia.

Hence, the crux of the argument between Paul and the Jews, who did not accept his message, was whether or not the Messianic Age was truly begun and the World to Come would appear soon. All other differences were derived from this basic issue. Most un-Jewish as Paul's career seems to Jewish scholars today, he was utterly sincere when he claimed: "I have committed no offense either against Jewish Law or the Temple or Caesar" (Acts 25:8).

The exclusivism of the Apostolic community is understandable in this context: "Neither is there salvation in any other; for there is none other name under heaven given among men, whereby we must be saved" (Acts 4:12). In the End of Days, we are told, "the Lord will be one and His Name One" (Zech. 14:9).

Understandable also is the revelation concerning the Covenant, the Law, the formation of a new Israel, the concept of a high priest in heaven, and the idea of the Messiah "sitting on the right hand of God." The last notion, frequently described as blasphemous, is attributed to Rabbi Akiba (d. 135 C.E.) (*Hagigah* 14a).

In brief, the first perspective I would urge is that Paul be understood as far as possible within the context of his Jewish upbringing, though unconsciously he might well have absorbed the teachings of the "mystery" religions.

As the second perspective, I urge that neither the New Testament in general nor Paul in particular teaches that the Jews were "rejected" and the Gentiles were chosen in their place. Where such references occur, the meaning is that Judaism as such will no longer suffice in the coming Day of Judgment, inaugurating the World to Come.

Jews, on this view, are like the rest of mankind, that is "guilty" of the sin of Adam. Living under the Law, they were more conscious of their sinfulness. Indeed, a common motif in the High Holiday liturgy is "we and our fathers have sinned."

According to Luke in Acts, the nonacceptance of Jesus as the Messiah makes one "guilty" of human sinfulness and of the blood of Jesus. So, Stephen, addressing himself to a Jewish crowd, speaks of the murderers of Jesus in the third-person plural, "they," and to his audience directly as facing the possibility of becoming guilty: "They killed those who foretold the coming of the Righteous One, and you now living have become his betrayers and murderers . . ." (Acts 7:52).

The "rejection," if any, will occur in the Parousia, in the Day of Judgment.

For this reason, Paul says to Jews who did not believe: "Your blood be upon your own heads; I am clean; from henceforth I will go to the Gentiles" (Acts 18:6). But then he goes to the Jews in the very next town. And at the end of the book, he is still speaking to the Jews of Rome.

The third perspective is a recognition that the issue between Paul and his Jewish opponents was not universalism or humanism vs. Jewish particularism or ethnicism, but whether the Law remained valid in the new eschatological age, prior to the Second Coming.

It was not universalism as such, because the Jews accepted the "fearers of the Lord" in the fellowship of the synagogue and as candidates of the World to Come. Also, the acceptance of Gentiles in the Christian dispensation was qualified. So, at Pisidian Antioch (Acts 13:42–52), Luke writes: "As many as were destined for eternal life believed." Later he reports James as saying: "For the Gentiles to take out of them a people for his name" (Acts 15:14). Also, the Exodus of the Israelites from Egypt provided a paradigmatic image of redemption, and Israel then included a mixture of many peoples (Exod. 12:38).

The Apostles were surprised to find that the Holy Spirit fell upon Gentiles also, though they had not accepted the Law.

The issue was not admittance into the *national* community of Israel, but into the Covenant. The rabbinic expression for entering into the Covenant was "to come under the wings of the divine Presence."

Luke's writing is understandable from the standpoint of the second generation, which was impressed by the preponderance of Gentiles in the Christian churches. So, we read of Jewish "jealousy" (Acts 13:45), and we get the general feeling that somehow, by a fresh divine fiat, the Gentiles were substituted for the Jews as the newly chosen people. The very word *Gentiles* is meaningful only in a Jewish context. Out of the Jewish context, the word *Gentile* places the Jews apart from the rest of humanity, as if they were metaphysically superhuman or subhuman, not like other people.

The Apostles and Jesus and the classical prophets, speaking to their own people, demanded more from them—hence, the tone of bitterness and frustration. But this intra-Jewish family feeling must not be perverted by removing it from its historical context.

The couplet "Jews rejected, Gentiles accepted" must be put in its historical context. Paul finds the nucleus of his adherents in every city among Jews and their associates, the "God-fearers," *sebomenoi, yirai Adonai*. They were prepared by the synagogue for the understanding of the Gospel. When Paul preaches to a Roman like Festus, the Roman governor in Caesarea, the latter exclaims: "Paul, thou art beside thyself; too much learning doth make thee mad" (Acts 26:24).

Agrippa is not converted, but, as Jew, he understands what Paul is saying.

The number of Jews in the Roman Empire was between 5 and 10 percent of the total population. Suppose the Christian church obtained twice as large a percentage of converts among Jews as among Gentiles; the percentage of Jews within the churches would vary from 10 to 20 percent.

To illustrate the devious reasoning of some scholars—eager to maintain the simplistic couplet "Jews rejected, Gentiles accepted"—may I refer you again to Johannes Munck's comment in the *Anchor Bible* on Acts 11:1–18: "This Pauline view, which may suitably be named 'representative universalism,' represented a Semitic outlook. Where a part had accepted the Gospel, then, the whole, that is the nation concerned, had accepted it, and where a part had rejected it, the nation as a whole had rejected it."

Translated it means that the Jews rejected it, because a part did so; *the* Gentiles accepted it, not *some* Gentiles, because the part equals the whole. How even-handed! How Semitic!

The fourth perspective that is frequently ignored by Jewish as well as Christian scholars is that Pauline Christianity grew out of opposition to Temple Judaism, not the modified post-Temple Judaism that is reflected in the Mishnah and Talmud.

The theology of Paul and of the Letter to the Hebrews operates with the notion of forgiveness of sin through the supreme sacrifice of the "Son of God." Post-Temple Judaism maintains in practice the sufficiency of repentance, on the part of man, and forgiveness, on the part of God. However, in theory it cherished the hope of a reinstitution of the Temple and its sacrifices. Also, it speculated that in the heavenly Temple, "not built by human hands," the sacrifices of the righteous are even now being offered in the shape of "lambs of fire" and the officiating priest is either Michael or Metatron (*Hagigah* 12b, *Menahot* 110a).

The latter speculation was never raised to the rank of a dogma. Interesting is a *baraitha* which reflects the gulf between Temple Judaism and that of the rabbinic period: "A sinner, what is his punishment?—They asked this question of Wisdom. It responded, 'a sinner, he shall die'; they asked it of prophecy, it responded, 'evil pursues the sinner'; they asked it of Torah, it responded, 'let him bring a sacrifice and his sin will be forgiven'; they asked it of God, He answered, 'let him repent and all will be forgiven.' "[2]

Here, then, is a policy, representing the true intent of God, which is superior to the Divine Will, as it is found in the Torah.

A similar thought is presented in the name of Rabban Yohanan ben Zakkai, who assumed the leadership of Judaism after the destruction of the Temple (*Abot di R. Nathan* IV). He said to his disciple who wept over the destruction of the Temple: 'We have an atonement of equal efficacy, deeds of lovingkindness."

Now we know that many pietists were embittered by the administrators of the Temple.

The Talmud notes the popular resentment of the high priests and their aides.[3] The Samaritans were implacable in their hostility, and Stephen may have been a Samaritan. The Samaritans referred to themselves as Hebrews, and the Epistle by this name may have been written to Samaritans.

More to the point, the Qumran community shows us a group of ardent pietists who disdained the high priests of the Temple as usurpers, since they did not belong to the family of Zadok. The Qumran *Hassidim* were organized by their Righteous Teacher, *Moreh Zedek*, as a holy community, in which God dwelt, a living sanctuary that could serve as a substitute for the Holy Temple. This community, or its governing council, *azat hayahad*, was "the true Israel." Their sacred meals were probably modeled after those in the Temple. They looked forward to the descent of the heavenly Temple, the one not built with human hands. (As Bertil Gärtner comments: "We have seen that the Qumran texts contain a consistent Temple symbolism, in which the community is represented as the new Temple, and in which the true sacrifice is seen as being spiritual in character, offered in the holy and pure lives, the praise and prayer of the members of the community.")[4]

The Temple symbolism of Paul in I Corinthians 3:16 and I Timothy 3:15 and of the author of Hebrews is paralleled by similar symbolism in the Qumran community and by rabbinic speculations concerning the heavenly Temple.

The frustrations of many Jews with the Temple ritual are reflected in Paul's and Luke's criticism of the Law and its supposed inefficiency. A large portion of the Law dealt with the Temple and the laws of "purity," which related to it.

The complaints that the Law could not be observed fully cut to the heart of many Jews—mostly in the Diaspora, but also in Galilee. The offering of *olah* was to be brought for "meditations of the heart."[5] How often could a Jew from the Diaspora go up to Jerusalem? The bringer of a sin-offering or a burnt-offering had to lean with both hands on the animal, prior to its sacrifice *(semikhah)*.[6] The laws of "purity" placed all Diaspora Jews in the category of the "impure," requiring a week of purification. Also, the commercialism of the priestly families and the legitimacy of the high priest were frequently questioned.

Apparently, before R. Akiba's time, the assumption was that anyone who did not observe *all* of the precepts of the Law was doomed. R. Akiba maintained that the observance of even one *mizvah* was sufficient to secure a share in the World to Come (*Makkot* 24a).

In brief, in Temple Judaism, many believed that "there is no forgiveness save in blood" (*Yoma* 5a). For the Apostolic community, the blood of Jesus has taken the place of the blood of lambs: "Him hath God exalted with His right hand to be a Prince and a Savior, for to give repentance to Israel, and

forgiveness of sins" (Acts 5:31). Rabbinic Judaism asserted that both repentance and forgiveness required no sacrificial intermediary.

The greatest sin in Temple Judaism was *pigul*, to entertain idle thoughts
while the sacrifice was being offered. Hence, Paul in I Corinthians (11:27)
warns of punishment for thoughtless participation in the eucharist. It was
the reenactment of a sacrifice.

The author of Hebrews argues that any sin committed after conversion
cannot be forgiven: "For if we sin willfully after that we have received the
knowledge of truth, there remaineth no more sacrifice for sins" (Heb. 10:26).

Temple Judaism was not identical with the Sadducee mentality, but the
two attitudes were certainly very close. So, the Sadducees, especially the
Temple functionaries, persecuted the early Christians, while the Pharisees
defend Peter and John: "But if it be of God, ye cannot overthrow it . . ."
(Acts 5:39). Paul too was defended by the Pharisees: "We find no evil in this
man; but if a spirit or an angel hath spoken to him, let us not fight against
God" (Acts 23:9).

Fifth, the perspective of universal history. If we look at the course of
human history, as it unfolds in the succession of centuries, it is clear that
some form of ethical monotheism, embracing the insights of Hebrew prophecy and Hellenic philosophy, was due to emerge in the Roman Empire.
Paganism was spiritually bankrupt. Judaism appealed powerfully to the
pagan population, but it was, after all, the religion of an ethnic community
that was emotionally withdrawn, socially insulated, and politically subju-
gated.

The logic of spiritual development was directed decisively toward an
integrated cosmos, governed by One God, Who is revealed in man's heart
and mind. As Greek philosophy superseded previous speculations, so Jewish
biblical thought advanced inexorably within the Roman Empire. Variations
of Persian dualism and Chaldaic Gnosticism captured for brief moments the
fancy of the populace, but they could not deflect the main current which
aimed at the harmonization of all the demands of man's spirit.

A new synthesis was needed that included the impact of Judaism, with its
antiquity and prestige, and yet was a new revelation, which non-Jews could
enter on the ground floor.

As Toynbee pointed out, the external proletariat tends to embrace the
culture of the nuclear people in some heretical form, which reflects their
ambivalence of both admiration and contempt.

So, the Samaritans embraced Judaism, but with a difference; the Germanic tribes took up the Arian form of Christianity; the Persians, the Shiya

form of Islam; the Russians, their own variation on Byzantine Orthodoxy. Religiously speaking, Judaism was the nuclear community. The time was ripe for a form of Jewish monotheism that would embrace its living core and at the same time dispute its legitimacy.

This historic role was carried out by Christianity, with Paul laying down the two basic lines of acceptance and rejection toward the mother faith. In Romans 9–11, he acknowledged in his own way that the nonacceptance of Christ by the Jews was providential. The ambivalent love-hate relationship between Judaism and Christianity was itself dynamic and restless, with the Gnostics stressing the anti-Judaic side and the second-century apologists emphasizing the pro-Jewish elements.

The rapid spread of Christianity in the pagan world was due to its serving as the vehicle of the biblical faith. In the case of the Jewish people, no such historical function existed, for they had experienced this development in the biblical period. Hence, the appeal of Christianity to Jews was comparatively modest. Its anti-Temple mood was neutralized by rabbinic Judaism, which in practice substituted prayer and good deeds for the sacrifices of the Temple but maintained the hope of the restoration of the Temple.

The sixth and final perspective that I urge is the personal attempt of Paul and other Apostles to overcome the isolation of the Jew and to eliminate the scourge of Antisemitism. Paul's complex personality contained a keen feeling for the broad sweep of history along with a deep concern for the destiny of his own people. He spared no effort to bring salvation to all men, but he loved the Jewish people with a passion.

Paul was a theologian, and all his actions had to be consciously systematized and related to his central conviction of "Christ crucified." He was also a great Jewish personality, who was deeply concerned with the endemic hostility between Jews and Greeks in the Eastern Mediterranean, especially in Syria and Egypt. Doubtless, he felt deeply the anguish of his fellow Jews when Caius Caligula ordered that his picture be worshipped in the Temple (39 C.E.) The anti-Jewish riots in Alexandria, Egypt (38–40 C.E.), and the anti-pagan riots in Jamnia, Palestine, provoked outbreaks in many parts of the empire. Antisemitism had become a murderous mass-phenomenon (Josephus, *Wars of the Jews* II:18).

It was inevitable that Paul, a native of the Hellenistic Jewish Diaspora, would be deeply concerned with the need of bridging the tragic rift between the Jews and the Greeks. His conviction that the Eschatological Age had already dawned reenforced his determination to hasten the day when all ethnic rivalries and hatreds would be overcome. With fierce resolve, he battled against the notion of retaining the line of demarcation between Jews and Greeks within the Christian community. He would not allow the Law to enforce Jewish insularity within the community that was already living in spirit in the Messianic Age. Hellenistic Jews were keenly conscious of the social consequences of the Law, which surrounded them with an "iron curtain," as it were (*Letter of Aristeas*, 139). They bore its restrictions with amazing courage, so long as its educational function was necessary. But in the time of fulfillment, the prophetic vision of the fraternity of peoples could no longer be postponed.

Paul felt called upon to prepare the way for the coming with power of the Messiah—hence, to insist that in Christ all divisions shall no longer be tolerated. "There is neither Jew nor Greek, there is neither bond nor free, there is neither male nor female; for ye are all one in Christ Jesus" (Gal. 3:28).

In sum, the perspectives that emerge out of Jewish scholarship are:

1. The bi-polarity and dynamism of the Jewish faith would be raised to the breaking point when the Eschaton was at hand.
2. The Day of Judgment was impending, but no "rejection" of the Jewish people had already taken place.
3. The core of the argument between Paul and the loyal Jews was not ideological but factual—had the Messiah arrived or not?—It was not universalism vs. particularism.
4. Temple-Judaism was the stem out of which Pauline Christianity and Pharisaism diverged.
5. The macroscopic view of world-history, in which Paul's career is to be seen.
6. The microscopic view of Paul's complex personality and his dedication to the unity of the community of the newly "chosen people."

## Notes to "Perspectives for the Study of the Book of Acts"

[1] Jer. *Yoma* 1, "Why did the priests serve in white garments?—As the service is above, so it is below."
[2] Jer. *Makkot* 2.
[3] *Yoma* 71a, *Pesachim* 57a.
[4] *The Temple and the Community in Qumran and the New Testament* (Cambridge University Press, 1965), p. 47.
[5] *Taanit* 26a. "How can a person's sacrifice be offered when he is not present?"
[6] "Always an *olah* is brought only for meditation of the heart" (*Lev. Rabba* 7:3). (We can understand Paul's predicament in Romans 7.)

# THE FUTURE OF JEWISH MESSIANISM

THE MESSIANIC vision is probably the most potent drive in the collective spirit of the Jewish people. Yet, it is strangely protean, assuming different shapes in various ages and inspiring the efforts of mystical radicals as well as those of unworldly mystics. It is so many-splendored that only a fraction of its component elements may glow on the intellectual horizon of any one period. It functions most powerfully when it is barely affirmed on the conscious level. It hovers uncertainly in the twilight zone between the immanent and the transcendent—now close at hand, now gleaming in the distance.

To view it in the perspective of history and to hazard some reflections concerning its manifestations in the future, I suggest the following categories: Affirmation, Negation, Fragmentation.

The category of Affirmation points to that firm assurance that the patterns of the messianic age are even now emerging out of the web of history. A nationalist may see it chiefly or even exclusively in the wondrous emergence and astonishing career of the State of Israel. A humanist may recognize it in the many-sided achievements of the post-war era—the marvelous advance of human rights, the amazing growth of education, the ever expanding dominion of reason and freedom. A Lurianic mystic will see it chiefly in the inner dialectic of the hidden currents of holiness, of which only occasional hints appear in the open pages of the book of general history, especially in the history of the Jewish people.

But along with this profound assurance, there operates within the messianic complex the corrective and contradictory force of Negation—to wit, the Messiah is not here and all our achievements are flawed. The vision is too many-sided and magnificent to be manifested even in part in this mundane world. It comprises the perfect realization of spiritual as well as physical attainments, the vindication of Jewish destiny as well as the

Originally published in *Human Responses to the Holocaust*, ed. by Michael D. Ryan (Texts and Studies, vol. 9; New York, 1981).

redemption of mankind. How can any age, or movement, or person measure up to its superlative promise?—In this mood, the open sores of mankind move into the focus of attention. There is too much that is wrong and raw in our modern world for it to qualify even as proto-messianic. We suspect that even our successes may later turn out to be a prelude to disaster.

This cautious negation is reinforced in the minds of informed Jews by the memory of many sad frustrations which followed in the wake of pseudo-messianic eruptions: Bar Kochba, David Alroy, Solomon Molcho, Sabattai Zevi, Jacob Frank.

The inner turbulence between the perceptions and sentiments of Affirmation and Negation may lead to the deceptive calm of mutual nullification. But in many epochs, various segments of the Jewish people favored only certain aspects of the messianic vision. As a result, those aspects preempted the psychic energy of the historic hope, while other aspects were allowed to sink into oblivion.

The fragmentation of the messianic vision upsets the balanced tension within the traditional conception, channeling pent up fervor into a one-sided ideology. Consequently new utopias occasionally burst upon the horizon, imposing modern shapes upon age-old yearnings. The external expressions of pseudo-messianic movements were generally fresh and unprecedented, but they often masked an inner reality that was deep and ancient. The long-awaited "great shofar" of redemption has been heard in the depths of the soul—"the voice of my Lover—here, he comes."

To be sure, the surprising turns of the course of history tended to restore a sense of balance to the messianic vision. Also, the profound feelings of mutual concern among the various sections of Jewish people tended to make *all* Jews share vicariously in the experience of *some* Jews. So, in time, the separated strands of messianism were reclaimed and woven into the texture of Jewish history as a whole.

Without delving far into the past, we may note the functioning of the three categories in modern Jewish history.

In the middle of the seventeenth century, two fascinating personalities brought the two polar aspects of the messianic vision to climactic heights: Benedict Spinoza at one end of the spectrum, Sabbatai Zevi at the other end.

Spinoza represented the long tradition of Jewish rationalism, raising it to its highest peak of logical development. The Messiah is absolute Reason, capable of reigning supreme within the lives of individuals and in the structure of societies. Spinoza projected the vision of a free society, untrammeled by religious dogma and political tyranny. In the name of "true religion," he sought to break the yokes of the contending official religions on the long suffering population of Europe. True religion can flourish only in freedom. With the ardor of a biblical prophet, he preached the gospel of salvation through the disciplines of selfless Reason. It is the irrational passions and the hereditary prejudices that most bedevil nearly all societies. But these diseases of the mind can be overcome by the rigors of clear thinking and by a love of God, so intense, so intuitive, and so unerring as to assure the triumphs of philosophic serenity and peace. The "intellectual love of God," blending the dictates of reason with the ardent quest of God, is alone capable of steering the frail bark of the soul through the bewildering storms of passion and toward the safe haven of joy and peace.

Spinoza's philosophy of redemption was socio-political as well as theological. He transferred the dynamic power of messianism from the supernatural and the dogmatic domains to the sphere of personal fulfillment, by way of philosophic meditation, and to a social peace through the building of a society dedicated to freedom. People can give up many rights for the sake of their common security, he contended, but in opposition to Hobbes he argued, they cannot surrender their freedom to think without violating their dignity as human beings.

Spinoza's messianism included a solution to the unique problems of his own people. If Jewish people will curb their reliance on supernatural visions and devote themselves to the task of building their own state, they will succeed and become a free people. Here, then, was the germ of the modern Zionist movement. [*Theological Political Tractate*, ch. 3.] To be sure, it was stated as an ideal for others to realize. For himself and others like him, the path of redemption led through the building of free societies in the lands of Europe.

Spinoza was excommunicated by the rabbis of Amsterdam, but he refused to accept the protective covering of Christianity. He lived in a no-man's land, as the prophet of a world still unborn. His was "the voice crying in the wilderness," calling for the building of the pathway of reason toward the Kingdom of God.

Sabbatai Zevi gathered the fragments of the messianic vision which Spinoza ignored, and blended them into an unquenchable flame. He saw the real world as an unreal copy of the true world, in which scattered "sparks of holiness" contended against the ubiquitous "shells of pollution." The natural course of events was a mirage, masking but also pointing to the true reality, which the Kabbalist Isaac Luria had seen in his visions. Lurianic Kabbalah had postulated that already in the seventeenth century people were living at the dawn of the new age. The inner process of regeneration was approaching its predicted culmination. The spiritual stature of the heavenly Messiah was all but liberated with only the "heels" of the generation needing some additional labors. When the "prophet" Nathan of Gaza proclaimed that Sabbatai Zevi was the hoped for Messiah, a mass-hysteria gripped the widely dispersed Jewish diaspora, unsettling the "establishment" in many communities. From Hamburg in the Northwest to Yemen in the Southeast, the tides of mystical assurance that redemption was imminent carried everything before them. Movements of penitence, ecstatic prayer, ascetic mortification, sharing one's possessions with the poor and similar acts of moral heroism reached climactic heights. No pseudo-Messiah of the past had ever attained so vast a following and, considering the slowness of communication, the rapid spread of this "good news" bordered on the fantastic.

The "believers" assumed that a sudden intervention by God would usher in a new and marvelous age, in which the laws of nature would be suspended and human nature would be metamorphosed; in which the people of Israel would be uplifted above the rest of humanity, with the wicked being annihilated, the good Gentiles being converted, the dead being resurrected, the Messiah and his companions ascending their respective thrones. The old hope, formulated in the letters of Paul, had re-emerged with amazing social force, all the more resplendent because it was so long repressed.

Indeed, so overwhelming was the Sabbataian experience that the masses of Jewish people were hard put to return to a normal state of mind. The after-glow of messianism dominated the horizon. A century later, the Frankist movement and almost simultaneously the Hasidic movement encountered little difficulty in stirring up the embers of messianic hope and in projecting new pathways to redemption.

The Sabbataian-Spinozist polarity of the seventeenth century was paralleled in the eighteenth century by the Enlightenment-Hasidism messianic polarity, headed respectively by Moses Mendelssohn of Gemany and Rabbi Israel Baal Shem Tov of Russian Poland. Both men were animated by messianic fervor, with one pointing to the rational and universal components of Messianism, the other stressing its popular, supernatural, mystical aspects. Both men were highly revered by different segments of contemporary Jewry; both embraced polarized fragments from the messianic spectrum of traditional Judaism.

Moses Mendelssohn managed to remain at home in both the Jewish and European worlds. He retained the high regard of the Jewish masses even as he moved in the rarefied strata of the enlightened Christian elite. He and his followers thought of the Age of Enlightenment as the dawn of the messianic era. Jewish redemption would be part of the universal redemption, liberating mankind from the follies and hatreds of the unhappy past. While he lived before the ideals of progress and evolution had captured the European imagination, he believed that the oppression and humiliation of Jewish people would be among the first evils to be eliminated by a spiritually resurgent Europe, newly converted to the ideals of reason and humanity. He was not interested in a Zionist solution of the Jewish problem, though, like Spinoza and like Maimonides, he could see the possibility of a return to Zion being achieved through the normal processes of history. As a philosopher, he thought of redemption in terms of an intellectual-moral victory, transpiring within the hearts of individuals and the inner life of societies. It is a triumph which must be won again and again in every generation. For in his essential nature, man does not change.

Rabbi Israel Baal Shem Tov launched a mass-movement of mystical piety that provided an approved outlet for the superheated messianic ardor of the hidden Sabbataians and Frankists. In the famous letter to his brother-in-law, he told of his "ascents to heaven" and his conversations with the soul of the Messiah. In these visions, he was commissioned to teach his disciples certain mystical exercises ("unifications") that would enable them to ascend to the academies on high or at least to receive messages from heavenly beings. The masses of the people would "bind themselves" to be guided totally by the saints (zaddikim) and thus to share vicariously in the mystical "unification" of the spiritual elite.

So, we read in this letter:

> On Rosh Hashono of 5507 (1747) I experienced an ascent of the soul, following an oath, and I beheld wondrous events in a vision, things which I have never seen before . . . and I asked my teacher and master [his heavenly guide was Ahiya of Shiloh, the reputed teacher of Elijah the Prophet] to go with me for it is very dangerous to rise up to the higher worlds . . . and so I came to the palace of the Messiah . . .
> Then, I asked the Messiah, "when will the Lord come?" And he answered,
> "This is how you will know; when your teaching will become widely known and accepted, and the learning which I conveyed to you will become widely known and followed, with your fountains bursting out, so that others, too, will be able to attain unifications and ascents, even as you, then the dominion of shells will end, and there will ensue a time of favor and salvation." [R. Jacob Joseph, *Ben Porat Joseph*, published by Mefitzai Torah, New York, 1954, p. 255.]

Briefly, the Hasidic movement was a massive pietistic movement, dedicated to the hastening of the advent of the Messiah. The "saints," who served as the vital centers of the movement were viewed as messianic precursors. In their personalities, evil had already been overcome and the dominion of holiness foreshadowed. Through their "unifications" and their association with their followers, the "sparks of holiness," imprisoned by the demonic "shells," will be liberated and the pathway for redemption will be readied.

When a Hasidic teacher was asked, "weren't our forefathers pious enough? Why is a new way needed?", he replied, "did they bring the Messiah?" This was the decisive test for these pietistic enthusiasts. Jewish people cannot wait any longer for redemption to come. They must hasten "the end of days" through all the ways that are legitimate.

Mendelssohn and the Baal Shem Tov represented the opposite poles of messianism within the context of the Jewish religion—the former working within the tradition of the philosophers, preeminently Maimonides and Spinoza; the latter within the dreamy mythology of Kabbalah.

As the secular mentality began to dominate the imagination of modern man, the messianic polarity took on more realistic and more subtle forms. The mystical vision was incarnated in the Zionist movement, while the rational current assumed either the shape of political liberalism or of socialist utopianism.

The mystical overtones of Zionism were discernible in the early decades of the movement, when only the eyes of faith could glimpse the dawn of redemption in the few, economically unviable colonies, which dotted the map of the Holy Land. Those colonies were dependent on the largesse of Baron Edmond Rothschild and surrounded by an oppressed and bitterly hostile population. Only a tiny fraction of the idealistic young people, who gave up promising careers in the Diaspora and took up menial tasks as agricultural workers and day-laborers, remained in the land. The hardy pioneers were sustained by the romantic cadences of the biblical prophets, even when they professed to be hard-bitten secularists. They spoke of the natural union of "the land without a people" with "the people without a land," refusing resolutely to take account of the Arabs dwelling in the land. In the first three decades of the twentieth century, no responsible Zionist seriously contemplated the possibility of six to nine hundred thousand Arabs vacating the land of Israel in the war of 1948 and another four hundred thousand leaving in the war of 1967. Yet, without those masses deserting their homes in panic, a Jewish state would have been an unviable entity, even after the Holocaust and even after the United Nations' vote on partition in November 1947.

But where the calculations of sober statesmen were confuted by the twists and turns of modern history, the mystical visions of the masses of Jewish people proved to be solidly realistic. Following the establishment of the State of Israel, the remaining Jews of the central European countries and of all Arab lands were transported to Israel. In respect of those parts of the Dispersion, the Zionist solution of "the Jewish problem" proved to be right. The messianic dream has come true, though in part only. In the prayer of thanksgiving for the state, composed by the Chief Rabbi of Israel, gratitude is expressed for "the beginning of the growth of our redemption."

The messianic character of European liberalism and socialism is not so self-evident, since these movements affected so many nations. Yet, it is worth noting that the Jews in the West embraced these ideologies with special fervor. The Liberal outbursts of 1789, 1830, and 1848 in France were hailed by Jewish thinkers as redemptive events, manifestations of the light of the Messiah. The Antisemites of Western Europe scorned the ideals of the French Revolution as products of the "Jewish spirit." In Bismarck's Germany, the leaders of the Liberal party were Jewish. Some theologians attributed the philosophy of liberalism, affirming the innate goodness of men and women, to the intellectual impact of the Hebrew Bible, which does not stress the melancholy doctrine of man's total depravity. Also, liberalism is essentially cosmopolitan, envisioning society in terms of citizens banding together to form states, rather than as natural tribes and races, formed in primeval times by ties of blood and unconscious forces, utilizing armies and states in a fierce struggle for existence.

Liberalism appeared in Europe first in opposition to the doctrine of the "divine right of Kings," then in opposition to the principle of historical "legitimacy"—"whatever was, must be right"; then, as a nominalistic philosophy, treating individuals as sources of right and wrong, rather than states; then, in opposition to the romantic glorification of the Middle Ages as the time when society was stratified by castes and everybody knew his place; then, against folkism, jingoistic nationalism and the glorification of military power. In respect of all these issues, Jewish citizens fell naturally and inevitably, through self-interest as well as idealism, into the camp of the liberals.

In keeping with this ideology, they revised their faith and their sense of identity.

Reform and Conservative Judaism arose out of the "internalization" of the liberal philosophy of life. What people have in common is far more decisive in their makeup than what sets them apart. The past of Jewish people is no exception to the general rule, and in the future, the Jewish people must not be set apart from the rest of humanity. In the history of Divine revelation, there cannot have been a Jewish monopoly, and the teaching of the Holy

Bible must be interpreted accordingly. The entire history of the Jewish people must be reconstructed in terms of all-human categories. Hence, it must be demonstrated that the biblical philosophy of life arose by stages out of the sentiments and thoughts of ancient nations. Such concepts as a "Jewish genius," a "Semitic psyche," or "a Hebraic soul" are valid only tangentially and metaphorically. The leading ideas of the Bible are meaningful for all men and women. The Israelites were "chosen," in the sense of *example* rather than of *exception*. In religion as in respect of every other quality, some people may at any time be ahead of others, but none is set aside to live in isolation. God addressed himself to all people in the past. And in the present, redemption must be sought on an all-human basis. The Messiah will come for the Jews as part of a universal redemption. As residents of their respective countries, they will be redeemed when the lot of the common man will be uplifted from poverty and distress. The course of history runs toward ever wider horizons of freedom. Biblical religion considered man's freedom to be "the image of God." In modern liberalism, this doctrine is articulated in all the domains of public life. In a sense, all liberal states belong to the same "great society" advancing together toward the goals of well-being and brotherhood. In this course of unflagging progress, "the light of the Messiah" is revealed.

The fervor of messianism is all too apparent in the socialist movement, which may be regarded as an extension of the liberal philosophy from the domain of politics to that of economics. And the impact of socialism within the Jewish world reverberated with the millennial echoes of the messianic vision. The Messiah will be the proletariat come to power. Did not the prophet Zechariah picture him as "a poor man, riding on a donkey"? The "pangs of the Messiah" is the class-struggle, constantly increasing in ferocity. All the evils of contemporary society are due to the vain effort of doomed classes to resist the irresistible course of history. The religious concept of Providence is but a projection of the economic forces, which operate by way of a built-in dialectic. The final result will be not only the triumph of the proletariat, but the elimination of all the manifold evils of society. The underlying malaise of society is due to the "alienation" of modern man and his subjection to a soul-less machine, a Moloch-like juggernaut. In the socialist paradise, men and women will be metamorphosed into a new human breed, because their inner freedom will correspond to the necessities of the objective world.

Not all forms of socialism embodied the messianic dream of Jewish people. The movement drew its social power from several sources: first, from the resentment felt by the oppressed classes; secondly, from the appeal of a restructuring of society on the basis of social justice; thirdly, from the felt contradiction between the goodness of people as individuals and the failure of society as a whole to be equally good; fourthly, from the technocratic ambition to control totally every aspect of social life and the corresponding intolerance of every deviation from the centrally guided plan.

The motif of resentment in socialist circles was at times turned against Jews, as a predominantly commercial class. So, Fourier and Proudhon in France, Adolf Stoecker in Germany, Nicholai Bakunin in Russia, represented proletarian resentment allied with Antisemitism. The ideal of social justice and the appeal of an elite dedicated to the improvement of the lot of the poor fitted in with the Jewish tradition. St. Simonism in France was especially dear to talented Jews, including its call for a new religion that would embrace the social idealism of the Judeo-Christian tradition. The notion that a rational approach untrammeled by the momentum of prejudice, can tackle and resolve every social issue was especially appealing to Jews, since the main component of the Jewish tradition was humanistic and rationalistic. Some Jewish theologians found support in Savigny's "positive-historical" school, which assumed that institutions evolved slowly and unconsciously through the dim centuries of history, being supra-rational in inspiration and reflecting the deeper psyche of the folk. But essentially such theories, in France as in Germany, were invariably reactionary and Antisemitic. As recent entrants into the mainstream of public life, by the grace of rationalism, young Jews rebelling against the rigidities of their own tradition, were minded to promote the rational approach in every sphere of life.

However, the fourth motif, the quest of total control, was ambivalent toward the Jewish heritage, from the very beginning. Socialists like Kautsky in Germany and Otto Bauer in Austria led the fight against Antisemitism, but they also resisted the craving of Jewish people to preserve their cultural heritage. And in the Soviet Union the potency and ruthlessness of this drive toward uniformity were revealed in all their horror.

In art, philosophy, science or social concern, any deviation from the norm is bitterly resented by the Soviet ruling circles. The spell of an entire society marching in step, without anyone stepping out of line, must not be broken. The Jewish community, which cannot be pressed into any one category, is invariably ill at ease in a society which tolerates no "dissidents."

In sum, the messianic vision of Jewish people was fragmented in the modern world, first by the polarity between naturalism-supernaturalism, then, with the progressive dominance of the secularist mentality, by the polarity between Zionism, aiming to redeem Jews first, and liberalism-socialism, putting the redemption of the Jew within the universal surge toward the redemption of mankind.

We now have before us the experience of the first generation after the Holocaust and of the State of Israel. What can we say regarding the fragmented vision of the Messiah? Are we perhaps approaching a fourth category of the messianic ideal—that of Convergence, when the fragmented vision is made whole once again?

We have sketched out the basic lines of the fragmentation of the Jewish messianic vision in the modern world. The many-sided vision broke into *divergent* ideals. Is a progressive *convergence* likely to take place in the coming generation?

Such a development might be predicted on the ground of the partial fulfillment of the Zionist dream in Israel and the profound devotion of nearly all Jews in the Diaspora to the Jewish state. At least on the surface-level of leadership, there is greater unity in regard to Israel than there has been in the pre-state era, though in the domain of religion, the lines of demarcation cut deeper than ever before. But this facade of political unity is due to the bitter war of survival in which Israel has been engaged virtually without interruption. With the coming of peace, it may reasonably be questioned whether the old ideological divisions are likely to reappear.

We cannot predict the future. Yet, with due reverence for the momentum of history, we may assume that the inner contradictions within the messianic vision will be manifested in possibly novel forms. The Israeli are likely to break through the boundaries of state-worship in their quest of spiritual values and in their endeavor to share with their neighbors the burden of building a just order for the peoples of their region. Israel's veneration of "blood and soil" was the consequence of a reaction to European Antisemitism and the Holocaust, reinforced by the implacable hostility of the Arabs. But the humanist tradition of Judaism is also nurtured by the same history and the same memories. Can we look forward to a reintegration of the humanist and the ethnic elements in the consciousness of the Israeli? To be sure, the Israeli cannot in the foreseeable future rest at east in Zion, with the rising tide of Arab nationalism engulfing them from all sides. At best, the military confrontation of the past three decades will give way to a non-violent rivalry. The best that we can hope for is that the component of militant nationalism in the messianic vision will be blended with and balanced by the humanist component of messianism which so clearly predominated in the Jewish world of the pre-Holocaust era. At the same time, the Israeli Jews will continue to draw moral as well as material sustenance from their brethren in the Diaspora. Their sense of identity as Jews, not merely Israeli, forming a vital center of the global fellowship of the Jewish faith, will be stimulated by the continual endeavor to retain their distinctiveness amidst an alien sea of self-conscious Arabs. With the increase in tourism, the bonds of kinship between Israel and the Diaspora will be deepened and extended. These bonds are likely to be spiritualized, moving beyond the symbolism of ritual, the accents of language and the cadences of folk-music in Israel and the endless campaigns in the Diaspora. Israeli Jews will seek to define themselves in terms of the moral-religious heritage of Judaism, which can lay claim to the loyalties of the majority of American Jewry and the secularist majority of Israeli Jews. So, there is likely to be a renewal of the humanist-universalist component of messianism, balancing the national-political elements which hitherto preempted the attention of the Israeli.

In the case of American Jewry, the dominant tension is likely to be between the national-political sentiments, focused on the struggling state of Israel, and the humanist-spiritual trends of messianism. The emergence of a generation for whom the Holocaust is ancient history and Israel is not a resplendent dream of the future but a concrete fact of the present, may allow the messianic impulse to seek fulfillment in the general, all-embracing path of human progress—"to improve the world by the Kingdom of God." Can we look forward to a *convergence* of Jewish and Christian efforts to usher in the messianic age? Can there be a concurrence in regard to means, when there is no agreement on the shape of the future?—We recall that the first generation of Christians called themselves a "way" and the rabbinic sages called their laws—*Halichot olam*, pathways into the world. We can only know our tasks, not our ultimate goals. Hence, our pathways into the future may run in parallel lines and even converge at times. One example from recent years is the union of religious and academic forces, which was galvanized by the issues of civil rights and Vietnam. Such efforts on a wide scale may well lie ahead of us. Naturally, this development will depend on the emergence of new issues in public life and on the silent inner struggle within the hearts of western intellectuals, especially the leaders of the churches. Has the time arrived when Christians and Jews can join in efforts to build God's Kingdom?

Can we now think in terms of the unifying goals of the future rather than in terms of the divisive dogmas of the past?

And what of the nay-saying phase of the vision that must guard against the delusions of pseudo-messianism?—Negation is after all as important as affirmation in turning the wheels of history. For no goal is perfect, no ideal is unexceptionable. The drive toward ecumenism in social action will have to be paralleled by an equal and opposite emphasis on the distinctiveness of diverse theological traditions, thereby counterbalancing a one-sided emphasis on immanentism. The three categories of the Messanic vision—

Affirmation, Negation, Fragmentation—apply to our tasks in the future, as well as to our understanding of the past.

An ecumenical world-embracing movement of Jews, Christians, and Moslems may well become the "wave of the future," but only if the danger of messianic utopianism is taken into account along with its golden promise. And the holy places of these faiths in Jerusalem, reminders of tragedy as well as of triumph, will mirror the ambivalence of mankind in its quest of holiness.

# INDEX